HANSONS
MARATHON
METHOD

HANSONS
MARATHON
METHOD

2ND EDITION

RUN YOUR FASTEST MARATHON

LUKE HUMPHREY WITH KEITH & KEVIN HANSON

VELO press

an imprint of Ulysses Press
PO Box 3440
Berkeley, CA 94703
www.velopress.com

VeloPress is the leading publisher of books on sports for passionate and dedicated athletes around the world. Focused on cycling, triathlon, running, swimming, nutrition/diet, and more, VeloPress books help you achieve your goals and reach the top of your game. V

Library of Congress Cataloging-in-Publication Data

Names: Humphrey, Luke, 1981-
Title: Hansons marathon method: run your fastest marathon / Luke Humphrey
with Keith and Kevin Hanson.
"Distributed in the United States and Canada by Ingram Publisher Services"—T.p. verso. |
Includes index.
Identifiers: LCCN 2015046279 | ISBN 9781937715489 (Paperback: alk. paper)
Subjects: LCSH: Marathon running—Training.
Classification: LCC GV1065.17.T73 H86 2016 | DDC 796.42/52—dc23
LC record available at http://lccn.loc.gov/2015046279

Cover design by Charles Chamberlin
Interior design by Jessica Xavier

24 25 / 10   9   8   7

Contents

Foreword

As one of the privileged few who have run for the Hansons-Brooks Distance Project, I can tell you that my years as a member of the team were some of the best of my life. I was able to learn from two of the best marathon coaches the United States has ever known, Kevin and Keith Hanson, and I was able to train every day with some of the toughest athletes I've ever encountered.

One of those athletes was none other than *Hansons Marathon Method* author Luke Humphrey. Even as rookies, Luke and I shared several common bonds. First, we were both human sponges, soaking in everything Kevin and Keith had to say about marathon training. We also both fell head over heels in love with the event from the start. And we both believed in the Hansons training methods because we saw success, not only in our own careers but everywhere we turned as our teammates continued to shock the running world.

Fast-forward 10 years, and I now coach a professional training group of my own in Flagstaff, Arizona. I am proud to say that many of our accomplishments—including multiple national championships, representing the United States at the international level, and a slew of world-class times in events ranging from the 5K to the marathon—can be directly attributed to the training methods I learned from Kevin and Keith. And now you can learn them too. Luke, a 2:14 marathoner who has used this system himself for more than a decade, explains the training in a way that only an insider could. Luke has suffered (in a good way) through workouts like 3 × 3 miles, 2 × 6 miles, and the 26.2-km Simulator so often that he can break these sessions down like a

Harvard professor. But perhaps the best part of the book is that he breaks the program down not only for elites but for anyone and everyone who is willing to work toward their running goals.

The Hansons Marathon Method is an invaluable resource for runners of all ages and abilities. I've witnessed its success firsthand as an athlete in the Hansons program, as an observer of the training groups based out of the Hansons running stores, and as a coach of my own athletes. Is the method easy? Heck, no. It requires a lot of focus and commitment. But the results will make it all worthwhile. And from a lifetime in our sport, I can tell you this: Runners are tough, no matter what their speed. The Hansons method is not afraid to challenge runners by giving them exactly what they want: rigorous, effective training plans that will make them faster!

—BEN ROSARIO, HEAD COACH,
NORTHERN ARIZONA ELITE PROFESSIONAL RUNNING TEAM

Preface

Kevin and Keith Hanson were fixtures in the Detroit running scene for many years. In fact, if you were ever at a group run, a clinic, or at one of their running shop events, you would find it tough to question their success at the local level. However, at the national level the Hansons method was significantly less well known. So in 2011, when VeloPress approached us about writing a book about the program, we realized it was the perfect opportunity to share our program with a wider audience. And it has been an honor to provide a different way of training to a larger group of runners who, judging by the overwhelming success of the first edition, have proven that they are hungry for a fresh approach to the marathon.

The response to the book has been tremendously positive. We get e-mail after e-mail from people thanking us for the programs and telling us their PR stories. We never get tired of hearing inspiring stories of hard work, dedication, and then ultimately reward for those efforts. It is a humbling experience.

The best part of this process has been the opportunity to grow as coaches and educators. With thousands more people now using the program, we've gotten a lot of questions and in answering them, we've been able to refine the program even more. Writing a second edition has given us a chance to consider those questions and comments, and address as many as possible in this new edition. I am pleased to announce the inclusion of a Just Finish Program, designed to help new runners who are attempting their first marathon but aren't quite ready (yet) for the more difficult workouts in the Beginner and Advanced Programs. Finally, we've also introduced more structured supplemental training, including flexibility and strength, and shown you how these can enhance your run training. One thing, however, has not changed and never will, and that is our goal: to meet you, the runner, where you are, and give you solid information that you can put into use now, as well as for years to come as you grow in your running.

With this second edition, the Hansons Marathon Method will continue to help more and more runners reach their goals. Kevin, Keith, and I cannot thank you enough for your support and your belief in the method!

—LUKE HUMPHREY

Acknowledgments

When it comes to the exciting path my life has taken into the sport of running, I have to credit Kevin and Keith Hanson. They are talent scouts, coaches, and mentors, all rolled into one. Time and again they have identified potential in runners who no one else would think twice about. For the runners in the Hansons-Brooks Distance Project, it is through Kevin and Keith that countless opportunities have been offered and goals realized. Without them, dozens of "just not quite good enough runners" wouldn't have gotten shoe contracts, elite-level coaching, and support from some of the greatest experts in the running business. The world would know nothing of Brian Sell, Desiree Linden, or many others on a long list of athletes who represented the United States at the World Championships over the years. To be sure, a big thanks is also owed to all the runners who have come through the Hansons-Brooks Distance Project. We all shared similar running backgrounds, and hopefully the chapter dedicated to how you train will show the world just what it takes.

While the Hansons' success with elite marathon runners has gained them national attention, their roots are with the hardworking people of Detroit. Through the Hansons' unconventional training methods, runners of all abilities have experienced marathon success since the 1990s. Kevin and Keith have given me a wonderful opportunity to share this program with the world, and I humbly thank them for that.

Much appreciation also goes to my wife, Nicole, who was eternally patient with me while I worked on this project. And I have to give a big shout-out to my right-hand man, Corey Kubatzky. While I was writing, he took over many of the day-to-day activities of Hansons Coaching Services and made sure we never missed a beat. He has been a guiding force in making this endeavor as successful as it has been.

The fine folks at VeloPress are wonderful and I cannot thank them enough, in particular Casey Blaine, Dave Trendler, and Connie Oehring. VeloPress has given Kevin, Keith, and me a wonderful opportunity to provide all the details of the Hansons Marathon Method that magazine articles simply don't have room to offer.

Much appreciation is also owed to Brooks Sports for all its support over the years of the sport of distance running and the Hansons Marathon Method in particular.

Finally, thanks to all the runners who take a leap of faith and try this program. Breaking tradition isn't an easy thing to do and we understand that. While we're providing the guidance, you're the one who has to do all the heavy lifting (and hard running).

INTRODUCTION

I COME FROM SIDNEY, MICHIGAN, a nondescript, rural Midwestern village with a population of 927. Actually, I'm from a couple of miles outside of town. As in most towns in the Midwest, cross-country and track and field aren't exactly popular, mainly because they interfere with football and baseball seasons. As a kid, that was just fine with me, since baseball was, without a doubt, my first love. By eighth grade, I was 6 feet tall, with a father who was 6 feet 8 inches. In terms of athletics, the sky seemed to be the limit.

Although baseball was something I would have loved to play, my algebra teacher, who was also the track coach, "suggested" that I run track instead. Clearly he suspected I could run better than I could hit a baseball. It was there on the track that I truly found my place, discovering I had some natural talent when it came to running—so much so that I was convinced by my teachers that I should abandon my other activities and focus on running. I am forever grateful to the people who encouraged me in those early days of my running career. Without them, I wouldn't have had the opportunity to train with an elite group, run in the Olympic Trials, travel around the world racing, or write this book.

After a successful high school running career, I enrolled at Central Michigan University and walked onto the cross-country team. During my tenure, our team won several conference titles and earned top-25 rankings. We even managed to take ninth place at the NCAA Division I Cross-Country Championships one year. I graduated in 2004 with a bachelor's degree in exercise science and a collegiate running record I was proud of. But while I was happy with all I had accomplished, and felt good overall about my time spent in the world of collegiate running, I always had a lingering notion that I had more to give. That led me to begin dreaming big about the possibilities of running longer distances and competing at the postcollegiate elite level.

Enter Kevin and Keith Hanson. As luck would have it, the Hansons-Brooks Distance Project is located in Michigan. So after my eligibility at Central Michigan came to a close, I asked the Hansons if they would consider taking me on. While other coaches would have likely overlooked me, they saw some potential, thinking that I might end up being a decent marathoner. That is where the adventure truly began. In August 2004, I packed all my possessions in my car and moved from Mount Pleasant to Rochester, ready to begin training for my first marathon under the tutelage of Kevin and Keith.

In October 2004, I made my debut at the LaSalle Bank Chicago Marathon, finishing in 2:18:48, the 5th American and 17th overall. As soon as I crossed the finish line, I swore I'd never do it again. Ten years later I had run 10 more marathons. Guess I was wrong.

Affirming my entrance into the professional running world, 2006 was a major turning point in my running career. I distinctly remember the two weeks leading up to the Boston Marathon that spring. A group of us from the Hansons-Brooks Distance Project who were training for that race headed down to Florida to acclimate to running in the heat. The day before we took off, I defended my thesis before my committee members, my last official duty in completing my master's degree in exercise physiology from Oakland University. It had been a long, challenging academic road, and it felt like a weight had been lifted from my shoulders. I knew the marathon would be nowhere near as difficult as standing in front of three professors who were a hundred times wiser than I as I defended my humble work.

After months of training through the depths of the Michigan winter and then acclimating to the sunny temperatures of Florida, the team was more prepared than ever to take on Beantown 2006 in force. Members of our group ended up taking 4th, 10th, 11th, 15th, 18th, 19th, and 22nd places in the men's race. I finished 11th with a new personal best of 2:15:23. With the performances of Meb Keflezighi, Alan Culpepper, and Pete Gilmore, Americans managed to seize 7 of the top 15 places. It was clear the tide of U.S. running mediocrity was changing, with American marathoners making significant steps to once again be competitive on an international level. There hadn't been this much excitement about American marathon runners since the Bill Rodgers, Frank Shorter, and Greg Meyer days in the late 1970s and early 1980s.

In addition to a renewed excitement for my own training, that race prompted me to take over the Hansons' annual marathon training clinics through the Hansons Running Shops. While I had a good job as an exercise physiologist at the local hospital, this was an opportunity I couldn't pass up. It not only allowed me to utilize my academic degrees but also gave me the chance to become further immersed in the sport I had come to love. Most rewarding was being in a position to transmit my passion for running to other people through the Hansons Marathon Method. As it turned out, coaching was a perfect fit for me.

As my experience—and clientele—grew, Kevin and Keith encouraged me to open a coaching business, called Hansons Coaching Services, which I did in 2006. With feature articles about their unique method in countless magazines and newspapers, the brothers became nationally recognized for their coaching of elites and everyday distance runners alike. As their methods gained increased attention, I served as the go-to guy for answering questions and guiding runners via these time-tested training methods.

In the meantime, my own running has also taken off. I have qualified for three Olympic Marathon Trials (2008, 2012, and 2016), finished 11th at the ING New York City Marathon and 12th at the LaSalle Bank Chicago Marathon, and recently lowered my marathon PR to 2:14:39, all under the tutelage of Kevin and Keith. It has been quite a ride.

Most exciting for me has been watching the successes of the runners I've coached over the years. Every year during marathon season, the brothers and I take great pleasure in reading the many e-mails from our athletes who have just completed a marathon after utilizing the Hansons Marathon Method. Shaving 20–30 minutes off personal bests is not uncommon for runners who have come on board with us. We often hear that they spend much of their 26.2 miles waiting to hit the wall, but never do. Even better, most are eager to run another marathon in the future. While every finisher is a feather in our coaching caps, their success is really more of a testament to the power of strategic training backed by science and common sense. The Hansons Marathon Method really works. I have used it, I have coached it, and I will continue to preach the success it brings for years to come.

PART I

THE APPROACH

1

HANSONS TRAINING PHILOSOPHY

KEVIN AND KEITH HAVE BUILT their marathon business with the help of exercise science research and physiological evidence. I came on board as one of their athletes in 2004, and two years later I was presenting the brothers' training programs to runners across the country. The Hansons rolled out their first marathon training programs in 1992 for the Detroit Marathon, so the Hansons Marathon Method was time-tested by the time I came into the picture. The inception of these plans was driven by a frustration the brothers had with the existing programs on the market. "We felt that those programs didn't prepare runners properly for the demands of the marathon," explains Keith. "Most focus on minimal training during the week and then pile on the mileage over the weekends when people have more time. We wanted well-rounded programs."

In the years since the Hansons first introduced their training schedules, the sport has experienced what some call a "second boom." After the jogging craze hit in the 1970s, marathon mania followed a couple decades later. Consider this: In 1976, there were roughly 25,000 marathon finishers in the United States. By 1990, the number had increased nearly tenfold to 224,000 finishers. It didn't end there. In 1995, 2000, and 2005 there were 293,000,

353,000, and 395,000 marathon finishers respectively. By 2013, there were 541,000 marathon finishers in the United States, with more than 1,100 marathons in the U.S. alone.

As the number of finishers has increased, so too have the finishing times. From 1980 to 2010, the average time for men went from 3:32 to 4:16. Since 2010, that average finish time has held steady at 4:16. Women's numbers tell a more encouraging story. From 1980 to 2002, the average time for women faded from 4:03 to 4:56. Since then, however, their times have gradually improved to 4:41 in 2013 (www.runningusa.org). The slower times and the higher finishing numbers are certainly related. In the 1970s and 1980s, the smaller marathon population largely consisted of hard-core pavement pounders who trained with time goals in mind. Today, the demographic has evolved. What was once a sport solely for serious elites and subelites is now an activity accessible to the masses, many of whom simply want to cross the finish line.

In my time both as a runner and a coach, I have encountered three types of marathon hopefuls:

- **Veteran runners:** This group has logged plenty of miles over the years and has probably run a marathon or two in the past. They are looking to take their previous marathon performances to the next level.

- **Recreational runners:** This group might or might not be new to marathoning, but they are not running newbies, as they have done a number of shorter races. This group is looking to establish a marathon baseline, usually with plans to run more marathons in the future.

- **Just Finishers:** This group includes new runners looking to knock "26.2" off their bucket list as well as those running for charity groups. Many of these runners plan to leave marathoning behind once they finish a race.

Kevin and Keith are actively involved in Team In Training, and I coach for Southeastern Michigan's DetermiNation through the American Cancer Society, so we are well acquainted with runners who are new to the marathon distance and whose goals are noncompetitive. The main issue with Just Finishers and new runners is that they are oftentimes convinced through popular media that running three days a week is the best way to train for a marathon. These approaches work to persuade them that marathon training can be done with relatively little priority shifting: Buy a new pair of shoes, make time for a run a few days a week, and you'll be ready to make the 26.2-mile journey several months down the line. But the truth is that even for those looking simply to finish the race, running only three days a week is not the optimal way to develop, regardless of aspirations. It not only creates a mass of harriers who are ill prepared for the marathon distance, but also doesn't encourage retention within the sport.

As I spoke to Kevin about this third group, he pointed out the fact that every three years, about 50 percent of the customer base of a running specialty store consists of new runners. So, if a store serves 40,000 runners, every three years 20,000 of these runners are new to the sport. While it is great that so many people are motivated to begin running, one is left to wonder what simultaneously accounts for such a high attrition rate. As we spoke, it became obvious. A good number of runners are lured into the sport by promises of big payoffs with few sacrifices. They are told they can complete a marathon with minimal adjustments to their existing schedule and lifestyle—thus the attraction of a minimalist training plan. Since these runners often have a rotten marathon experience because they are undertrained, it is no wonder so few of them return to the marathon distance.

When looking at the most popular of the minimal training programs, a number of similar characteristics arise:

- **Low mileage:** Beginning runners are assigned 35–40 miles for a couple weeks at the highest, and advanced runners hit 45–55 miles.

- **Low frequency:** Beginners are told to run 3–4 days per week and advanced runners 5–6 days.

- **Megalong runs:** Most of the programs reach 20 miles and a few max out at 26 miles. These long runs are generally prescribed during the peak mileage weeks. Most of the programs place a major run on Saturday before the long run, so that 60–75 percent of the weekly mileage is run in two days.

- **Very long duration:** Most of these plans span 24–32 weeks. This is unsurprising, because with such low mileage, the body needs that long to adapt.

- **Misplaced intensity:** In the three-day-per-week programs, all runs are very high on the intensity scale (70 percent and higher of VO_2max) and are accompanied by a long run that is 40–50 percent of the weekly mileage.

A training plan with minimal mileage and three running days per week can be a great way for a novice to ease into the sport of running and build a foundation without getting injured. But once a runner decides to jump into a marathon, this simply isn't enough training. These plans usually assist runners in reaching their main goal, which is to finish, but unfortunately, the by-product is oftentimes a dislike for the sport. Since the greatest predictor of adherence to any type of exercise is enjoyment, this certainly isn't a recipe for long-term success in running.

By charting a course for a strong, successful, and enjoyable marathon experience, the Hansons Marathon Method seeks to encourage the crossing of many marathon finish lines. Unlike a number of the other popular training plans out there, our approach will transform you not only into a marathon finisher, but also into a long-time marathoner. We take a straight-talk approach when it comes to teaching you about marathon training: We won't sugarcoat, offer any supposed shortcuts, or treat you with condescension. Indeed, the marathon wouldn't be a big deal if it didn't require a little blood, a lot of sweat, and perhaps a few tears.

 Cumulative fatigue is the accumulation of fatigue over days, weeks, and even months of consistent training.

What follows is a closer look at the philosophies that lay the groundwork for the Hansons Marathon Method. These building blocks rest on the teachings of famed coach Arthur Lydiard. Widely credited with popularizing the sport of running, Lydiard led a long line of runners to realize their Olympic dreams. As a result, his ideas about training had a major influence on the development of our methods. The Hansons use Lydiard's idea of cumulative fatigue as a foundation for their training plans. Put simply, cumulative fatigue results from repetitive training that doesn't allow for full recovery between training days. It emphasizes a concerted, strategic approach to marathon training, rather than a number of disparate training days strung together at random. You will notice the fundamental principle of cumulative fatigue runs throughout the Hansons Marathon Method. Without one component of the cumulative fatigue philosophy, you interfere with the others, creating a domino effect that limits physiological adaptations necessary for successful marathoning. These components include:

- Mileage
- Intensity
- Balance
- Consistency
- Recovery

Mileage: Strategic Weekly Volume

The biggest problem with many marathon training plans is that they are tailored to fit what average runners want, not what they need. These programs often place a majority of the weekly mileage on Saturday and Sunday, when runners have the most time. Roughly the same amount of mileage is then spread over a few days of the workweek. This can mean that all of the prescribed weekday runs are higher-intensity workouts, leaving few opportunities for easy runs and the accumulation of important marathon mileage. Since the weekday runs are mostly high intensity, it takes a runner longer to recover, causing the easier runs to fall to the wayside. Even if these plans did instruct runners to run on the interim days, they would likely be too tired from the previous workouts.

Adequate weekly mileage plays an important role in the cumulative fatigue process. Increasing mileage comes along with increasing training between 3 and 4 days a week to 6 days a week. This doesn't necessarily mean adding intensity, but rather more easy mileage. The Hansons Marathon Method will show you how to add that mileage, while keeping your pace in check to avoid overworking yourself. Consider the fact that runners training for a 5K will put in 4–6 times their actual race distance in mileage each week. It then makes sense that people training for a marathon would increase their mileage (see Table 1.1). Although the average marathoner won't put in 4–6 times the marathon distance on a weekly basis (100–150 miles), it is reasonable to run 2–3 times the distance per week (50–70 miles).

Most runners preparing for the marathon realize they need an increased volume of mileage to be ready to toe the starting line. What they lack is confidence. New runners will look at the distance they are scheduled to run 12 weeks into the plan and doubt their ability to reach that point. "Start at the ridiculous and work back until you reach something manageable," suggests Kevin. "Right now, 60 miles in a week may seem ridiculous, but what are you supposed to do today? Focus on today and you will be surprised at what you can handle a few months down the line."

TABLE 1.1 WEEKLY MILEAGE BASED ON LEVEL AND EVENTS	BEGINNER	COMPETITIVE	ELITE
5K	20–30	40–50	90+
Marathon	40–50	60–70	110+

In addition to the intimidation factor, training errors can make a certain volume of mileage seem impossible. Inappropriate intensities, unbalanced training, old shoes, and adding too much mileage too soon can all doom a runner from the get-go. Again and again we have seen our athletes give their bodies adequate time to adapt to new training stresses, allowing them to tolerate much more than they ever imagined possible. Our programs work to take you up the mileage ladder one rung at a time, starting with lower mileage and gradually increasing both mileage and intensity. As I like to say to our athletes, "If you want to build a house, you must first create a structure to hold it up." The volume of mileage builds a foundation that allows all the other variables to work.

Intensity: Physiological Adaptations

In addition to increased mileage, our plans stand apart from the rest in terms of pace and intensity. These factors are inextricably linked because if workouts are too hard, you're going to be too tired to reach your weekly mileage quotas. In the Hansons-Brooks Distance Project, the competition can be fierce among our elite athletes. Teaching proper pacing is perhaps our biggest struggle as coaches. During workouts, Kevin and Keith always seem to know when an athlete has developed an "I know you're fast, but I'm just a little bit faster" mentality toward another runner. As a means of emphasizing the importance of pace and punishing runners who run faster than they are instructed, the Hansons dole out push-ups for every second someone is too fast. After a few push-ups, runners always fall into step and pull back on the reins.

While we won't make you do push-ups every time you falter in your pacing, it remains an important part of the implementation of cumulative fatigue. The majority of our suggested mileage is at anaerobic threshold (lactate threshold) pace or slower. You may wonder, "How am I supposed to get faster if I'm running slower?" In Chapter 2, we will discuss the many adaptations that come with endurance training, such as mitochondria development, muscle-fiber adaptations, ability to burn fat as fuel, and more. Exercise physiologists have discovered that those adaptations are best elicited through slower-than-anaerobic-threshold pace. It improves your running by pushing the aerobic threshold, anaerobic threshold, and aerobic capacity up from the bottom, instead of trying to pull them up from the top. Whether it is an easy running day or a hard workout, executing the task at the appropriate pace is integral to our entire marathon training system.

Easy runs are often misunderstood as junk mileage or filler training. The truth is, easy runs are a big percentage of the training week and when they are run at the optimal intensities, they promote a wide array of favorable physiological adaptations. Despite this fact, both novices and experienced runners struggle with properly pacing these relaxed workouts. Newer runners tend to run their easy days too hard because the gradual training plan feels too easy. Most of the time, the intensity evens out as mileage increases and the runner is too tired to maintain that pace throughout the week. However, as a coach, I would prefer to have you adjust the pace to your marathon goal and train properly from day one. This allows you to increase your mileage and intensity safely over weeks and months. More experienced runners tend to get over-zealous in their training, believing that faster is better, especially for those moving up from running competitively at shorter distances. Runners in this situation will quickly be benched as a result of overtraining if they don't temper their excitement and allow easy runs to truly be easy. Regardless of what level you're at, when we instruct you to run "easy," we really mean easy. Once you add in hard workouts, these easy days will serve as active recovery to allow your body to bounce back and prepare for the next workout.

Proper pacing during hard workouts is equally vital. We cannot stress enough that workouts are designed to spur specific physiological adaptations; they are not to be run as hard as you can to see who will be the last runner standing. Tempo runs and strength workouts develop the anaerobic threshold; however, that doesn't mean you should be running a tempo workout faster than anaerobic threshold pace. Speed workouts develop aerobic capacity and should be run just under your maximal aerobic capacity, not beyond it. For instance, imagine if you are instructed to run 6 × 800-meter repeats at 5K pace. Let's say this pace is 6:00 minutes per mile or 3:00 for 800 meters. If you do the first three intervals at 2:45, 2:45, and 2:55, there's a good chance the last three will be around 3:10, 3:15, and perhaps 3:10. While you averaged 3:00, you failed to hit a single interval at the prescribed pace. This means that you didn't accumulate any training at the desired pace, which was specifically set to stimulate aerobic capacity. The first three were too fast, which exceeded VO$_2$max, producing anaerobic energy and lactic acid. The last three were then progressively slower due to that fatigue and lactic acid buildup. In the end, you drove yourself into the ground without gaining any major physiological benefits.

Now you can see why Kevin and Keith assign push-ups. By keeping your pace in check across the training spectrum, you'll be able to tolerate higher training volumes. You'll also be more consistent in training because you won't be so worn out that you need to take unscheduled days off or modify workouts. Cumulative fatigue is designed to make you tired, but running paces faster than prescribed will put you beyond the point of being able to recover sufficiently. That really is junk mileage.

Balance: Training Equilibrium

One of the major downfalls of existing marathon training plans is that they lack balance. There tends to be a standard emphasis on the long run, with the remainder of the week spent recovering from that one workout. When the long run serves as the primary focus, training consistency, weekly volume, recovery, and intensity are all lost. To fully reach your potential as a runner, all the physiological systems must be incorporated into training. "Nothing is make or break," explains Kevin. "The long run is not going to make your marathon if that's the only thing you are doing. There have to be other variables."

The Hansons Marathon Method will present you with two types of runs: Easy and Something of Substance (SOS). SOS runs include speed workouts, strength workouts, tempo runs, and long runs. As Kevin and Keith indicate, "They are runs that require more effort than an easy day." By varying the training, you reap the necessary physiological benefits, in addition to maintaining motivation. If variety is the spice of life, you better include a good amount of it in marathon training.

In the same way your mind gets bored with repetition, so does your body. On the other hand, when you cycle your workouts and stress each individual system, you stimulate a steady rate of physiological adaptation. By giving time and energy not just to the long run, but also to easy days, strength days, speed days, tempo days, and recovery days, you'll be a stronger, more balanced marathoner. There is such a thing as too much of a good thing. When you balance your training, you'll be sure to get just the right amount of each of those things.

Consistency: Sticking to the Game Plan

As a coach, I find many runners struggle with training consistency. One week they run three days, the next four days, and the next week maybe only two days. This is unsurprising as each week brings its own challenges and issues: Your boss imposes a last-minute deadline, your car breaks down, or your child gets sick. The unpredictability of life can make sticking to a training plan difficult. While training adjustments are necessary at times, a regular running schedule remains important.

Physiologically speaking, inconsistency in training makes for a never-ending struggle to maintain even a baseline of fitness. While adaptations can occur rapidly with proper training, they can also be lost with just a week or two of inconsistent running. For instance, if a runner trains five days a week for three weeks, a noticeable improvement in fitness will take place, but if those weeks are followed by two weeks of training only two or three days a week, fitness gains will begin to retreat. It then requires two more weeks of consistent running to get back to the previous level of fitness. In the end, six to eight weeks of running went by just to get back to where you were at week 3. If life does intervene, modify training, but don't skip it. Something is always better than nothing.

In order to achieve this consistency, you must establish attainable goals and plan ahead. If you set your sights too high, you're likely to get discouraged when you discover you have too much on your plate. Conversely, when you set your sights too low, you get bored. Properly placed goals will keep you motivated to get out the door each day, even when running feels like the last thing you want to do. Planning your weekly running schedule in advance also aids commitment. Rather than looking at the training schedule the morning of a workout, know what to expect for the next five to seven days. By penciling your runs into your day planner or posting them on your refrigerator, you can plan for hurdles that may be thrown at you throughout the week. If you have an early meeting Tuesday morning, plan on running after work. If your kids have a soccer tournament all weekend, find an opening to fit your run in. When you schedule your runs, you are far more likely to stick to the plan and remain consistent in your training.

Recovery: Partial Rest

When it comes to cumulative fatigue, you walk a fine line between training enough and overtraining. The goal of the Hansons Marathon Method is to take you close to the line, but not over it. The training you do during the program is tough, but it will lead to a better, more enjoyable race-day result. Incomplete recovery is an important part of the training, as it allows you to perform well, even when you aren't 100 percent.

Whether it is a speed, strength, tempo, or long run, there is a general preoccupation with the idea of being "fresh" for workouts. That freshness, however, requires days off before and after workouts, which takes away from the crucial aerobic adaptations that easy runs offer. While we don't put hard workouts back to back, we do employ the idea of active recovery. This means that harder workouts are often followed by easy running days. This allows you to recover for the next hard workout without taking the day off from running. Think about it this way: After a hard workout, your muscles are depleted of glycogen and feel supremely fatigued. At this time it is important to replace that glycogen, hydrate, and allow the muscles to heal. This, however, doesn't mean you should lie on the couch for the next 24 hours. Easy running is done at low enough intensities that you are primarily burning fat, allowing your body time to rebuild the lost carbohydrate (glycogen) stores. In addition, your muscles learn to more efficiently burn fat because they are running at a pace that promotes fat, rather than carbohydrate, burning.

While this recovery is important, cumulative fatigue calls for only partial recuperation. Even after an easy run day, your muscles may still be somewhat fatigued and glycogen stores only moderately refueled, causing you to feel slightly sluggish. Remember, this is normal. You are training your body to withstand many miles. Just as you will feel sluggish toward the end of the marathon, it is important to learn to push through and keep moving forward. This makes cumulative fatigue an integral part of your long runs. Although you'll have the last few days of training still in your legs, you'll be recovered enough to run the long run as desired. "It all comes back to the long run," Kevin says of plans that are solely focused on the long run. "It doesn't teach your body anything except how to be completely fatigued after the first 20 miles. Instead, we want to put fatigue in your legs and teach your body how to run at the end of a long run."

He continues, emphasizing, "In training we want to simulate running the last 16 miles of the marathon, not the first 16 miles." That said, the stress is not so great that you will need the following week to recover. Instead, the next day will be easy and a few days later there will be a harder workout. Through a number of physiological adaptations, cumulative fatigue trains your body to be fully prepared for the physiological stress imparted by the marathon distance. As you look at our training schedules, you'll notice that every four weeks, the mileage increases slightly via easy days, tempo runs, and long runs. As your body adapts, you vary the stress and continue the progression upward.

Leading up to the big day, you will finally allow your body to fully recover, giving you that fresh feeling as you toe the line. Our programs are designed this way to help you to feel your best during the race, not during training. After all, you never want to execute your best performance in practice.

Cumulative Fatigue Versus Overtraining

The various elements of the cumulative fatigue formula work in concert; in essence, it is a fine balancing act. Take away one of the variables, and the whole formula becomes null. The parts are interrelated, building on and reinforcing one another. When you work to create balance in training by putting equal importance on the different aspects of running, you end up creating more mileage. If you need a long run, an easy run, a tempo run, and a speed or strength run, then you already put yourself in the four to five days per week range. But strict pacing is a key factor in the formula, as well. When you run too hard on every run, you often are forced to take time off, losing consistency and teetering toward overtraining. Adhering to the paces prescribed ensures balanced training. So while the volume may be higher than what you are used to, the intensity is spread out and that can be the biggest difference between adapting to a new workload and simply becoming overtrained.

Will you be tired? Certainly. "Fatigue" is a key word in cumulative fatigue. But tired is not the same as overtrained. Here's a real-world example of the program in action: A local athlete, Celeste, came into our office seeking a plan to prepare her for a marathon in the spring. She had some marathon experience and was looking for a way to get a new personal best. She did a VO_2max test in December 2014. Her VO_2max occurred at 49 ml/kg/min. She was able to get to 7:40 per mile at the maximum level. In May 2015, after following Hansons Advanced marathon training plan (with a few personal tweaks), she was tested again. Her VO_2max was 60 ml/kg/min. She was able to run 6:40 per mile. Incredible! Just by following a consistent, appropriately paced, balanced, moderate mileage plan, she saw massive increases in overall fitness. Certainly it was not easy, and she admitted many times that she felt tired. But she ran every workout within her guidelines, hitting her paces as planned. Had she been overtrained, she would not have been able to hit those paces. That is the difference between cumulative fatigue and overtraining. A few weeks after the test, she ran her marathon and set a personal best by almost 8 minutes.

Training for a marathon isn't easy and it shouldn't be taken lightly; a few curse words may be uttered, favorite television shows missed, and social outings forgone, but you will regret nothing when you successfully cross that finish line. This entire program is just that: a program. Developed by great coaches who have learned from other great coaches, it is a philosophy that can transform you from a person who wants to run a marathon into a bona fide marathoner. We're here to get you there.

2

MARATHON PHYSIOLOGY

ONE OF MY PERSONAL GOALS in writing *Hansons Marathon Method* was to take the physiology chapter that we see in all running books and turn it into something that runners can really understand and employ. Sometimes when I read a journal article or a textbook, I have a hard time seeing the practical application for the average runner. I'd often find myself wondering, "does doing this or that even make sense for the average person?" I figured if I had these questions, then a lot of other people did too. So I set out to write a chapter on physiology that gives readers "aha" moments. I want you to be able to close the book, take a breath, and say, "This all makes sense now. I know what I need to do and why I need to do it."

It can all get a little confusing. And we (and by we, I mean coaches, exercise physiologists, lab rats, and brainiac runners) tend to overthink training processes. We oftentimes know too much for our own good. But you don't need a Ph.D. in exercise physiology to train better. This chapter will help you learn the basics of the physiology involved so that you can direct your attention toward the training itself. By grasping the basic physiological justification for each day's run in the Hansons Marathon Method, you will gain confidence in your training, sans information overload.

Now, as both an exercise physiologist and a coach, I know that sometimes there can be disagreement between what the science says and what the real world dictates. With this chapter, my goal is to bridge that gap, by not just telling you about science-based principles but, more importantly, by helping you connect them to your own real-world performance.

You will find that we tailor our plans specifically to entertain the many physiological adaptations your body needs to make to run a successful 26.2 miles. Keep in mind the following principles as you dive into our methods:

- Marathon muscles
- VO_2max
- Anaerobic threshold
- Aerobic threshold
- Running economy

Marathon Muscles

When it comes to physiological movers and shakers, the musculature system is king. More than 600 muscles in your body work to create motion and force. They allow your heart to beat, your eyes to move, your food to digest, and your legs to run. The three main types of muscle fibers are: cardiac, smooth, and skeletal. While the cardiac muscle makes your heart beat and the smooth muscle lines your intestines, pushing food through your system, the skeletal muscle plays the biggest role in human locomotion. Skeletal muscles make running possible.

Not only are the skeletal muscles responsible for generating physiological movement, they are also where the majority of energy is stored. These muscles include slow-twitch fibers and fast-twitch fibers, the latter of which has several subcategories. Each muscle contains both types of muscle fiber, which are bound together like bundles of cable, each bundle consisting of a single type. Thousands of these bundles constitute a muscle, and each individual bundle is controlled by a single motor neuron. The motor neurons are located in the central nervous system, where they work to control muscles, and in turn, movement.

Altogether, the fibers and the motor neuron make up the motor unit. Since each bundle contains only one type of fiber, a bundle of slow-twitch fibers and a bundle of fast-twitch fibers will receive information from the brain via separate motor units. If one motor neuron is activated, a weak muscle contraction occurs. If multiple motor neurons are activated, however, a more powerful muscular contraction is created.

Why is all this important? Ultimately, the structure of the skeletal muscle system dictates marathon ability. The better understanding you have of your own physiology, the smarter your training will be. Let's look more closely at the muscle types.

TYPE I FIBERS (SLOW-TWITCH FIBERS)

Your family tree plays an important part in determining your marathon potential. If your parents endowed you with an abundance of slow-twitch muscle fibers, you have a leg up on the competition. These slow-twitch fibers, also called type I fibers, are particularly important for endurance events because of their efficient use of fuel and their resistance to fatigue. Slow-twitch muscle fibers are aerobic, which means they use oxygen to transfer energy. This is a result of their large capillary area, which provides a much greater available supply of oxygen than fast-twitch fibers. Additionally, these fibers have the machinery necessary for aerobic metabolism to take place. Known as the mitochondria, this machinery is often referred to as the "powerhouse of the cell." Thanks to the mitochondria, you are able to use fats and carbohydrates as fuel sources to keep your body running.

True to their name, the slow-twitch fibers also have a slower shortening speed than the other types of fibers, which serves an important function for endurance runners. While these fibers cannot generate as much force as the others, they supply energy at a steady rate and can generate a good amount of power for an extended period. They also have smaller motor neurons, which require less neural impulse to make them contract, so the slow-twitch fibers are first to start contracting when you begin running. In addition to being slower to contract, type I fibers are only about half the diameter of fast-twitch fibers. Although they are smaller and slower, they are also more efficient and persistent, warding off fatigue during a long haul on the roads.

TYPE II FIBERS (FAST-TWITCH FIBERS)

Fast-twitch fibers, also known as type II fibers, are also genetically determined and are the slow-twitch fibers' more ostentatious counterpart. They are bigger, faster, and pack a powerful punch, but they also fatigue rapidly. Since these fibers have very few mitochondria, they transfer energy anaerobically, without the use of oxygen. These forceful contractions use such large amounts of adenosine triphosphate (ATP), basically a high-energy molecule, that they quickly tire and become weak. That is precisely why an Olympic 100-meter champion can run a record-setting pace for the length of the homestretch, while a marathon champion can maintain record-setting pace for 26.2 miles. Two different muscle-fiber types; two different results.

The type II fibers are further divided into subgroups. Two of the most common are type IIa and type IIb, also known as the intermediate fibers. The type IIa fibers share several characteristics with slow-twitch fibers, as they have more mitochondria and capillaries than other types of fast-twitch fibers. As a result, type IIa fibers are considered to be aerobic, although they still provide a more forceful contraction than slow-twitch fibers. By contrast, type IIb fibers contract powerfully, transfer energy anaerobically, and fatigue quickly. See Table 2.1 for a brief comparison of fiber types.

A WORKING SYSTEM

All humans have both type I and type II muscle fibers, but the distribution varies greatly. Most people, regardless of gender, have a type I fiber distribution of 45–55 percent in their arms and legs. Individuals who are fitness

TABLE 2.1 COMPARISON OF MUSCLE-FIBER TYPES

	TYPE I	TYPE IIA	TYPE IIB
Contraction time	Slow	Fast	Fastest
Fatigue resistance	High	Medium	Low
Force production	Low	High	Highest
Mitochondria density	High	High	Low
Capillary density	High	Medium	Low
Oxidative capacity	High	High	Low

conscious, but not completely devoted to training, can see a type I distribution of around 60 percent. Meanwhile, trained distance runners tend to have a type I distribution of 70 percent, and elite marathoners have an even greater percentage than that. Herein lies the challenge. When it comes to running a marathon, Runner A, who has a high proportion of type I fibers, will naturally be better off than Runner B, who has a low type I and low type IIa distribution. So how does Runner B get around his own physiology?

Luckily for both runners, the body is an amazing machine capable of adapting to myriad stresses. In the field of exercise physiology, "stress" denotes the repeated and intense training that leads to certain physiological adaptations. Researchers have long sought the key to muscle-fiber conversion, hoping they might discover how a person like Runner B could actually change the composition of his or her muscles via training stress. Although much of the research remains inconclusive, it is agreed that elite distance runners have a greater proportion of type I fibers than the average recreational runner, and that those type I fibers are necessary for a fast marathon performance. (See Table 2.2 for a comparison among different types of runners.) What we don't know is if you are genetically bound to a particular muscle-fiber arrangement or if you can change it with physical training through

TABLE 2.2 COMPARISON OF TYPE I AND II FIBERS

	TYPE I	TYPE IIA	TYPE IIB
Sprinter	20%	45%	35%
Sedentary	40%	30%	30%
Average active	50%	40%	10%
Middle-distance runner	60%	35%	5%
World-class marathoner	80%	20%	‹1%

certain training stresses. Although it may be too early to make any definite statements about conversions from type I to type II fibers, it has been shown that transformations can take place within the type II fibers. Even after a relatively short training block of 10–12 weeks, a runner can display a transition from anaerobic, fatigable type IIb fibers to the more aerobic, fatigue-resistant type IIa fibers. This is great for an endurance runner. It shows that training elicits tangible physiological changes that create performance advantages and real improvements. There is much hope for Runner B.

MAXIMIZING MUSCLE FIBERS

Regardless of genetics, training remains a vital predictor of running performance. To get your muscles to respond the way you want them to on race day, you must train them to fire in a particular manner. It all starts with a signal sent from the motor units in the central nervous system, which begins by recruiting the slow-twitch fibers. You continue to rely heavily on those fibers unless one of these three things happens:

- You increase your pace.
- You encounter a hill or another force that creates resistance.
- You run long enough to exhaust the slow-twitch fibers.

Depending on fitness level, some runners can go an hour at a modest pace before they begin to recruit the fast-twitch fibers; others can go up to two. It is likely that you'll rely on type I fibers almost exclusively during the first half or so of the marathon. As those fibers tire, the body will begin to employ the type IIa fibers, those slightly larger, aerobic fast-twitch fibers. If you have trained properly, you'll have enough leeway to get through the rest of the marathon using these fibers. While they aren't great for endurance running, they are a good substitute for the exhausted type I fibers. Issues arise when the undertrained runner is forced to go to the third line of defense: type IIb fibers. Remember, these are built for power, and they fatigue quickly. If you are relying on these fibers to get you to the finish line, things will not end well.

What the Hansons Marathon Method seeks to do is teach you how to maximize the use of the type I and type IIa muscle fibers, without having to resort to the type IIb fibers. While genetics dictates what kind of work you may be innately suited for, the right training helps you maximize your individual potential. We will show you how this can be done, no matter what your DNA might say.

VO$_2$max

If muscle fibers are in the driver's seat when it comes to marathon endurance potential, VO$_2$max works in the pit, constantly providing assistance. VO$_2$max stands for "volume of oxygen uptake," defined as the body's maximum capacity to transport and utilize oxygen while running. When a person's VO$_2$max is described as 50 ml/kg/min, you would read "50 milliliters of oxygen per kilogram of body weight per minute." Basically, the higher the number, the better. (For a discussion on measuring your VO$_2$max, see "Ask the Coach" on page 40.) Although VO$_2$max is often considered the gold standard of fitness, it should be noted that it doesn't always serve as the best predictor of marathon performance. In fact, elite marathon runners tend to have a slightly lower VO$_2$max than elite 5K and 10K runners. But although it isn't the single most important predictor of marathon potential, it remains a significant piece of the puzzle.

 VO$_2$max is the maximal rate at which oxygen can be brought in and used by exercising muscle.

Since blood carries oxygen to the muscles, one must look at the heart when considering VO$_2$max. Just like the skeletal muscles, the heart muscle can be strengthened with work, thus allowing it to pump more blood and push more oxygen to the muscles. The heart adapts to training stress in the same way the muscles in your legs do. There are a number of positive adaptations related to the heart that occur as a result of endurance training. Four of these adaptations, shown in Figure 2.1 and described below, are considered the central components of VO$_2$max:

Circulation of the coronary arteries improves. Since these are the arteries that supply the heart, improved circulation means more blood reaches it.

Ventricle walls thicken, particularly the left ventricle. This is the area of the heart that pushes blood out to be circulated around the body. As the ventricle walls thicken, the force of the contractions becomes greater, pumping more blood into the circulating arteries.

The ventricle chamber enlarges. This allows for more oxygenated blood to be stored within the ventricle, which is then circulated throughout the body.

Pulse rate decreases. When the cardiac muscle is strengthened, it doesn't have to work as hard to do its job.

FIGURE 2.1 IMPROVEMENTS WITH ENDURANCE TRAINING

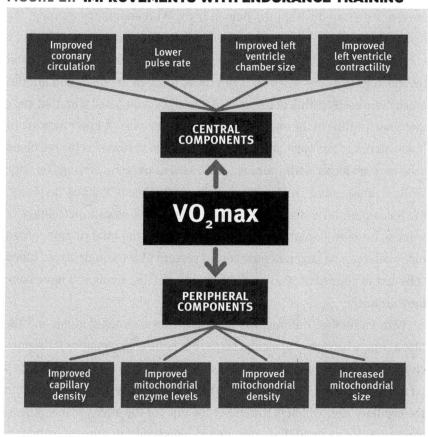

In sum, more blood is pumped with greater force and less effort. Since the heart has bigger chambers that hold more blood, heart rate slows across all running paces, making the entire system more efficient and healthier.

The heart supplies blood to the body, and the better it can deliver large amounts of blood into the bloodstream, the more efficiently the oxygen in the blood reaches the running muscles. What's more, the adaptations don't stop with the heart; they also affect the blood itself. In fact, blood volume has been shown to increase with endurance training. Red blood cells, the most common type of blood cells, are the main means through which oxygen is delivered within the human body. With endurance training, the hematocrit level, or the amount of red blood cells within the total volume of blood, decreases. This means that since total blood volume is higher and the blood itself is less viscous, it can travel through the heart and arteries much more easily. Think of the new oil in your car compared with that gunk that's been sitting in the engine for the last 15,000 miles. A lower hematocrit level equates to less wear and tear on your system because, as the red blood cells become larger with training, you lose less oxygen-carrying capacity. While it may sound counterproductive, since plasma volume increases, the hematocrit level decreases because it is expressed as a percentage of volume. So even though the percentage is lower, the total number of red blood cells can be larger. Remember, 20 percent of 100 equals 20 red blood cells and 15 percent of 500 equals 75 red blood cells, giving you more bang for your buck.

With endurance training, the heart becomes a stronger pump and the blood supply becomes bigger and better, but none of that matters if the muscles cannot use the massive amount of oxygen that is now being dropped off at their doorstep. The actual delivery of oxygen to the muscle happens in the capillary bed, which is the end of the line for the artery. Some of these capillaries are so small that only one red blood cell can drop off its bounty of oxygen to the muscle at a time. From there, the red blood cell begins its journey back to the heart and lungs where it is reloaded with oxygen. During rest, many of these capillary lines lie dormant. As you begin running, the lines open up, allowing muscles to accept an increasing amount of oxygen to meet the demands of exercise.

While improving the central components of VO_2max is important, having a bigger left ventricle to pump more blood doesn't do much good if the muscles that are being used can't handle the changes. Luckily, our running muscles, as we discussed, adapt simultaneously. These adaptations, shown in Figure 2.1 and which we will call peripheral components, include:

Increased capillary density. A greater density of capillaries means that oxygen can move among cells faster and more efficiently. This allows the exercising muscle to receive the oxygen it needs to continue to exercise.

Improved mitochondrial enzyme levels and activity. Think of an enzyme as a tool that makes work easier, rather like the ramp you'd use to push a heavy box up the front steps. They reduce the amount of energy required to make a reaction occur. With higher levels, reactions within the mitochondria can allow more work to be done at the same rate.

Improved mitochondrial density. The mitochondria are where fats and carbohydrates are presented as fuel for exercise, so the more mitochondria we have, the more fat can be used as fuel to maintain aerobic intensity.

Increased size of existing mitochondria. Bigger mitochondria allow more fuel to be processed at a single site. If we can process more fatty acids through more and bigger mitochondria, we reduce the need for carbohydrates to be used and increase the intensity it takes to prompt the anaerobic system (which relies on carbohydrates for energy).

The bottom line is that the body is remarkable at adapting to training. It will do everything it can to support a given activity and become better at it. VO_2max is the ceiling for your aerobic potential, but it is not the overall determinant of potential performance. When your aerobic capacities are maxed out, your anaerobic faculties are right on their heels. As a result, other physiological variables contribute to how well a person can run a marathon.

Anaerobic Threshold

Marathon running relies heavily on the oxygen supplied by the aerobic system, which is more efficient and provides greater endurance than the anaerobic system. While powerful and explosive, the anaerobic system functions without oxygen and therefore can only provide short bursts of speed before energy stores are depleted, lactic acid builds up in the muscles, and running ceases. While lactic acid, or lactate, has gotten a bad rap as a soreness-inducing, fatigue-causing by-product of high-intensity exercise, it actually serves as an energy source for the muscles, allowing them to squeak out a bit more work before bonking. Research now tells us that the fatigue that occurs at that point is caused by another physiological phenomenon. The real culprits are the electrolytes: sodium, potassium, and calcium. These electrolytes are positioned along the muscles, each with its own electrical charge that triggers muscle contractions. At high intensities and over time, the potassium ion outside the cell builds up, clogs the passageway, and cannot switch places with the sodium ion inside the cell. This leads to weaker and weaker muscle contractions, or neuromuscular fatigue, and it will soon slow your body to a sputtering halt.

Not only is blood lactate not the villain we once thought it to be, we've also come to realize that it plays an important role in marathon running. The aerobic system supports a moderate pace for long periods because the lactate that is produced is simultaneously processed and removed. However, as the aerobic system fatigues or the intensity increases, you become more dependent on the anaerobic system, and in turn reach a point where you produce lactate faster than your body is able to get rid of it. Referred to as lactate threshold, onset of blood lactate, or anaerobic threshold (AT), it is the tipping point where lactic acid starts to build up in your bloodstream.

Anaerobic threshold is particularly important because it has been identified as perhaps the best predictor of endurance performance. It occurs at anywhere between 60 and 90-plus percent of a person's VO_2max, so as you get closer to your VO_2max, blood lactate begins to accumulate. The best of the best tend to have an anaerobic threshold exceeding 70 percent of VO_2max. While training may raise your VO_2max only a few points, it can have a significant impact on anaerobic threshold. A group of elite marathon runners

> **Anaerobic threshold** is the pace at which lactic acid will begin to accumulate exponentially, despite running at a steady pace.

may have similar VO$_2$max levels. What tends to separate first place from 10th place is anaerobic threshold. While VO$_2$max may separate the national class from recreational runners, anaerobic threshold separates the champions from the contenders.

Remember that anaerobic threshold is the point at which the aerobic pathways are still providing energy for muscle contraction, but they cannot do it fast enough to provide all the required energy. This is where the anaerobic pathways begin to make up the difference. As a result, we can push the threshold higher via training. By running farther and faster, we teach our bodies to rely more heavily on the aerobic pathways, thus improving endurance and increasing the time it takes to reach that point of anaerobic reliance. One of the big differences in the Hansons Marathon Method, compared with traditional training programs, is that we teach you to stimulate aerobic metabolism through a large volume of aerobic training, not high-end anaerobic work.

Aerobic Threshold

All this talk about energy systems may have you wondering where that energy comes from in the first place. The short answer: fats and carbohydrates. As a marathon runner, you should focus on training the body to use fat as the primary source of energy. Why? Because fat is high in energy, providing nearly twice as many calories per gram as carbohydrates. And while our bodies store very small amounts of carbohydrates for quick energy, the fat stores are nearly endless. Even if you have a small percentage of body fat, your system has plenty of fat for fuel. The only problem is that the oxidation of fat to energy is slow compared with the oxidation of carbohydrates. For most people, fat serves as the main source of energy up to about 50 percent of VO_2max because the fat can be processed fast enough through the mitochondria to supply the demands that running requires up to that point. Bear in mind that for most runners, 50 percent of VO_2max is painfully slow. After that point, whether as a result of distance or intensity, the body looks to burn carbohydrates. Since fat cannot be burned without oxygen, that point at which the body begins to burn through carb stores is called the aerobic threshold. See Figure 2.2 for a graph that illustrates the contribution of fat and carbohydrate based on running intensity.

Aerobic threshold is considered the pace at which fats and carbohydrates are being consumed at approximately the same rate (50/50).

This is the reason carbohydrates (glycogen) provide the majority of energy at faster paces. The downside of relying on glycogen stores for energy is that you have only about two hours' worth and once they are gone, your run is over. When you burn through your stored glycogen, the body will draw on the glucose in your blood, which runs out even more quickly. The result is often called "hitting the wall" or "bonking." If you've ever watched a marathon, you have likely seen runners at the front of the pack, the back of the pack, and everywhere in between who smacked right into that wall. They're the ones who have slowed to a slog and look as if they are dragging a 300-pound anchor behind them. Although this was once thought to be an unavoidable rite of passage for marathon finishers, a smart training plan will help you skirt the wall altogether. It's all about burning fat for a longer period of time to put off drawing on those limited carbohydrate stores.

Somewhere within the fat-burning range is your optimal marathon pace. If you're a beginning runner, your range may be between 50 and 60 percent

FIGURE 2.2 FAT AND CARB USE BASED ON INTENSITY

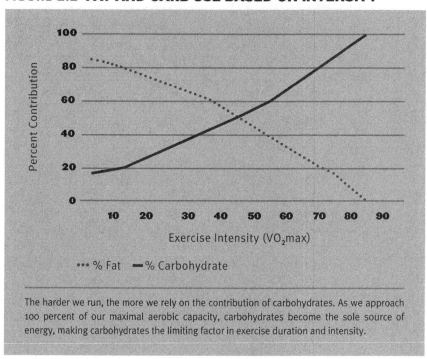

The harder we run, the more we rely on the contribution of carbohydrates. As we approach 100 percent of our maximal aerobic capacity, carbohydrates become the sole source of energy, making carbohydrates the limiting factor in exercise duration and intensity.

of your VO₂max. Trained recreational runners usually range between 55 and 65 percent, and faster runners range between 60 and 80 percent.

Luckily for the aspiring marathoner, it is possible to train the body to burn fat longer. The speed at which fat can be processed doesn't change with training, so in order to be able to use more fat, we have to burn a higher volume of it. To burn a high volume, we need more metabolic factories (the mitochondria, which, as mentioned earlier, are the powerhouse of the cell). Aerobic training, such as running, helps to add mitochondria, which in turn introduces new enzyme activity and oxygen to the system. While the mitochondria are not necessarily producing energy more quickly, they are bigger and more plentiful, which allows fat to be oxidized and turned into energy for muscle contraction. With the increase in energy

FIGURE 2.3 VO₂MAX RESULTS FROM TREADMILL TEST

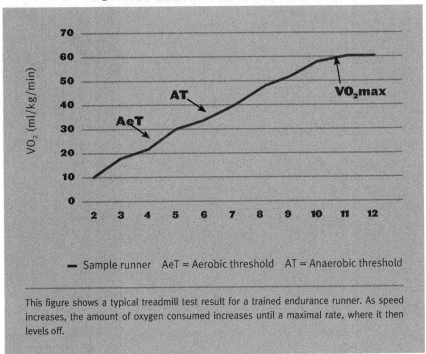

— Sample runner   AeT = Aerobic threshold   AT = Anaerobic threshold

This figure shows a typical treadmill test result for a trained endurance runner. As speed increases, the amount of oxygen consumed increases until a maximal rate, where it then levels off.

from fat, the glycogen in the muscles isn't tapped until later, saving it for faster paces. Basically, the wall is pushed back and, with any luck, never reached.

Figures 2.3 and 2.4 illustrate our discussion. Figure 2.3 represents the results of a VO₂max treadmill test of a trained recreational runner. Note a linear increase in the amount of oxygen used as intensity increases. At our threshold points, we see slight deflections on the graph. The first represents the aerobic threshold. The second represents the anaerobic threshold. Figure 2.4 represents the actual blood lactate measurements from the same test. By graphing the amount of lactate in the blood at set intervals of a test, we can again see the deflection points that coincide with our threshold points.

FIGURE 2.4 LACTATE PRODUCTION AND CLEARANCE

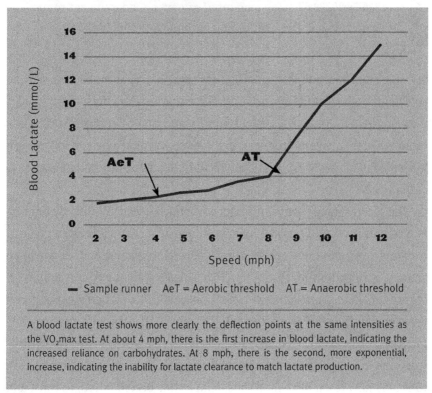

— Sample runner   AeT = Aerobic threshold   AT = Anaerobic threshold

A blood lactate test shows more clearly the deflection points at the same intensities as the VO_2max test. At about 4 mph, there is the first increase in blood lactate, indicating the increased reliance on carbohydrates. At 8 mph, there is the second, more exponential, increase, indicating the inability for lactate clearance to match lactate production.

Running Economy

Running economy, which is a term used to describe how much oxygen is required to run a certain pace, is the final physiological topic marathoners should understand. Consider this scenario: Runner A and Runner B both have the same VO_2max of 70 ml/kg/min. It might take Runner B 55 ml/kg/min to run a 6:30 mile, while it takes Runner A 60 ml/kg/min to run the same pace. Given this, Runner B is more economical than Runner A, but more importantly, probably faster too. See Figure 2.5 for a graphic example.

Although there has been much debate over the effects of running economy, two facts are clear. First, running economy depends on a high training volume.

Running economy is the amount of oxygen a runner utilizes to run a certain pace. The less oxygen required, the better.

You don't need to pound out 140-mile weeks, but your mileage should be sufficient for the distance for which you are training. You must also consider the amount of training over weeks, months, and years. Beginners will be less economical than veteran runners, in the same way that a person following a low-mileage plan will be less economical than a person running most days of the week.

The second component of running economy is speed training. By training at a certain pace, you become more economical at that pace. Since the goal is to improve running economy at race pace, you must spend an adequate amount of time training at race pace. This also solidifies why it is important for runners not to run workouts faster than prescribed. When you opt to run faster than suggested, you are training at a level that you may not be ready for, based on actual race performances. Training above suggested paces turns workouts into something they were not intended to be; for example, easy runs may now resemble tempo runs, tempo runs become strength runs, and strength runs become speed runs. These paces may feel achievable at first, but it is our experience that the majority of people who train too fast end up overtrained, burned out, or injured. If you feel strongly about training at a faster pace, then it is important to run (or simulate) a race to confirm that you are ready to move to a more aggressive pace goal.

A Physiologically Based Method

If you understand all of the physiological factors involved in optimal marathon training, you can see the underlying reason for each and every workout. As muscle fibers adapt to running stress, VO_2max is optimized, anaerobic threshold improved, and the ability to burn fat at higher inten-

FIGURE 2.5 COMPARISON OF VO₂MAX FOR SIMILAR RUNNERS

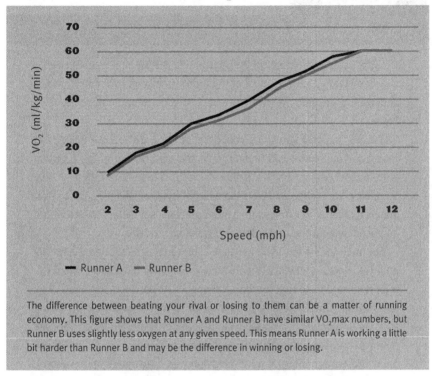

The difference between beating your rival or losing to them can be a matter of running economy. This figure shows that Runner A and Runner B have similar VO₂max numbers, but Runner B uses slightly less oxygen at any given speed. This means Runner A is working a little bit harder than Runner B and may be the difference in winning or losing.

sities is increased. In the end, improved running economy is the result of consistent, optimal training. It all comes down to the tiny, biological happenings of the human body: Increased capillarization, an increase in the number and size of mitochondria, and greater mitochondrial enzyme activity equate to less oxygen being necessary to run the same paces. All of these factors are implemented in the Hansons Marathon Method as you run your way to your best 26.2.

ASK THE COACH

Should I get my VO₂max tested?

The most common type of physiological test is a VO_2max test. Though it is called VO_2max testing, most of the time you also get your aerobic and anaerobic thresholds, as well as your corresponding heart rates, from the test.

Testing can give you some cool data, but how do you use it? In most cases, all you'll know is if those thresholds are improving. The problem is that most testing uses a protocol that increases the intensity only by raising the incline on the treadmill, not by increasing the pace. That makes it difficult to extrapolate a more practical set of data, which would be paces that correspond with the physiological data.

For me, that's a letdown, because I want practical information for my athletes. Now, I know many would say that if they have heart rate data, then they could use that for their training. True, but there are some cons to consider. One is getting people to go to their maximal effort in the test. Could you wear a mask while breathing through a tube, all while trying to run your absolute hardest effort and trying not to fly off the back of the treadmill? It's tough and involves a learning curve. Second, the test is typically done in controlled environments—indoors and on a treadmill. So those numbers may not equate to the same intensities when training in the real world. Overall, I would describe the testing as one tool in your toolbelt, or better, a method of creating a starting point or checkpoint.

If you decide on testing, I suggest getting the Respiratory Exchange Ratio (RER) collected as well. This data will help you determine what percentage of your calories are coming from fat and from carbohydrate, and how many calories you expend at a given intensity level. This information allows you to dial in your fueling, break it down to manageable parts, and even determine if your goal pace is too aggressive.

In sum, getting numbers and data is fun, but at the end of the day, you have a fairly good idea of your fitness without it. Testing has a place, but make sure you are obtaining the right data, and then, take it with a grain of salt.

PART II

THE PROGRAM

3

TRAINING PROGRAM COMPONENTS

THERE IS AN ALL-TOO-COMMON misconception that one can prepare sufficiently for a marathon by simply running three days per week, provided one
of those days includes a grueling 20-mile (or more) long run. That sounds
simple, but the truth is that there's a lot more to successful preparation than
that. All runs are not created equal, and the long run, while key, is merely
one component of a larger system that prepares you for success in the marathon distance.

The Hansons program has become known for the "16-mile long run" and
a six-day-per-week running schedule that includes several types of workouts. This has sometimes been perceived as renegade when compared with
status quo programs on the market, and some runners have had their doubts
when we promise they'll PR with our program. In fact, in the first edition of
this book, we shared the story of Kevin Hanson's wife performing marvel-
ously using our method, albeit all the while intending to prove the method
wrong. Since then, I've gotten similar e-mails, with runners who had been
fired up to write a scathing "I told you so" instead thanking us for their PR
and confessing that they never should have doubted the process. I don't
write these stories to gloat, but rather to show by example that there is more

to successful marathon training than a few runs a week plus a long run. And while people tend to have laser focus on our 16-mile long run, they really have to embrace the whole picture of what the method entails.

In this chapter, we will dissect our training schedules, considering the various components that make up our Just Finish, Beginner, and Advanced Programs. Runs are organized in one of two categories: Easy Days and Something of Substance (SOS) workouts. The SOS workouts include long, speed, strength, and tempo runs. (See Figure 3.1 for a breakdown of weekly mileage by workouts.) By varying the training plan from one day to the next, you train different bodily systems, all working in concert to optimize your marathon potential.

The basis for this approach stems from the overload principle, which states that when the body engages in an activity that disrupts its present state of homeostasis (inner balance), certain recovery mechanisms are initiated. As we discussed previously, different stresses work to overload the system, stimulating physiological changes. These adaptations, in turn, better prepare the body for that particular stress the next time it is encountered. This is where the principle of cumulative fatigue, which underscores our entire training philosophy, comes in. Cumulative fatigue is all about challenging the body without reaching the point of no return (overtraining).

Easy Running

Misconceptions abound when it comes to easy running. Such training is often thought of as unnecessary filler mileage. Many new runners believe that easy days can be considered optional, as they don't provide any real benefits. Don't be fooled: Easy mileage plays a vital role in a runner's development. That's

The **overload principle** is the idea that regular exposure to a specific exercise will enhance certain physiological functions and therefore include a training response: You become more fit.

FIGURE 3.1 WEEKLY MILEAGE BREAKDOWN

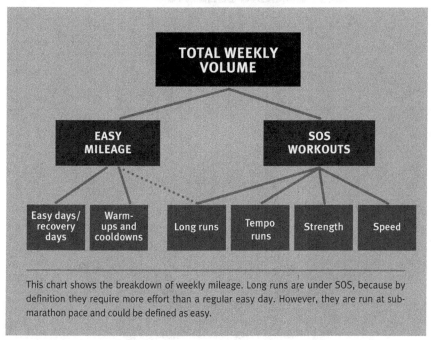

This chart shows the breakdown of weekly mileage. Long runs are under SOS, because by definition they require more effort than a regular easy day. However, they are run at sub-marathon pace and could be defined as easy.

good news because it means that not every run needs to be a knockdown, drag-out experience. Easy runs dole out plenty of important advantages without any of the pain by providing a gentler overload that can be applied in a higher volume than SOS workouts. This keeps the body in a constant state of slight disruption, helping to prevent injuries while simultaneously forcing your body to adapt to stress to increase fitness.

In the Advanced Program's peak week, we prescribe a ceiling of 63 miles in a week. Looking closer, 31 of those miles, or 49 percent, are classified as easy. Figure 3.2 provides justification for why nearly half of your weekly mileage is devoted to this type of training. To understand why easy running is important, you must consider the physiological adaptations that it stimulates in muscle-fiber development, energy utilization, capillary development, cardiovascular strength, and structural fitness.

FIGURE 3.2 EASY RUNNING BENEFITS

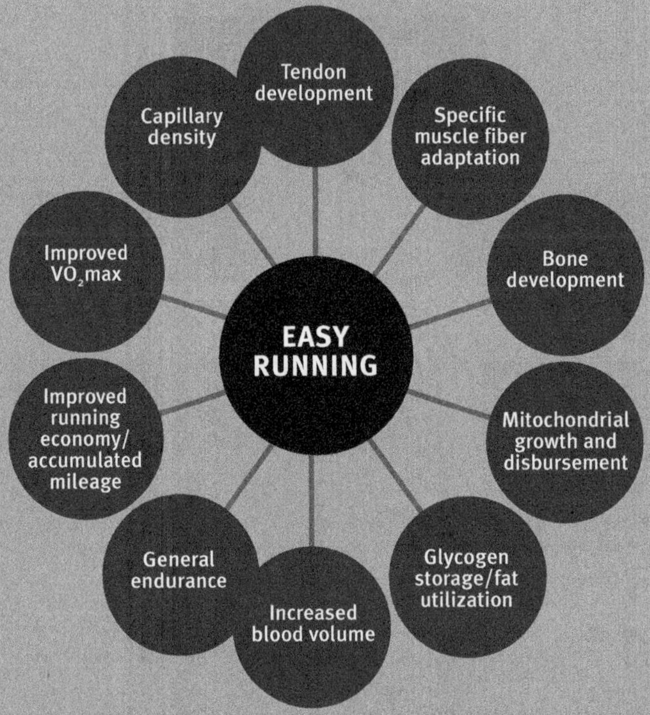

Tendon development

Capillary density

Specific muscle fiber adaptation

Improved VO$_2$max

Bone development

EASY RUNNING

Improved running economy/ accumulated mileage

Mitochondrial growth and disbursement

General endurance

Glycogen storage/fat utilization

Increased blood volume

Check out all the benefits that occur with easy running. Still think easy running is junk mileage?

THE PHYSIOLOGY OF EASY RUNNING

When considering why easy running is important, look at what it does for your muscle fibers. As discussed in Chapter 2, while the number of slow-twitch fibers you are genetically endowed with will ultimately define your potential as a marathoner, training can make a difference. Easy running recruits a whole host of slow-twitch fibers because they have a lower "firing," or contraction, threshold than the more powerful fast-twitch fibers. Like any other muscle, the more they are used, the more they develop. Along with resistance to fatigue, slow-twitch muscles can be relied upon for more miles so that the fast-twitch muscles are not fully engaged until down the road. In the end, easy running helps to develop slow-twitch fibers that are more fatigue resistant and fast-twitch fibers that take on many of the characteristics of the slow-twitch fibers.

Plus, the more slow-twitch fibers you have, the better you'll be prepared to use fat for energy. We now know this is a very good thing because the body contains copious amounts of fat to burn and only a limited supply of carbohydrates. The greater length of time you burn fat, rather than carbohydrate, the longer you put off glycogen (carb) depletion and an encounter with the dreaded wall. When you run at lower intensities, you burn somewhere around 70 percent fat and 30 percent carbohydrate. With an increase in pace comes an increase in the percentage of carbohydrate you burn. Your easy running days serve as catalysts to develop those slow-twitch muscle fibers and consequently, teach your body to burn fat instead of carbohydrates. Slow-twitch fibers are better at burning fat than fast-twitch fibers because they contain larger amounts of mitochondria, enzymes that burn fat, and capillaries.

In response to the need for fat to provide the lion's share of the fuel for training, the mitochondria grow larger and are dispersed throughout the muscles. In fact, research has indicated that just six to seven months of training can spur the mitochondria to grow in size by as much as 35 percent and in number by 5 percent. This benefits you as a runner because the higher density of mitochondria works to break down fat more effectively. For instance, if you burned 60 percent fat at a certain pace a year ago, training may have increased that percentage to 70 percent. This is one of the many improvements training will elicit.

Thanks to easy running, your body will also see an uptick in the enzymes that help to burn fat. Every cell in your body contains these enzymes, which sit waiting to be "turned on" by aerobic activity. No pills or special surgeries are needed: This is simply your body's natural way of burning fat. These enzymes work by making it possible for fats to enter the bloodstream and then travel to the muscles to be used as fuel. With the help of the increased mitochondria and fat-burning enzymes, the body utilizes fat for a longer period of time, pushing back the wall and keeping you running longer.

Capillary development is another benefit of easy running. Since running requires a greater amount of blood to supply oxygen to your system, the number of capillaries within the exercising muscles increases with training. After a number of months of running, capillary beds can increase by as much as 40 percent. It should also be noted that the slow-twitch fibers contain an extensive network of capillaries compared with the fast-twitch fibers, supplying those slower fibers with much more oxygen. As the density of capillaries increases throughout those muscles, a greater amount of oxygen is supplied in a more efficient manner to the muscles.

Easy running also results in a number of adaptations that happen outside the exercising muscle. As you know, your body requires more oxygen as it increases workload. The way to deliver more oxygen to your system is to deliver more blood. With several months of training, much of which is easy running, an athlete will experience an increase in hemoglobin, a.k.a. "the oxygen transporter," in addition to a 35–40 percent increase in plasma volume. This increased volume not only helps deliver oxygen, but also carries away the waste products that result from metabolic processes.

Easy running also creates certain structural changes to your physiological system that you'll find advantageous for good marathoning. But none of these adaptations makes much difference if there isn't a good pump to move all of this blood and oxygen through the system. Just like skeletal muscle, the heart gets stronger with exercise. More specifically, the heart's left ventricle increases in size and thickness, providing a bigger chamber to pump more blood from the heart to the arterial system. This gives the heart a break, as it won't be required to beat as often to deliver the same amount of blood, regardless of rest or exercise intensity. If you compare your heart rate from the beginning of a training cycle to the end, you'll be surprised by how much lower it can be. Again, this means that your system is becoming more efficient.

Another major physiological adaptation comes from within the tendons of the running muscles. As you may be aware, the body lands at a force several times the runner's body weight, and the faster you run the greater that force becomes. The resulting strain on tendons and joints, applied gradually through easy running, allows these tendons to slowly adapt to higher impact forces to later handle the greater demands of fast-paced running.

Collectively, the adaptations stimulated by easy running prompt a higher VO_2max, anaerobic threshold, and running economy. While fast anaerobic workouts provide little improvement in the muscles' aerobic capacity and endurance, high amounts of easy running can bump aerobic development upward by leaps and bounds. Whether you're looking to strengthen your heart, transport more oxygen to the working muscles, or simply want to be able to run longer at a certain pace, all signs point to including high amounts of easy running in your training.

Metabolic Efficiency 101 and Easy Running

Metabolic efficiency (ME) is a popular buzzword, but what does it really mean? It is basically the body's ability to utilize its storage of fat and carbohydrate at the proper times. As it relates to our purposes, ME is an important measure of how well we burn fat and save carbohydrate at higher and higher intensities. In brief, the more metabolically efficient you are, the more fat you can utilize across the spectrum of paces.

Poor metabolic efficiency results in the body processing carbohydrate in higher amounts at lower intensities. This is the opposite of what we want for optimal marathon performance. Poor ME will ultimately limit our ability for prolonged running at even moderate paces because carbohydrate stores are depleted much more quickly than fat.

Figure 3.3 shows the metabolic efficiency of two very different athletes, with data taken during their VO_2max tests. The figure showcases the relationship between poor ME and the onset of early fatigue. With

CONTINUES

Continued

Runner A, we see a textbook example of what good fueling looks like. Early on, during light intensity, he is burning primarily fat. As intensity increases, his reliance on carbohydrates increases. By the end of the test, he is running at VO_2max effort and using almost all carbohydrate as his fuel source. Runner B illustrates a very different scenario. He is not as well trained and works out sporadically. The result of that lack of aerobic training is significant because we see that right away, at the lightest intensity, he is already relying on carbohydrate as a significant fuel source. As he approaches and surpasses marathon pace and moves into greater intensities, that number only increases. In sum, Runner A is preserving carbohydrate, while Runner B is burning through them at a high rate, even at marathon pace. The result for Runner B is that he will need to take in exorbitant amounts of carbohydrate to supplement what is being lost, or be forced to slow down from his goal pace.

How do easy runs fit into this?

Studies show that easy runs help runners develop ME. One study looked at the rate of fatty acid mobilization and fat usage as exercise intensity increased. The study showed the usage of fat versus carbohydrate after 12 weeks of endurance training. At 64 percent VO_2max, the subjects increased their fat usage from 60 percent to 65 percent of the fuel contribution. This may not seem like a huge increase, but think of it like this. Say you burn 100 calories per mile, and 40 calories of those come from carbohydrate stores. With improved ME, you burn 35 calories per mile worth of carbs. That's a difference of 5 calories, which over 26.2 miles, is about 132 calories of glycogen saved. Divide that by 35 calories and you get 3.79. That's almost 4 more miles that you could run without taking any extra calories in through gels, sports drink, or other supplements.

Looking at ME and this study shows us that 12 weeks of endurance training at intensities of 65–85 percent of your VO_2max promotes big increases in the ability to use fat as a fuel source. It just so happens that 65 percent is right around the effort that your easy runs will be at.

Easy runs are junk miles? Far from it.

FIGURE 3.3 METABOLIC EFFICIENCY OF TWO ATHLETES

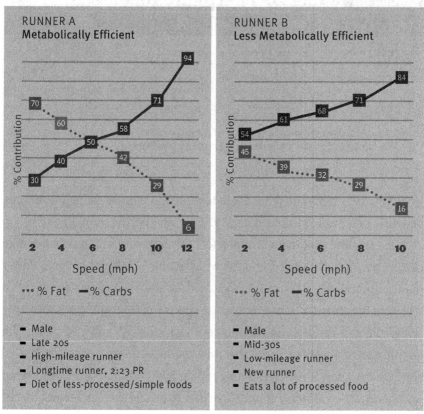

RUNNER A
Metabolically Efficient

RUNNER B
Less Metabolically Efficient

% Contribution / Speed (mph)

••• % Fat   — % Carbs

- Male
- Late 20s
- High-mileage runner
- Longtime runner, 2:23 PR
- Diet of less-processed/simple foods

- Male
- Mid-30s
- Low-mileage runner
- New runner
- Eats a lot of processed food

EASY RUNNING GUIDELINES

An easy run is usually defined as a run that lasts anywhere between 20 minutes and 2.5 hours at an intensity of 55–75 percent of VO_2max. Since most of us don't have the means to get VO_2max tested, the next best thing is to look at pace per mile. The Hansons Marathon Method calls for easy runs to be paced 1–2 minutes slower than goal marathon pace. For example, if your goal marathon pace is 8:00 minutes per mile, then your easy pace should be 9:00–10:00 minutes per mile. While easy running is a necessary part of marathon training, be sure not to run too easy. If your pace is excessively

TABLE 3.1 HOW EASY RUNS FIT INTO THE BIG PICTURE

SUN	MON*	TUES	WED
Long 10 miles	Easy 6 miles	Speed	OFF
Long 10 miles	Easy 5 miles	Speed	OFF
Long 15 miles	Easy 7 miles	Speed	OFF

*Monday and Friday pacing should be treated carefully and sensibly.
**Saturday is a day to consider the faster end of your easy pace range.

slow, you are simply breaking down tendon and bone without any aerobic benefits. Refer to Table 3.5 on page 92 for your specific guidelines.

Keep in mind that there is a time for "fast" easy runs (1 minute per mile slower than marathon pace) and "slow" easy runs (2 minutes per mile slower than marathon pace). Warm-ups and cooldowns are two instances when you will want to run on the slower end of the spectrum. Here the idea is to simply bridge the gap between no running and fast running, and vice versa. The day after an SOS workout is another time you may choose a pace on the slow side. For instance, if you have a long run on Sunday and a strength workout on Tuesday, then Monday should be easier to ensure you are recovered and ready to run a good workout on Tuesday. By running the easy runs closer to 2:00 minutes per mile slower than marathon pace, beginning runners will safely make the transition to higher mileage. More advanced runners will likely find that they can handle the faster side of the easy range, even after SOS workouts. The day following a tempo run and the second easy day prior to a long run both provide good chances to run closer to 1 minute per mile slower than marathon race pace.

Whether you are a novice or an experienced runner looking for a new approach, stick to the plan when it comes to easy running. In fact, have fun with the easy days, allowing yourself to take in the scenery or enjoy a social run with friends. Meanwhile, you'll be simultaneously racking up a laundry

THURS	FRI*	SAT**	WEEKLY TOTAL
Tempo 5 miles	Easy 5 miles	Easy 6 miles	43 mi.
Tempo 8 miles	Easy 6 miles	Easy 5 miles	45 mi.
Tempo 8 miles	Easy 5 miles	Easy 8 miles	54 mi.

list of physiological benefits. What's more, after a nice, relaxed run, your body will be clamoring for a challenge, ready to tackle the next SOS workout.

Table 3.1 gives you an idea of how easy runs fit into the overall schedule. This snapshot is taken from weeks 7–9 of the Beginner Program. You'll notice a variety of things going on throughout each week. On Mondays, you see distances ranging from 5 to 7 miles, followed the next day by a speed session and in front of a longer run on Sunday. Also, look at the easy days that land on Fridays, following the tempo runs on Thursdays. This is where overtraining can occur, because those easy runs are sandwiched between SOS workouts. It is common for this to happen during the first part of the training plans when runners are still feeling pretty fresh, causing them to run faster than prescribed. Remember, these are not the days to worry about how fast you are running; time on your feet is the focus, not pace.

For the Saturday easy run, you can be a little more flexible with pace. If you feel good, run on the faster end of your easy running spectrum. The metabolic adaptations will happen throughout the pace range, but injury can occur if you make a habit of always running faster, so be sure to moderate your pace. The above sample also shows that you get to a point where it is not logical to keep adding workouts to your training week, and if progression is to take place, then it must come from either adding another easy day (Wednesday) and/or adding mileage to the easy days, not from simply running harder. You will notice in the

Hansons Marathon Method training schedules that once the workouts peak in mileage, the easy days are what adds to the weekly mileage.

SOS Workouts

THE LONG RUN

The long run garners more attention than any other component of marathon training. It has become a status symbol among runners in training, a measure by which one compares oneself against one's running counterparts. It is surprising, then, to discover that much of the existing advice on running long is misguided. After relatively low-mileage weeks, some training plans suggest backbreaking long runs that are more akin to running misadventures than productive training. A 20-mile long run at the end of a three-day-a-week running program can be both demoralizing and physically injurious. The long run has become a big question mark, something you aren't sure you'll survive, but you subject yourself to the suffering nonetheless. Despite plenty of anecdotal and academic evidence against such training tactics, advice to reach (or go beyond) the 20-mile long run has persisted. It has become the magic number for marathoners, without consideration for individual differences in abilities and goals. While countless marathoners have made it to the finish line using these programs, the Hansons Marathon Method comes to the table with a different approach (Figure 3.4). Not only will it make training more enjoyable, it will also help you cover 26.2 more efficiently.

While our long-run approach may sound radical, it is deeply rooted in results from inside the lab and outside on the roads. As I read through the exercise-science literature, coached the elite squad with Kevin and Keith, and tested theories in my own training, I realized that revisions to long-held beliefs about marathon training, and in particular long runs, were necessary. As a result, a 16-mile long run is the longest training day for the standard Hansons program. But there's a hitch: One of Kevin and Keith's favorite sayings about the long run is, "It's not like running the first 16 miles of the marathon, but the last 16 miles!"

FIGURE 3.4 LONG-RUN BENEFITS

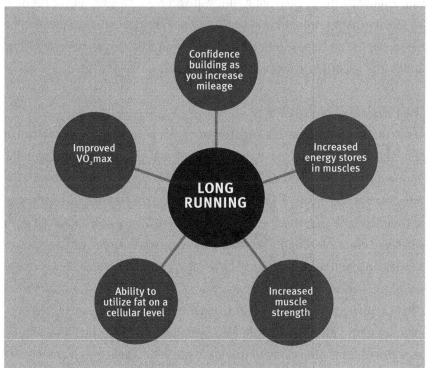

What they mean is that a training plan should simulate the cumulative fatigue that is experienced during a marathon, without completely zapping your legs. Rather than spending the entire week recovering from the previous long run, you should be building a base for the forthcoming long effort.

Take a look at a week in the Advanced Program, which includes a 16-mile Sunday long run (see Table 4.4, page 120). Leading up to it, you are to do a tempo run on Thursday and easier short runs on Friday and Saturday. We don't give you a day completely off before a long run because recovery occurs on the easy running days. Since no single workout has totally diminished your energy stores and left your legs feeling wrecked, you'll feel the effects of fatigue accumulating over time. The plan allows for partial recovery, but it is designed to keep you from feeling completely fresh going into a long run. Following the Sunday long run, you will have an easy day of running on Monday and a strength workout Tuesday. This may initially appear to be too much, but because your long run's pace and mileage are tailored to your ability and experience, less recovery is necessary.

The Physiology of Long Runs

Long runs bring with them a laundry list of psychological and physiological benefits, many of which correlate with the profits of easy running. Mentally, long runs help you gradually build confidence as you increase your mileage from one week to the next. They help you develop the coping skills necessary to complete any endurance event. They also teach you how to persist even when you are not feeling 100 percent. Since you never know what is going to happen on marathon day, this can be a real asset. Most notable, however, are the physiological adaptations that occur as a result of long runs. Improved VO_2max, increased capillary growth, and a stronger heart are among the benefits. Long runs also help to train your body to utilize fat as fuel on a cellular level. By training your body to run long, you let it adapt and learn to store more glycogen, thereby allowing it to go farther before becoming exhausted.

In addition to improving the energy stores in your muscles, long runs also increase muscle strength. Although your body first exploits the slow-twitch muscle fibers during a long run, it eventually begins to recruit the fast-twitch fibers as the slow-twitch fibers fatigue. The only way to train those fast-twitch fibers is to run long enough to tire the slow-twitch fibers first. By strengthening all of the fibers, you'll avoid bonking on race day. By now the majority of these adaptations are probably starting to sound familiar. You can expect many of the same benefits reaped from easier work from long runs too.

Long-Run Guidelines

Advice from renowned running researcher and coach Dr. Jack Daniels provides a basis for our long-run philosophy. He instructs runners never to exceed 25–30 percent of their weekly mileage in a long run, whether they are training for a 5K or a marathon. He adds that a 2:30–3:00-hour time limit should be enforced, suggesting that exceeding those guidelines offers no physiological benefit and may lead to overtraining, injuries, and burnout.

Dr. Dave Martin, running researcher at Georgia State University and a consultant to Team USA, goes one step further, recommending that long runs be between 90 minutes and 2 hours long. While he proposes 18–25-mile long runs for high-level marathoners, one must take into consideration that a runner of this caliber can finish a 25-mile run in under 3:00 hours. This highlights the importance of accounting for a runner's long-run pace. Dr. Joe Vigil, a Team USA coach and scientist, further supports this notion, advising that long runs be increased gradually until the athlete hits 2:00–3:00 hours. Certainly a 25-mile run completed in less than 3:00 hours by an elite runner will provide different physiological adaptations than a 25-mile run that takes a less experienced runner 3:30 hours or more.

According to legendary South African researcher and author, Dr. Tim Noakes, a continual, easy-to-moderate run at 70–85 percent VO_2max that is sustained for 2:00 hours or more will lead to the greatest glycogen depletion. Exercise physiologist Dr. David Costill has also noted that a 2:00-hour bout of running reduces muscle glycogen by as much as 50 percent. While this rate of glycogen depletion is acceptable on race day, it is counterproductive in the middle of a training cycle, as it takes as many as 72 hours to bounce back. When you diminish those energy stores, you can end up benched by fatigue, missing out on important training, or training on tired legs and potentially hurting yourself. Instead of risking diminishing returns and prescribing an arbitrary 20-mile run, the Hansons Marathon Method looks at percentage of mileage and total time spent running. While 16 miles is often the suggested maximum run, we are more concerned with determining your long run based on your weekly total mileage and your pace for that long run. It may sound unconventional, but you'll find that nothing we suggest is random; it is all firmly based in science with proven results.

Long-Run Mileage: Training to Adapt or Training to Survive?

Recreational marathoners are often told to do 20-plus-mile long runs as a way to prepare themselves mentally. And while I understand that argument, I doubt that it's worth the possible consequences. In 1985, researchers studied 40 trained males who had just completed a marathon. All had muscular damage in their legs, which was not surprising. What was surprising, however, was the damage to mitochondria and capillaries. After a week, glycogen levels were back to normal, but the damage remained. After eight weeks, there was still evidence of damage. If you are doing several 20-mile runs in preparation, then you are likely doing similar damage to your legs. Mitochondria and capillaries are crucial for performance. If we continually do damage to these components, then are we boosting adaptations or are we simply taking away what we spent the past months building? If we continually take away from this supply, then we end up merely surviving from long run to long run, not to mention greatly increasing our chance for injury. By backing down a little, we get the physiological benefits, and we are training to adapt, not just to survive.

As stipulated by Dr. Noakes, it is widely accepted among coaches that long runs shouldn't exceed 25–30 percent of weekly mileage. Even so, that guideline manages to get lost in many marathon-training programs in the effort to cram in mileage. For instance, a beginning program that peaks at 40–50 miles per week and recommends a 20-mile long run is violating the cardinal rule. Although the epic journey is usually sandwiched between an easy day and a rest day, there is no getting around the fact that it accounts for around 50 percent of the runner's weekly mileage. Looking at Table 3.2, you can see how far your long run should be based on your total mileage for the week.

TABLE 3.2 LONG RUN BASED ON TRAINING VOLUME

	25% OF VOLUME	30% OF VOLUME
40 miles/week	10 miles	12 miles
50 miles/week	12.5 miles	15 miles
60 miles/week	15 miles	18 miles
70 miles/week	17.5 miles	21 miles

The numbers illustrate that marathon training is a significant undertaking and should not be approached with randomness or bravado. They also make apparent the fact that many training programs miss the mark on the long run. If you are a beginning or low-mileage runner, your long runs must be adjusted accordingly. What is right for an 80-mile-a-week runner is not right for one who puts in 40 miles a week.

In addition to running the optimal number of miles on each long run, you must also adhere to a certain pace to get the most benefit. Since we don't all cover the same distance in the same amount of time, it makes sense to adjust a long run depending on how fast you'll be traveling. The research tells us that 2:00–3:00 hours is the optimal window for development in terms of long runs. Beyond that, muscle breakdown begins to occur. Look at Table 3.3 to see how long it takes to complete the 16- and 20-mile distances based on pace.

The table demonstrates that a runner covering 16 miles at a 7:00-minute pace will finish in just under 2:00 hours, while a runner traveling at an 11:00-minute pace will take nearly 3:00 hours to finish that same distance. It then becomes clear that anyone planning on running slower than a 9:00-minute pace should avoid the 20-mile trek. This is where the number 16 comes into play. Based on the mileage from the Hansons marathon programs, the 16-mile long run fits the bill on both percentage of weekly mileage and long-run total time.

TABLE 3.3 LONG RUN DURATIONS BASED ON PACE

	16 MILES	20 MILES
7:00/mi.	1 hr. 52 mins.	2 hrs. 20 mins.
8:00/mi.	2 hrs. 8 mins.	2 hrs. 40 mins.
9:00/mi.	2 hrs. 24 mins.	3 hrs.
10:00/mi.	2 hrs. 40 mins.	3 hrs. 20 mins.
11:00/mi.	2 hrs. 56 mins.	3 hrs. 40 mins.
12:00/mi.	3 hrs. 12 mins.	4 hrs.

ASK THE COACH

At what pace should I do my long run?

We generally coach runners to hold an easy-to-moderate pace throughout a long run. Instead of viewing your long run as a high-volume easy day, think of it as a long workout. If you are new to marathoning, err on the easy side of pacing as you become accustomed to the longer distances. More advanced runners should maintain a moderate pace as their muscles have adapted to the stress of such feats of endurance. Refer to the pace chart (pages 92–93) for exact paces. In the long run (literally and figuratively), when you avoid overdoing these lengthy workouts, you reap more benefits and avoid the potential downfalls of overtraining.

SPEED WORKOUTS

With speed workouts, marathon training begins to get more interesting. When we refer to speed training, we are talking about interval sessions, also called repeat workouts. Speed workouts require you to run multiple bouts of certain distances at high intensities with recovery between each. Not only does this type of training play a role in prompting some of the important physiological changes we already discussed, it also teaches your mind to handle harder work. While easy days are typically low pressure, speed workouts require you to put your game face on and come ready to push hard. Discipline is one of many benefits (see Figure 3.5). While you may be able to complete an easy run the morning following a late night out on the town, if you want to get the most out of your speed work you're going to need to eat a hearty dinner and hit the hay at a decent hour. Whatever you give up to execute these workouts, optimally, the training will give back to you tenfold. Every speed workout you complete is like money in the bank when it comes to resources on which you can draw during the most difficult moments of the marathon.

Some marathoners have done little or no speed workouts in the form of repeats or intervals. If you are new to marathoning and your past speed workouts have consisted of simply running some days slightly faster than others, you are in the majority. Luckily, the speed workouts in our plans provide an introductory course on how to implement harder workouts, no matter what distance for which you are training. As you learn how to properly implement speed workouts, your training will be transformed from a somewhat aimless approach to fitness to a guided plan of attack. Speed workouts can also help you predict what you are capable of in the marathon. By implementing speed work, you can successfully race a shorter race, such as a 5K or 10K, and then plug that time into a race equivalency chart to determine your potential marathon time. (See Table 6.1, page 146.) Additionally, this can help to highlight weak areas so you can address them early on.

Surprisingly, advanced runners sometimes make the same mistakes that novices do in terms of speed training; namely, they neglect it. For instance, we have had runners come to us feeling stale after running two to three marathons in a year. Along with a flat workout tends to come stagnated finishing times. Digging into these runners' histories, we often find that they are running so many marathons that they have completely forgone speed training, spending all their time on long runs, tempo runs, and recovery. That's where we set

FIGURE 3.5 SPEED WORK BENEFITS

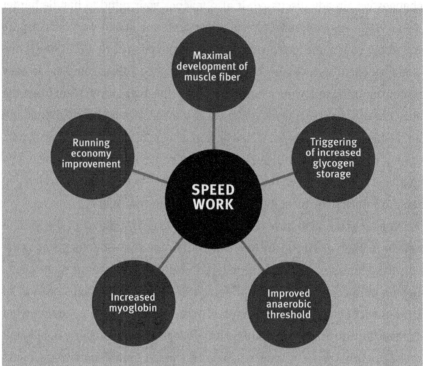

them straight by guiding them through the Hansons Marathon Method. As with the other types of workouts, speed training is an important part of constantly keeping your system on its toes, requiring it to adapt to changing workouts that vary in intensity and distance.

Physiology of Speed Workouts

The greatest beneficiaries of speed training are the working muscles. With speed sessions, not only do the slow-twitch fibers become maximally activated to provide aerobic energy, so too do the intermediate fibers. This forces the slow-twitch fibers to maximize their aerobic capacities, but when they fatigue, it also trains the intermediate fibers to step in. As a result of better muscle coordination, running economy also improves. Stimulated by everything from speed workouts to easy running, running economy is all about how efficiently your body utilizes oxygen at a certain pace. Remember, running economy is a better predictor of race performance than VO_2max, so improvements can have a great influence on marathon performance.

Another adaptation that occurs through speed work is the increased production of myoglobin. In fact, research tells us that the best way to develop myoglobin is through higher intensity running (above 80 percent VO_2max). Similar to the way hemoglobin carries oxygen to the blood, myoglobin helps transport oxygen to the muscles and then to the mitochondria. With its help, the increased demand for oxygen is met to match capillary delivery and the needs of the mitochondria.

Exercise at higher intensities can also increase anaerobic threshold. In short, the speed intervals provide a two-for-one ticket by developing the anaerobic threshold and VO_2max during the same workout. Finally, since speed sessions include high-intensity running near 100 percent VO_2max (but not over), glycogen stores are rapidly depleted. In fact, during these workouts glycogen is providing upward of 90 percent of the energy. This, in turn, forces the muscles to adapt and store more glycogen to be used later in workouts.

Speed Guidelines

You'll notice that the speed segments of our training plans are located toward the beginning of the training block, while later portions are devoted to more marathon-specific workouts. When you consider our contentions about building fitness from the bottom up, this may seem counterintuitive. However, if speed workouts are executed at the right speeds, it makes sense to include them closer to the beginning of your training cycle. As in other workouts, correct pacing is essential. When many coaches discuss speed training, they are referring to work that is done at 100 percent VO_2max. In reality, when you run at 100 percent VO_2max pace, it can only be maintained for 3–8 minutes. If you are a beginner, 3 minutes is likely more realistic, while an elite miler may be able to continue for close to 8 minutes. Running your

ASK THE COACH

Why is speed positioned early in the program?

Your most race-specific work should be done close to the race. For that reason, if you are preparing for a 5K, then yes, speed should be closer to your race. But in the case of marathon preparation, there is little purpose in doing fast repeats on a track to prepare for the feeling of being at 22 miles with more than 4 to go.

Also, putting speed work early in the program allows a runner to do some shorter races before transitioning into full-blown marathon-training mode. The speed is relative to the distance being raced. I typically prescribe 10K pace, which would be slower than in a traditional 5K or 10K training schedule. That said, at this pace, it is not as strenuous as speed work would be for an all-out assault on a 5K PR.

speed workouts at or above 100 percent VO_2max causes the structural muscles to begin to break down and forces your system to rely largely on anaerobic sources. Not only does this overstress the anaerobic system, it doesn't allow for the positive aerobic adaptations you need to run a good marathon. Our marathon programs base speed work on 5K and 10K goal times and these races both last much longer than 3–8 minutes. Rather than being at 100 percent VO_2max, you're probably between 80 and 95 percent VO_2max when running these distances. At these intensities, you aren't running fast enough to create an onset of severe acidosis (a condition when the muscles have a low pH brought on by high levels of blood lactate). Unlike other plans, we instruct you to complete speed workouts at slightly less than 100 percent VO_2max pace to spur maximum physiological adaptations. If you go faster, gains are nullified and injuries probable.

In addition to pace, duration of the speed intervals is important. Optimal duration lies between 2 and 8 minutes. If the duration is too short, the amount of time spent at optimal intensity is minimized and precious workout

ASK THE COACH

Should I adjust my speed workouts to stay within the optimal 2–8-minute range?

Probably not. For those using the Beginner Program, the repeats from 400 meters to 1 kilometer should not present an issue. The line becomes blurred for the 1200-meter and 1600-meter repeats. Here you may be conflating a speed workout with a strength workout. However, that's OK because it will help you transition from the speed workouts and the upcoming strength workouts. If, on the other hand, you are using the Advanced Program, then time will likely not be an issue because you'll probably be running the workouts under that 8-minute-per-repeat ceiling.

time wasted. However, if the duration is too long, lactic acid builds up and you are too tired to complete the workout at the desired pace. As a result, the duration of speed intervals should be adjusted to your ability and experience levels. For example, a 400-meter repeat workout, with each interval lasting around 2 minutes, may be the perfect fit for a beginner. Conversely, the same workout may take an advanced runner 25 percent less time to complete each 400-meter repeat, therefore resulting in fewer benefits.

Recovery is another important part of speed sessions, allowing you the rest you need to complete another interval. Guidelines for recovery generally state that rest should be between 50 and 100 percent of the repeat duration time. For instance, if the repeat is 2 minutes in duration, the recovery should be between 1 and 2 minutes. However, we tend to give beginners longer recovery time at the beginning of the speed sessions to sustain them through the entire workout. With further training, recovery time is shortened as an athlete is able to handle more work. When it comes to recovery, Kevin and Keith always say: "If you are too tired to jog the recovery interval, then you're running too hard!" It's a good rule of thumb. The session is designed to focus on accumulating time within the desired intensity range. If you run your repeats so hard that you aren't able to jog during your recovery time, you are unlikely to be able to run the next interval at the desired pace. In the end, these speed sessions should total 3 miles of running at that faster intensity, in addition to the warm-up, cooldown, and recovery periods. If you can't get through the intervals to hit 3 miles total, you're running too hard for your abilities and thereby missing out on developing the specific adaptations discussed.

The speed sessions that are utilized throughout the Hansons Marathon Method are provided in tables below. Typically, the schedules start with the lower-duration repeats (10–12 × 400 meters) and work up to the longer-duration repeats (4 × 1200 meters and 3 × 1600 meters). Once the top of the ladder is reached (from the shortest- to the longest-duration workouts) you are then free to do the workouts that fit best for your optimal development.

If you're new to speed work, we strongly encourage you to join a local running group. Coaches and more experienced runners can take the guesswork and intimidation out of those first speed workouts by showing you the ropes. Additionally, a local track will be your best friend during this phase, as it is marked, consistent, and flat.

Below is an outline of how speed workouts build on one other in the Advanced Program (the Beginner Program is similar but has fewer speed sessions, and the Just Finish Program does not have speed workouts). To determine the correct pace for your speed workout, use the pace charts that follow. Find your goal pace for 5K or 10K and run the designated interval as close to that pace as possible. Remember: Each session should include a 1.5–3-mile warm-up and cooldown.

Week 1: 400s
Week 2: 600s
Week 3: 800s

Week 4: 1 kilometer

Week 5: 1200s

Week 6: Ladder

Week 7: 1600s

Week 8/9: Repeats sessions of 800–1600 meters.

Decoding Speed Workouts

2-mile WU
6 × 800 m @ 5K pace with 400-m jog recovery
2-mile CD

Veterans of the sport and those who ran high school or college track might understand this workout immediately. For those who have never done interval workouts, it may appear to be a foreign language. Let's break it down:

2-mile WU: 2 continuous miles of easy running to warm up the body and prepare it for the hard workout.

6 × 800 m @ 5K pace with 400-m jog recovery: You will run 800 m (roughly a half mile) at your 5K goal pace, then, without stopping or walking, run 400 m (roughly a quarter mile) at an easy recovery jog. After the recovery jog, you'll run another 800 m at 5K pace, followed by another 400-m jog recovery. Repeat until you've run six 800-m segments at 5K pace.

2-mile CD: 2 continuous miles of easy running to cool down and shake out the legs after the hard workout.

Note: Warm up/cool down 1.5–3 miles each.

SPEED WORKOUTS

400s

12 × 400 m with 400-m jog recovery

All sessions should include a warm-up and cooldown (1.5–3 mi. each).

5K GOAL	10K GOAL	400 PACE
15:30	32:30	1:15
16:00	33:35	1:18
16:30	34:40	1:20
17:00	35:45	1:23
17:30	36:50	1:25
18:00	37:55	1:28
18:30	39:00	1:30
19:00	40:05	1:33
19:30	41:10	1:35
20:00	42:15	1:38
20:30	43:20	1:40
21:00	44:25	1:43
21:30	45:30	1:45
22:00	46:35	1:48
22:30	47:40	1:50
23:00	48:45	1:53
23:30	49:50	1:55
24:00	50:55	1:58
24:30	52:00	2:01
25:00	53:05	2:03
25:30	54:10	2:06
26:00	55:15	2:08
27:00	57:25	2:13
28:00	59:45	2:18
29:00	62:05	2:23
30:00	64:25	2:28

SPEED

SPEED WORKOUTS

600s

8 × 600 m with 400-m jog recovery

All sessions should include a warm-up and cooldown (1.5–3 mi. each).

5K GOAL	10K GOAL	600 PACE
15:30	32:30	1:52
16:00	33:35	1:55
16:30	34:40	1:59
17:00	35:45	2:03
17:30	36:50	2:06
18:00	37:55	2:10
18:30	39:00	2:14
19:00	40:05	2:18
19:30	41:10	2:21
20:00	42:15	2:25
20:30	43:20	2:29
21:00	44:25	2:33
21:30	45:30	2:36
22:00	46:35	2:40
22:30	47:40	2:44
23:00	48:45	2:48
23:30	49:50	2:51
24:00	50:55	2:55
24:30	52:00	2:59
25:00	53:05	3:03
25:30	54:10	3:06
26:00	55:15	3:10
27:00	57:25	3:17
28:00	59:45	3:23
29:00	62:05	3:30
30:00	64:25	3:36

SPEED

SPEED WORKOUTS

800s

6 × 800 m with 400-m jog recovery

All sessions should include a warm-up and cooldown (1.5–3 mi. each).

5K GOAL	10K GOAL	800 PACE
15:30	32:30	2:30
16:00	33:35	2:35
16:30	34:40	2:40
17:00	35:45	2:45
17:30	36:50	2:50
18:00	37:55	2:55
18:30	39:00	3:00
19:00	40:05	3:05
19:30	41:10	3:10
20:00	42:15	3:15
20:30	43:20	3:20
21:00	44:25	3:25
21:30	45:30	3:30
22:00	46:35	3:35
22:30	47:40	3:40
23:00	48:45	3:45
23:30	49:50	3:50
24:00	50:55	3:55
24:30	52:00	4:00
25:00	53:05	4:05
25:30	54:10	4:10
26:00	55:15	4:15
27:00	57:25	4:25
28:00	59:45	4:35
29:00	62:05	4:45
30:00	64:25	4:55

SPEED

SPEED WORKOUTS

1 kilometer

6 × 1 km with 400-m jog recovery

All sessions should include a warm-up and cooldown (1.5–3 mi. each).

5K GOAL	10K GOAL	1K PACE
15:30	32:30	3:06
16:00	33:35	3:12
16:30	34:40	3:18
17:00	35:45	3:24
17:30	36:50	3:30
18:00	37:55	3:36
18:30	39:00	3:42
19:00	40:05	3:48
19:30	41:10	3:54
20:00	42:15	4:00
20:30	43:20	4:06
21:00	44:25	4:12
21:30	45:30	4:18
22:00	46:35	4:24
22:30	47:40	4:30
23:00	48:45	4:36
23:30	49:50	4:42
24:00	50:55	4:48
24:30	52:00	4:54
25:00	53:05	5:00
25:30	54:10	5:06
26:00	55:15	5:12
27:00	57:25	5:24
28:00	59:45	5:36
29:00	62:05	5:48
30:00	64:25	6:00

SPEED

SPEED

SPEED WORKOUTS

1200s

4 × 1200 m with 400-m jog recovery

All sessions should include a warm-up and cooldown (1.5–3 mi. each).

5K GOAL	10K GOAL	1200 PACE
15:30	32:30	3:42
16:00	33:35	3:50
16:30	34:40	3:57
17:00	35:45	4:05
17:30	36:50	4:12
18:00	37:55	4:20
18:30	39:00	4:27
19:00	40:05	4:35
19:30	41:10	4:42
20:00	42:15	4:50
20:30	43:20	4:57
21:00	44:25	5:05
21:30	45:30	5:12
22:00	46:35	5:20
22:30	47:40	5:27
23:00	48:45	5:35
23:30	49:50	5:42
24:00	50:55	5:50
24:30	52:00	5:57
25:00	53:05	6:05
25:30	54:10	6:12
26:00	55:15	6:20
27:00	57:25	6:36
28:00	59:45	6:51
29:00	62:05	7:07
30:00	64:25	7:23

SPEED WORKOUTS

Training Ladder

400-800-1200-1600-
1200-800-400 with
400-m jog recovery

All sessions should include
a warm-up and cooldown
(1.5–3 mi. each).

SPEED

5K GOAL	10K GOAL	400 PACE	800 PACE	1200 PACE	1600 PACE
15:30	32:30	1:15	2:30	3:42	5:00
16:00	33:35	1:18	2:35	3:50	5:10
16:30	34:40	1:20	2:40	3:57	5:20
17:00	35:45	1:23	2:45	4:05	5:30
17:30	36:50	1:25	2:50	4:12	5:40
18:00	37:55	1:28	2:54	4:20	5:50
18:30	39:00	1:30	2:59	4:27	6:00
19:00	40:05	1:33	3:04	4:35	6:10
19:30	41:10	1:35	3:09	4:42	6:20
20:00	42:15	1:38	3:14	4:50	6:30
20:30	43:20	1:40	3:19	4:57	6:40
21:00	44:25	1:43	3:24	5:05	6:50
21:30	45:30	1:45	3:29	5:12	7:00
22:00	46:35	1:48	3:34	5:20	7:10
22:30	47:40	1:50	3:39	5:27	7:20
23:00	48:45	1:53	3:44	5:35	7:30
23:30	49:50	1:55	3:49	5:42	7:40
24:00	50:55	1:58	3:54	5:50	7:50
24:30	52:00	2:01	3:59	5:57	8:00
25:00	53:05	2:03	4:04	6:05	8:10
25:30	54:10	2:06	4:09	6:12	8:20
26:00	55:15	2:08	4:14	6:20	8:30
27:00	57:25	2:13	4:25	6:36	8:50
28:00	59:45	2:18	4:35	6:51	9:10
29:00	62:05	2:23	4:45	7:07	9:30
30:00	64:25	2:28	4:55	7:23	9:50

SPEED

SPEED WORKOUTS

1600s

3 × 1600 m with 600-m jog recovery

All sessions should include a warm-up and cooldown (1.5–3 mi. each).

5K GOAL	10K GOAL	1600 PACE
15:30	32:30	5:00
16:00	33:35	5:10
16:30	34:40	5:20
17:00	35:45	5:30
17:30	36:50	5:40
18:00	37:55	5:50
18:30	39:00	6:00
19:00	40:05	6:10
19:30	41:10	6:20
20:00	42:15	6:30
20:30	43:20	6:40
21:00	44:25	6:50
21:30	45:30	7:00
22:00	46:35	7:10
22:30	47:40	7:20
23:00	48:45	7:30
23:30	49:50	7:40
24:00	50:55	7:50
24:30	52:00	8:00
25:00	53:05	8:10
25:30	54:10	8:20
26:00	55:15	8:30
27:00	57:25	8:50
28:00	59:45	9:10
29:00	62:05	9:30
30:00	64:25	9:50

STRENGTH WORKOUTS

After you've spent a number of weeks performing periodic speed sessions, your muscle fibers and physiological systems have adapted quite well and are now ready for more marathon-specific adaptations. When strength workouts are added to the schedule, the goal of training shifts from improving the VO_2max (along with anaerobic threshold) to maintaining the VO_2max and preparing the body to handle the fatigue associated with marathon running (Figure 3.6). You'll notice that at the same time the strength segment begins, the tempo runs and the long runs become more significant. At this point, everything the runner is doing is solely focused on marathon preparation.

When we talk about strength workouts, we aren't referring to intense sessions in the weight room, pumping iron and flexing muscles. Strength workouts are runs that emphasize intensity, rather than volume, with the goal of stressing the aerobic system at a high level. While the speed sessions are designed to be short enough to avoid lactate accumulation, the strength sessions are meant to force the runner to adapt to running longer distances with moderate amounts of lactate accumulation.

The Physiology of Strength Workouts

Over time, strength sessions improve anaerobic capacities, which will allow your body to tolerate higher levels of lactic acid and produce less of it at higher intensities. While your body may have shut down in response to the lactic acid buildup at the beginning of training, strength sessions help your muscles learn to work through the discomfort of lactic acid accumulation. Additionally, strength sessions help train your exercising muscles to get better at removing lactic acid, as well as contributing to improving your running economy and allowing you to use less oxygen at the same effort. Strength workouts also spur development of something called fractional utilization of maximal capacity. In practical terms, this allows a person to run at a higher pace for a longer period of time, which leads to an increase in anaerobic threshold. For the marathon, this means

FIGURE 3.6 STRENGTH WORKOUT BENEFITS

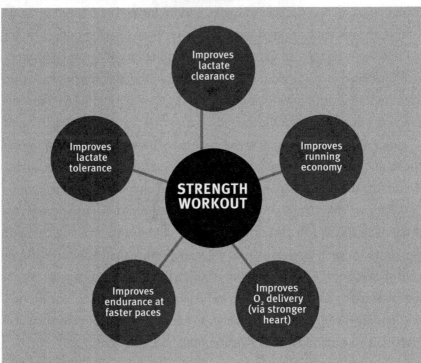

that glycogen will be conserved, optimal marathon pace held longer, and fatigue delayed.

These adaptations all begin with an increase in the heart's ventricle chamber size. During a strength workout, the heart is required to pump faster and with more force than during easier runs. While it is not being worked quite as hard as during a speed session, it works at a fairly high intensity for significantly longer. The end result is a stronger heart muscle with a larger chamber area, which means an increased stroke volume. (The stroke volume is the amount of blood pumped from the left ventricle per beat.) The benefit of this is that more blood is sent to the exercising muscles, and more oxygen is delivered. In addition, strength workouts help to involve the intermediate muscle fibers, increasing their oxidative capacities. Within the muscles, less lactate ends up being produced at faster speeds, and the lactate that is produced is recycled back into usable fuel. The practical purpose of all this is that running faster paces, especially near anaerobic threshold, begins to feel easier, you become more economical, and your stamina increases.

Strength Guidelines

For most runners, the strength repeats will fall somewhere between 60 and 80 percent of VO_2max, which will be slower than the speed sessions. However, while the speed sessions are relatively short (3×1600 m) with moderate recovery, the strength sessions are double the volume (e.g., 6 miles of higher-intensity running) with much shorter relative recovery. Strength workouts are designed to be run 10 seconds per mile faster than goal marathon pace. If your goal marathon pace is 8:00 minutes per mile, then your strength pace will be 7:50 per mile. The faster the runner, the closer this corresponds to half-marathon pace, but for the novice, this pace is between goal marathon pace and half-marathon ability. Although this may not seem like a big increase in pace, take a look at overall marathon times and you'll see that it makes a significant difference. For example, if your goal pace is 8:00 minutes per mile, you will finish around 3:30. However, if you run 7:50 per mile, just 10 seconds faster per mile, you will finish in 3:25. This faster overall time brings along with it a large increase in lactic acid. Even though the strength workout may not feel hard from an intensity standpoint, the volume, coupled with short recovery periods, is enough to stimulate lactic acid accumulation and make way for positive adaptations. Refer to Table 3.4 for a quick guide to strength sessions.

TABLE 3.4 STRENGTH SESSION QUICK GUIDE	
Strength pace	10 sec./mi. faster than marathon goal pace
Strength recovery	Short relative to repeat duration
Repeat volume	1–3 mi. per repeat
Total strength volume	6 mi. at strength pace

STRENGTH WORKOUTS

6 × 1 mile

6 × 1 mile @ 10 seconds faster than race pace with ¼-mile jog recovery

All sessions should include a warm-up and cooldown (1.5–3 mi. each).

MARATHON GOAL	HALF-MARATHON GOAL	MILE PACE
2:28	1:14:00	5:30
2:33	1:16:30	5:40
2:38	2:17:00	5:50
2:42	1:21:00	6:00
2:46	1:23:00	6:10
2:50	1:25:00	6:20
2:55	1:27:30	6:30
2:59	1:29:30	6:40
3:03	1:31:30	6:50
3:08	1:34:00	7:00
3:12	1:36:00	7:10
3:17	1:38:30	7:20
3:21	1:40:30	7:30
3:25	1:42:30	7:40
3:30	1:45:00	7:50
3:34	1:47:30	8:00
3:38	1:49:00	8:10
3:43	1:51:30	8:20
3:47	1:53:30	8:30
3:51	1:55:30	8:40
3:56	1:58:00	8:50
4:00	2:00:00	9:00
4:04	2:02:00	9:10
4:09	2:04:30	9:20
4:13	2:06:30	9:30
4:18	2:09:00	9:40
4:22	2:11:00	9:50
4:26	2:13:00	10:00
4:31	2:15:30	10:10
4:35	2:17:30	10:20
4:39	2:19:30	10:30
4:48	2:24:00	10:50
4:53	2:26:30	11:00
4:57	2:28:30	11:10
5:01	2:30:30	11:20

STRENGTH

STRENGTH WORKOUTS

4 × 1.5 miles

4 × 1.5 miles @ 10 seconds faster than race pace with 0.5-mile jog recovery

All sessions should include a warm-up and cooldown (1.5–3 mi. each).

MARATHON GOAL	HALF-MARATHON GOAL	1.5-MILE PACE	PACE PER MILE
2:28	1:14:00	8:15	5:30
2:33	1:16:30	8:30	5:40
2:38	2:17:00	8:45	5:50
2:42	1:21:00	9:00	6:00
2:46	1:23:00	9:15	6:10
2:50	1:25:00	9:30	6:20
2:55	1:27:30	9:45	6:30
2:59	1:29:30	10:00	6:40
3:03	1:31:30	10:15	6:50
3:08	1:34:00	10:30	7:00
3:12	1:36:00	10:45	7:10
3:17	1:38:30	11:00	7:20
3:21	1:40:30	11:15	7:30
3:25	1:42:30	11:30	7:40
3:30	1:45:00	11:45	7:50
3:34	1:47:30	12:00	8:00
3:38	1:49:00	12:15	8:10
3:43	1:51:30	12:30	8:20
3:47	1:53:30	12:45	8:30
3:51	1:55:30	13:00	8:40
3:56	1:58:00	13:15	8:50
4:00	2:00:00	13:45	9:00
4:04	2:02:00	14:00	9:10
4:09	2:04:30	14:15	9:20
4:13	2:06:30	14:30	9:30
4:18	2:09:00	14:45	9:40
4:22	2:11:00	15:00	9:50
4:26	2:13:00	15:15	10:00
4:31	2:15:30	15:30	10:10
4:35	2:17:30	15:45	10:20
4:39	2:19:30	16:00	10:30
4:48	2:24:00	16:30	10:50
4:53	2:26:30	16:45	11:00
4:57	2:28:30	17:00	11:10
5:01	2:30:30	17:15	11:20

STRENGTH WORKOUTS

3 × 2 miles

3 × 2 miles @ 10 seconds faster than race pace with 0.5-mile jog recovery

All sessions should include a warm-up and cooldown (1.5–3 mi. each).

MARATHON GOAL	HALF-MARATHON GOAL	2-MILE PACE	PACE PER MILE
2:28	1:14:00	11:00	5:30
2:33	1:16:30	11:20	5:40
2:38	2:17:00	11:40	5:50
2:42	1:21:00	12:00	6:00
2:46	1:23:00	12:20	6:10
2:50	1:25:00	12:40	6:20
2:55	1:27:30	13:00	6:30
2:59	1:29:30	13:20	6:40
3:03	1:31:30	13:40	6:50
3:08	1:34:00	14:00	7:00
3:12	1:36:00	14:20	7:10
3:17	1:38:30	14:40	7:20
3:21	1:40:30	15:00	7:30
3:25	1:42:30	15:20	7:40
3:30	1:45:00	15:40	7:50
3:34	1:47:30	16:00	8:00
3:38	1:49:00	16:20	8:10
3:43	1:51:30	16:40	8:20
3:47	1:53:30	17:00	8:30
3:51	1:55:30	17:20	8:40
3:56	1:58:00	17:40	8:50
4:00	2:00:00	18:00	9:00
4:04	2:02:00	18:20	9:10
4:09	2:04:30	18:40	9:20
4:13	2:06:30	19:00	9:30
4:18	2:09:00	19:20	9:40
4:22	2:11:00	19:40	9:50
4:26	2:13:00	20:00	10:00
4:31	2:15:30	20:20	10:10
4:35	2:17:30	20:40	10:20
4:39	2:19:30	21:00	10:30
4:48	2:24:00	21:40	10:50
4:53	2:26:30	22:00	11:00
4:57	2:28:30	22:20	11:10
5:01	2:30:30	22:40	11:20

STRENGTH WORKOUTS

2 × 3 miles

2 × 3 miles @ 10 seconds faster than race pace with 1-mile jog recovery

All sessions should include a warm-up and cooldown (1.5–3 mi. each).

MARATHON GOAL	HALF-MARATHON GOAL	3-MILE PACE	PACE PER MILE
2:28	1:14:00	16:30	5:30
2:33	1:16:30	17:00	5:40
2:38	2:17:00	17:30	5:50
2:42	1:21:00	18:00	6:00
2:46	1:23:00	18:30	6:10
2:50	1:25:00	19:00	6:20
2:55	1:27:30	19:30	6:30
2:59	1:29:30	20:00	6:40
3:03	1:31:30	20:30	6:50
3:08	1:34:00	21:00	7:00
3:12	1:36:00	21:30	7:10
3:17	1:38:30	22:00	7:20
3:21	1:40:30	22:30	7:30
3:25	1:42:30	23:00	7:40
3:30	1:45:00	23:30	7:50
3:34	1:47:30	24:00	8:00
3:38	1:49:00	24:30	8:10
3:43	1:51:30	25:00	8:20
3:47	1:53:30	25:30	8:30
3:51	1:55:30	26:00	8:40
3:56	1:58:00	26:30	8:50
4:00	2:00:00	27:00	9:00
4:04	2:02:00	27:30	9:10
4:09	2:04:30	28:00	9:20
4:13	2:06:30	28:30	9:30
4:18	2:09:00	29:00	9:40
4:22	2:11:00	29:30	9:50
4:26	2:13:00	30:00	10:00
4:31	2:15:30	30:30	10:10
4:35	2:17:30	31:00	10:20
4:39	2:19:30	31:30	10:30
4:48	2:24:00	32:30	10:50
4:53	2:26:30	33:00	11:00
4:57	2:28:30	33:30	11:10
5:01	2:30:30	34:00	11:20

STRENGTH

Recovery is key to the success of your strength sessions. In order to maintain a certain level of lactic acid, the recovery is kept to a fraction of the repeat duration. For instance, the 6 × 1-mile strength workout calls for a recovery jog of a quarter mile. If the repeats are to be done at 8-minute pace, the quarter-mile jog will end up being between 2:30 and 3:00 minutes, less than 50 percent of the duration of the intervals. Since these are less intense intervals, you may be tempted to exceed the prescribed pace, but keep in mind that the adaptations you're looking for specifically occur at that speed, no faster.

Strength workouts cover a lot of ground. When gearing up for these sessions, consider finding a marked bike path or loop to execute them. While a track can be used, the workouts can get monotonous and injury is more likely. Remember to always include 1.5 to 3 miles of warm-up and cooldown.

TEMPO WORKOUTS

The majority of runners who have trained for a distance race have encountered tempo workouts. They are a staple of all endurance training plans. Tempo runs have been defined numerous ways, but in the Hansons Marathon Method, a tempo run is a marathon-pace run. These runs will help you get a feel for what it is like to run race pace through a variety of conditions. Over the course of training, your tempo runs will span a number of months, requiring you to maintain race pace through an assortment of challenges and circumstances.

Internalizing pace is one of the most difficult components of training. If you feel great at the start line and go out 30 seconds per mile faster than you planned, you'll likely hit the halfway point ready to throw in the towel. No significant marathon records have been set via a positive split (running the second half slower than the first). Put simply, if you want to have a successful marathon, you are better off maintaining a steady pace throughout the entire race, rather than following the "fly and die" method. Tempo runs teach an important skill: control. Even when the pace feels easy, tempo workouts train you to hold back and maintain. Tempo runs also provide a great staging ground for experimenting with fluids, gels, and other nutrition.

FIGURE 3.7 TEMPO WORKOUT BENEFITS

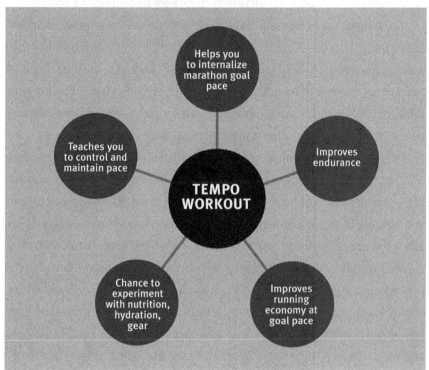

Since you'll be running at marathon pace, you will get a good idea of what your body can and cannot handle. The same goes for your gear. Use the tempo runs as dress rehearsals to try various shoes and outfits to determine what is most comfortable. Regardless of training, these things can make or break your race; tempo runs provide perfect opportunities to fine-tune your race-day plans.

The Physiology of Tempo Workouts

In the same way that easy and long runs improve endurance, so do tempo workouts. Although tempo days are faster than easy days, they are well under anaerobic threshold and thus provide many of the same adaptations. The longer tempo runs also mimic the benefits of long runs since the aerobic system is worked in similar ways. Specifically, from a physiological standpoint, the tempo run has a great impact on running economy at your goal race pace. One of the most visible benefits of this is increased endurance throughout a long race.

The tempo run has many of the same benefits as the strength workout, minus those that come from recovery between sets. Also, since it is slower than a strength workout, it elicits more aerobic benefits, similar to the long run. With tempo runs, the ability to burn fat is very specific to the workouts. The intensity is just enough that the aerobic system is challenged to keep up, but it's slow enough that the mitochondria and supporting fibers can barely keep up.

Over time it is the tempo run that will dictate whether or not you have selected the right marathon goal. With speed and strength sessions, you can in one sense "fake" your way through as a result of the relatively short repeats and ensuing breaks in between. However, with a tempo run, there is no break and if you are struggling to hit the correct pace for long tempo runs, then there may be a question as to whether you can hold that pace for an entire marathon.

Perhaps the greatest benefit that tempo runs offer is the opportunity to thoroughly learn your desired race pace through repetition. With time, your body figures out a way to internalize how that pace feels in heat, cold, rain, snow, and wind, which is incredibly valuable on race day. When runners cannot tell if they are on pace or not, then the tendency is to be off pace (usually too fast), setting their race up for unavoidable doom. Learning your pace and the feel of that pace can make the difference between a good race and a bad race.

Tempo-Workout Guidelines

In the Hansons Marathon Method, the tempo run is completed at goal marathon pace. For many other coaches, a tempo run is much shorter at paces closer to strength pace, but for our purposes, tempo and marathon pace are interchangeable. The pace should remain at goal pace. Never hammer a tempo run because it feels "easy." Not only are you compromising physiological gains, but you're also not learning to be patient and internalizing pace. It will take a good number of tempo workouts before you fully internalize the pace and can regulate your runs based on feel. What does change throughout training is the distance of these workouts. Tempo runs are progressive in length, adjusting every few weeks, increasing from 4 miles for a beginner and 5 miles for an advanced runner to 10 miles over the last few weeks of training. As an advanced runner begins to reach the heaviest mileage, the total volume of a tempo run, with a warm-up and cooldown, can tally 12–14 miles and approach 90 minutes in length (see tables below).

With the long run looming after a tempo run, that 16-miler might look a lot tougher than it did initially. This is a prime example of how the Hansons Marathon Method employs cumulative fatigue. Rather than sending you into the long run feeling fresh, we try to simulate the last 16 miles of the marathon, and there's nothing like a tempo run to put fatigue in your legs.

TEMPO PROGRESSION FOR BEGINNER PROGRAM

NUMBER OF WEEKS	TEMPO LENGTH
First 5 weeks	Easy mileage
3 weeks	5 miles
3 weeks	8 miles
3 weeks	9 miles
3 weeks	10 miles

TEMPO PROGRESSION FOR ADVANCED PROGRAM

NUMBER OF WEEKS	TEMPO LENGTH
First 2 weeks	Easy mileage
3 weeks	6 miles
3 weeks	7 miles
3 weeks	8 miles
3 weeks	9 miles
3 weeks	10 miles

TEMPO WORKOUTS

5-10 miles

All sessions should include a warm-up and cooldown (1.5–3 mi. each).

MARATHON GOAL	HALF-MARATHON GOAL	MARATHON PACE/ TEMPO
5:00:00	2:24:00	11:27
4:45:00	2:17:00	10:52
4:30:00	2:10:00	10:18
4:15:00	2:02:00	9:44
4:00:00	1:55:00	9:09
3:55:00	1:53:00	8:58
3:50:00	1:50:00	8:46
3:45:00	1:48:00	8:35
3:40:00	1:45:00	8:23
3:35:00	1:43:00	8:12
3:30:00	1:41:00	8:01
3:25:00	1:38:00	7:49
3:20:00	1:36:00	7:38
3:15:00	1:33:30	7:26
3:10:00	1:31:00	7:15
3:05:00	1:29:00	7:03
3:00:00	1:26:00	6:52
2:55:00	1:24:00	6:40
2:50:00	1:21:30	6:29
2:45:00	1:19:00	6:18
2:40:00	1:17:00	6:06
2:35:00	1:14:00	5:55
2:30:00	1:12:00	5:43
2:25:00	1:09:30	5:32
2:20:00	1:07:00	5:20
2:15:00	1:04:45	5:09
2:10:00	1:02:30	4:57

How to Pace Workouts

To help you better understand the intensity at which you should be running during the various components of the training plan, check out Figure 3.8. The diagonal line represents a sample VO$_2$max of a runner. The first line (Easy) on the left is for the easy running days and represents everything under the aerobic threshold. It is the largest, but also the slowest area. The next zone (L) is the long run and represents the fastest paces a person should run for the long run, but could also represent the fastest of easy days for beginners. The middle zone (T) denotes ideal tempo pace, and therefore, marathon goal pace. It is above aerobic threshold, but below anaerobic threshold. The strength zone (St) represents the high end of the "lactate" section, as strength runs should fall just below anaerobic threshold. Finally, there is the speed zone (Sp) that represents where speed workouts should fall, which is just below VO$_2$max for optimal development.

FIGURE 3.8 PACE VERSUS INTENSITY

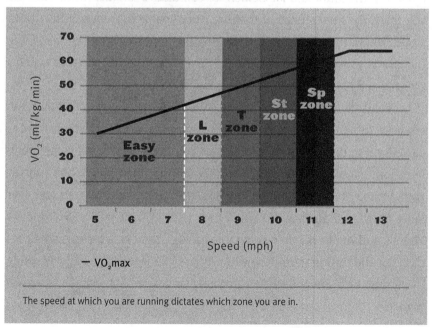

The speed at which you are running dictates which zone you are in.

With this continuum in mind, it becomes clear why running faster than you're instructed to run compromises development. Not only do you miss out on the benefits the workout was meant to provide when you go too fast, but you also increase fatigue. The essential point is this: Paces are there for a specific reason, and while some runners feel that paces sometimes hold them back, in reality proper pacing is what will propel you forward in the end. Fight the temptation to buy into the "if some is good, more is better" mentality and keep in mind the specific goal of that particular workout.

The Taper

Although we aren't generally in the business of telling folks to run less, cutting mileage and intensity is actually an integral part of marathon training when scheduled at the right times. For instance, while you may feel tired from the increased training two months into the program, avoid taking a day off and cutting your mileage that week. That is the wrong time, as it interferes with the foundational element of cumulative fatigue. However, when you reach the final stretch of training, your goal is to recover from all that work you put in, while also maintaining the improvements you made over the past few months. This is the right time to taper, or reduce your training volume, and it's one of the key steps in good marathoning.

The mistake many runners make with their tapering period is that they cut everything from training, including mileage, workouts, intensity, and easy days. In the same way we instruct you not to add these components too soon, we also suggest not abruptly cutting them out. When runners subtract too much training too quickly, they often feel sluggish and even more fatigued than they did when they were in their peak training days. There's nothing worse than going into an important race feeling more tired than you did during training, and a proper taper is the key to avoiding this. By cutting the training back in a gradual manner, you'll feel fresh and ready to race.

An SOS workout takes about 10 days to demonstrate any physiological improvement. That's right, it takes more than a week before you reap any benefits from a hard run. If you look at the training plans in the Hansons Marathon Method, you'll notice that the last SOS workout is done 10 days prior to the marathon, because after that point, SOS workouts will do nothing but make you tired for the big day. We also implement roughly a 55 percent reduction in overall volume the last seven days of the program. You will still run the same number of days per week, but with daily mileage reduced. Why the same number of days? Kevin and Keith liken it to being used to getting six hours of sleep every night and then suddenly getting 12 hours. You will feel pretty groggy the next day, even though you're well rested. The same can be said for being accustomed to running six days a week and then abruptly going down to only three or four days. It's a shock to the body. By continuing to run fewer miles, but still running every day, you reduce the number of variables that are adjusted. Instead of reducing frequency, volume, and intensity, you are tinkering only with the last two. Many other marathon training plans not only cut too much out of the schedule, but they also prescribe a taper of two to four weeks, causing a runner to lose some of those hard-earned fitness gains. By reducing the taper to just a 10-day period, you cut down on the risk of losing any of those gains, while still allowing adequate time for rest and recovery.

From a physiological standpoint, the taper fits well with the principle of cumulative fatigue, as the training program does not allow you to completely recover until you reach those final 10 days. Over the last couple months of the program, some of the good hormones, enzymes and functions in your body have been suppressed through incomplete recovery, while the by-products of fatigue have simultaneously been building. With reduced intensity and volume during the taper, these good functions flourish. Meanwhile, the by-products are allowed to completely break down and the body is left in a state of readiness for your best performance. We always warn runners not to underestimate the power of the taper. If you are worried about your ability to run a complete marathon at the pace of your tempo runs, consider this: The taper can elicit improvements of up to 3 percent. That is the difference between a 4:00 marathon and a 3:53 marathon. I don't know about you, but I'd be happy with a 7:00-minute improvement on my personal best.

Training Intensity Chart

To be utilized in determining how fast to run your workouts, Table 3.5 demonstrates pace per mile based on various goal marathon times. For easy runs, refer to the Easy Aerobic A and Easy Aerobic B columns. The faster end of the long-run spectrum is indicated in the Moderate Aerobic column. The Marathon Pace is the speed at which your tempo runs should be run. The Strength column will be your reference for strength workouts, and the 10K and 5K columns for your speed workouts. Keep in mind that actual 5K and 10K race times are going to be more accurate than this chart. If you have raced those distances, use your finishing times to guide your speed workouts. Our goal here is to provide you with guidance in your workouts, to help keep you focused and make the correct physiological adaptations throughout training.

Thoughts on Heart Rate Training

We don't prescribe by heart rate. We're not against heart rate (HR); rather we are in favor of treating all methods, from GPS devices to strength training to heart rate to shoes, as mere tools. Focusing too much on any one tool can throw off the balance in your training. Yes, heart rate training can have a place in your Hansons Marathon Method training—just not a primary one on your speed, strength, tempo, and possibly your long runs. There, pacing calls the shots.

With our training, pace, not heart rate, is key. Why? Because the entire system is based on a goal and/or race pace. In our system, easy runs are based on an amount of time slower than goal marathon pace. Tempo runs are based on that goal pace, and strength is a set amount faster than that goal pace. The majority of runners we coach have a time goal in mind. It may be a Boston Qualifier, a sub-2:30 or sub-4:00, or an Olympic Trials qualifier. To run the pace required to meet your time goal becomes incredibly important. If you can't run those paces, then you can't reach your goals. So is it more important that you know you've kept your heart rate at 75 percent or that you have run the 8:00-minute-per-mile pace you need to run your BQ? Let me just say, I haven't heard too many people cry out in joy at the finish line, "Yes! I kept my heart rate under 150!"

If you feel HR training is the way to go, then here are a couple of tips.

Be certain what your max heart rate is. Have it tested (a VO$_2$max test), and also get the HR ranges for your thresholds. The old standby equation to find HRmax (220 minus your age) is sufficient when looking at a large sample of people, but its individual accuracy can be questionable. Testing eliminates some of the guesswork.

Don't focus solely on HR; use all your tools. For example, GPS watches with HR monitors make this easy. Consider your tempo run. If you plan to run 8:00-minute miles, then it is helpful to know what your heart rate tends to be for those runs. If you see that heart rate trend climbing, take note. Are you feeling sick? Maybe it's something; maybe it's not. Use all the tools you have at hand—including your instincts—to know if you are training too hard. By relying on only one piece of data, you are at the risk of all kinds of variables. Better to look at the whole picture.

The main reasons we use heart rate are to gauge intensity and to monitor overtraining. In these regards, does it provide useful information? Potentially, but more in terms of tracking trends than in day-to-day numbers. If you use it, consider using it as an add-on to monitor your paces and give you an idea if you are getting fit enough to race what you want to. Should you wear a monitor

TABLE 3.5 TRAINING PACES

GOAL MARATHON TIME	RECOVERY	EASY AEROBIC A	EASY AEROBIC B	MODERATE AEROBIC/ LONG RUN
5:00:00	14:22	13:32	12:41	12:16
4:45:00	13:43	12:55	12:05	11:41
4:30:00	13:02	12:16	11:28	11:05
4:15:00	12:22	11:38	10:52	10:29
4:00:00	11:42	11:00	10:15	9:53
3:55:00	11:28	10:40	10:00	9:38
3:50:00	11:15	10:34	9:51	9:29
3:45:00	11:01	10:21	9:39	9:18
3:40:00	10:48	10:08	9:27	9:06
3:35:00	10:34	9:55	9:14	8:53
3:30:00	10:19	9:41	9:02	8:42
3:25:00	10:06	9:28	8:49	8:29
3:20:00	9:53	9:16	8:38	8:18
3:15:00	9:38	9:02	8:25	8:05
3:10:00	9:25	8:49	8:13	7:54
3:05:00	9:11	8:36	8:01	7:42
3:00:00	8:57	8:23	7:48	7:29
2:55:00	8:43	8:10	7:36	7:17
2:50:00	8:28	7:56	7:23	7:05
2:45:00	8:15	7:43	7:11	6:53
2:40:00	8:00	7:30	6:58	6:41
2:35:00	7:46	7:17	6:46	6:29
2:30:00	7:32	7:03	6:34	6:17
2:25:00	7:18	6:50	6:21	6:05
2:20:00	7:03	6:36	6:08	5:52
2:15:00	6:49	6:23	5:56	5:40
2:10:00	6:35	6:09	5:43	5:28

All paces are per mile.

MARATHON PACE/TEMPO	STRENGTH	10K SPEED	5K SPEED
11:27	11:17	10:30	10:04
10:52	10:42	9:58	9:34
10:18	10:08	9:27	9:04
9:44	9:34	8:55	8:33
9:09	8:59	8:24	8:03
8:58	8:48	8:13	7:53
8:46	8:36	8:03	7:43
8:35	8:25	7:52	7:33
8:23	8:13	7:42	7:23
8:12	8:02	7:31	7:13
8:01	7:51	7:21	7:03
7:49	7:39	7:10	6:53
7:38	7:28	7:00	6:43
7:26	7:16	6:49	6:33
7:15	7:05	6:39	6:23
7:03	6:53	6:28	6:12
6:52	6:42	6:18	6:02
6:40	6:30	6:07	5:52
6:29	6:19	5:57	5:42
6:18	6:08	5:46	5:32
6:06	5:56	5:36	5:22
5:55	5:45	5:25	5:12
5:43	5:33	5:15	5:02
5:32	5:22	5:04	4:52
5:20	5:10	4:54	4:42
5:09	4:59	4:43	4:32
4:57	4:47	4:33	4:22

every day? I don't recommend that. But nor do I recommend wearing a GPS every day. For those starting out, we know there are a lot of unknowns: Am I too fast? Too slow? What exactly is too fast or slow? Am I improving? These are legitimate questions. Having something to measure and provide feedback is great. However don't let that reliance keep you from learning to listen to what your body is telling you.

4

HANSONS TRAINING PLANS

WHILE SMALL REVISIONS have been made over the years, the training plans in this book are very similar to the first programs Kevin and Keith developed in the 1990s. When the brothers set out to create these plans, now collectively dubbed the "Hansons Marathon Method," they did so with average runners in mind, hoping to give them an alternative to the status quo programs already in existence. Since that time, thousands of runners have used our programs and found great success, a testament not only to Kevin and Keith's coaching know-how, but also to the programs themselves. Having been utilized many times over, the Hansons Marathon Method has withstood the test of time, while a laundry list of other training methods have come and gone.

In this chapter you will find our Beginner and Advanced Programs, as well as the Just Finish Program. Read through each to decide which might be the best fit for your experience and ability level. Miles logged, training history, goals, and race experience are all primary factors in making the decision. Whatever program you choose, following it faithfully will help you reach your marathon goals as so many others have over the past two decades since the Hansons Marathon Method came on the scene.

Just Finish Program

The Just Finish Program might be for you if:

- Your goal is to finish (i.e., you're less interested in performance)

- You are a new runner

- You have never run a marathon

- You have no experience with running workouts (such as the SOS days)

- You desire a simple but effective plan to get you to the finish line

When Kevin and Keith first developed the marathon programs, the idea of the average person running a marathon for fun was still relatively novel. From 1990 to 2014, the number of people running marathons has more than doubled. And it isn't just the number of people running marathons that has changed. The demographic has widened significantly, from a small, elite portion of the running population to a far broader spectrum of people of all ages, abilities, and goals. We have been thrilled to see this change. And it got us thinking about how we could ensure that the Hansons Marathon Method included this wider range. We asked ourselves: How can we take our method and philosophy and tailor it to people who are running to raise money for a charity that means the world to them or to the person who is simply looking to cross a long-term goal off a bucket list? With this in mind, we took the structure of the Beginner Program and used that as a template for our Just Finish Program (Table 4.2, page 112), which is designed for someone whose main goal is simply to get across the finish line, rather than being focused on a particular time goal. The Just Finish Program won't let you off easy, though! You still have to put in the work.

We started by thinking about what presents the biggest hang-ups to marathon training for people who might not consider themselves runners. For many people, the time factor involved in training is a barrier. To be honest, that is an issue for all marathoners, and I don't think we can ever truly get around that. As you will see, the Just Finish Program asks you to run several days a week, similar to the Beginner and Advanced Programs, but the mileage is significantly less. Another key difference to these miles is that they are less intense than in the other two programs, with a slow, careful buildup. Why? In my experience, it is not mileage that usually gets us hurt, but rather the intensities at which we run. Our aerobic system develops much faster than our bones and tendons, so it is easy to push harder than what our structural components can handle. With that often comes an Achilles' tendon injury, shin splints, or a stress fracture. In the Just Finish Program, we control the buildup of mileage for you. We also control the intensity, by prescribing easy runs throughout the program. A common mistake for new runners is thinking that they have to run fast. Hopefully, after our discussion of easy running in Chapter 3, you know that running easy and at a conversational pace will allow you to develop the vast majority of the components you need to cover the marathon distance.

When I've worked with new athletes running for their chosen charity, I found that many of them were not interested in running repeats on the track or suffering through strength workouts. They simply wanted to go run. And for most of those folks, this makes perfect sense because they are not trying to do anything but complete the marathon distance. So why make it more complicated or intimidating than it needs to be? If someone following this program gets bitten by the running bug, then the Just Finish Program serves as a perfect entry platform and that person may naturally gravitate to adding different components. But when it's the first program a runner is following, too much extra stuff can be overwhelming and a turnoff. Those are the last things we want to do to a new person attempting a very big race.

This program was designed to offer a lot of freedom. The intent is to get you to build your general endurance through a steady, but tolerable, increase in weekly mileage. With that said, there are a few key points regarding how to approach this program:

Run at an easy conversational pace for the majority of runs. Your goal is to build the amount of time you can run without stopping. The key to building endurance is time spent running as your first priority. Intensity is secondary.

If you feel like running hard, then run hard. Just make sure the next day is relaxed and easy.

This is not a walk/run program. Walk breaks are permitted, as long as it's a teaching opportunity—as in, teaching yourself that you aren't ready for that pace yet.

You should be able to handle 10 miles per week of running when starting this program.

The Just Finish Program offers newer runners the avenue to train properly for a marathon, while not having to worry about the extras that they may not be ready for or interested in.

The Beginner Program

The Beginner Program might be for you if:

- You are a performance-minded runner
- You have a certain time goal in mind
- This is your first marathon but you have experience racing other distances
- You are interested in moderate to higher mileage
- You have marathon experience, but are new to structured (SOS) training

The Beginner Program (Table 4.3, page 116) starts the runner at 15 miles per week and builds to the upper 50s during peak weeks. While the program includes the word "beginner" in the name, we have recommended it to many runners who have previously tackled the 26.2-mile distance. If you have experience with the marathon but have only trained with a minimalist-type program, then the Beginner Plan may be the logical next step in your training. Or perhaps you have never run high mileage, such as is prescribed in the Advanced Program. If so, the Beginner Program may be the best fit. One thing is certain: The marathon isn't something to treat lightly. A person who has never run a race before or even trained consistently should consider starting with the Just Finish Program to build up mileage and their readiness to take on the more rigorous schedule of the Beginner Program.

The initial five weeks of this program are designed to simply build weekly mileage. It's all about time on your feet and miles logged. The best way to bank mileage safely is to reduce intensity (no SOS workouts) and spread a moderate amount of mileage over a number of days. It is during those first five weeks that the body adapts to the stress of regular training, preparing it for the next phase. If you are already logging weekly mileage closer to the third or fourth week of training when you come into this training plan, just keep doing what you are doing and let the training program catch up with you.

Following the five-week base phase, we begin to turn up the heat, or rather, the intensity. You will notice two additions: speed and tempo. The speed workouts are executed at 5K or 10K pace (refer to Chapter 3 for specific workouts). These workouts include 12 × 400-meter repeats, 8 × 600-meter repeats, 6 × 800-meter repeats, and beyond. We throw different types of workouts at you to keep things interesting and get the desired physiological adaptations. While the total mileage that will be run at these faster paces equals 3 miles, the total mileage for the day will be greater once you add in the recovery intervals and a warm-up and a cooldown. Typically we instruct marathoners using this schedule to warm up and cool down for 1–2 miles. This remains one of the most important parts of training, as warming up and cooling down help to boost performance and speed the recovery process following workouts.

Some will question why the speed-oriented training block is scheduled prior to other phases, such as strength. In addition to the important physiological adaptations that occur as a result of speed training, it gives you an excellent opportunity to establish a baseline. If you do not have any idea what pace you should be shooting for in the marathon, complete several speed workouts and you will soon find out. If you have never run a 5K (or haven't done one in the recent past), much less a marathon, we encourage you to sign up for a 5K or 10K race following the base and speed phases. This will assist in determining an appropriate training goal for the more marathon-specific training block that is approaching in the coming weeks.

Another reason speed workouts are important is that they provide variety in training. While the higher-mileage weeks may appear daunting initially, we break up the miles into easy running, fast running, recovery intervals, and warm-ups and cooldowns. But it adds up fast: Before you know it, you have a significant number of miles in the bank, all of which will provide payouts on race day. Also, speed workouts make great dress rehearsals for the strength sessions. They allow you to make mistakes and learn lessons about pacing and recovery early on before starting those important marathon-specific strength workouts. Lastly, speed workouts help a runner develop supreme mental toughness. For those who are accustomed to lacing up their shoes and heading out the door for the same 30–60 minute jog each day, speed workouts provide new challenges for both the mind and body. These sessions force you to run at a higher-intensity pace for a longer period of time, drawing you out of your comfort zone and into new territory. Remember, the only way to improve fitness is by bumping it up from the bottom; each time you step slightly out of your comfort zone, your body responds to the new stimulus. When you learn to tolerate discomfort for longer and longer durations, the payoff is multifold: You gain speed, discover your true potential, and become comfortable with higher-intensity training. What's more, you also develop a higher anaerobic threshold and aerobic capacity without ever training beyond VO_2max and risking injury.

Around the time we add speed to the training schedule, tempo workouts also come into play. Assisting in self-regulation and pacing, tempo runs are to be completed at goal marathon pace. Look at the first week on the plan that includes a tempo run and notice it reads, "Tempo 5 miles + WU and CD." This means that the tempo run is 5 miles at goal marathon pace, and, like all SOS workouts, it also includes a warm-up (WU) and cooldown (CD). Just as we recommend before and after speed workouts, you should complete a 1–2 mile warm-up and cooldown. In the end, although the tempo run itself may be 5 miles, the total mileage will be closer to 7–9 miles. As the tempo distance increases, these workouts total somewhere in the neighborhood of 12–14 miles, 10 of which are at goal marathon pace. You may be surprised by the ease with which you complete the first few tempo runs. In fact, runners who are accustomed to lower weekly training volume often tell us that marathon pace is actually slower than what they run on their easy days. This is because many of these runners are running very few miles, thus allowing all mileage to be completed at a faster pace. Since they are only training a couple days during the week, they are running faster than they should because they always feel fresh. If you find yourself in that camp, you'll discover that these paces typically slow on their own as weekly mileage increases.

Once you have begun to master speed and tempo, you approach the more marathon-specific training. At this point, the speed workouts give way to strength workouts and the tempo runs become much longer. The long runs also peak in mileage and the weekly volume is at its highest. We won't sugarcoat this phase; it is difficult, and you will be tired. You'll find that strength workouts are similar in structure to speed sessions, with the main differences being volume and pace. While speed workouts totaled around 3 miles with the speed at a 5K–10K pace, strength workouts hit 6 miles and are completed at goal marathon pace minus 10 seconds per mile (also stated as MP minus 10). For instance, if your goal marathon pace is 10:00 minutes per mile, your strength workout pace will be 9:50 per mile. For exact speed and strength workouts, refer to Chapter 3.

As we suggested, this final section of SOS training is meant to be difficult and leave you feeling somewhat drained. Remember, though, that you've adhered to the principle of cumulative fatigue all along, so your body will be accustomed to handling new challenges on tired legs. Of course you do not want to enter this section overtrained. If you ran the previous blocks too hard, you won't have any fuel in the tank to tackle strength sessions. Through this section of training, the improvements will come from the larger weekly volume, which is why it is particularly important to stick to the paces we advise. Running too fast during high mileage weeks is sure to leave you injured or burned out.

You'll notice that the long runs are consistent in their placement throughout the program, although they become longer as you get further into training. It is this aspect of the program, the long run, that sparks the most questions, in particular about the progression and frequency of the long runs, which are scheduled on Sundays. We begin by gradually bringing you up to a 10-mile long run, increasing that Sunday run by no more than 2 miles from one week to the next. These increases are proportionate to the weekly mileage that is scheduled (the long run accounts for about 25 percent of your week's mileage). As the tempo runs begin to increase, so too do the long runs. For instance, during a week with a 15- to 16-mile long run, there is also a tempo run of 8–10 miles, but with warm-up and cooldown, that day will also total close to 15 miles. The reason we have a 15- to 16-mile long run one week and a 10-mile long run the next week is to accommodate those longer tempo runs. Without this adjustment, you'd essentially end up doing three long runs every eight days for more than a month, throwing off the balance of training and increasing your risk of injury. By doing a more traditional higher-mileage long run every 2 weeks, your body learns to handle the larger volume, while still running at least one run per week of significant distance.

ASK THE COACH

Why the big jump in mileage from week 5 to week 6?

You will notice in the Beginner Program that there is a significant jump in mileage between weeks 5 and 6. In week 5, the schedule calls for approximately 25 miles, while week 6 calls for about 41 miles.

The major difference between the two weeks is that you begin your SOS days in week 6. You also lose your Monday "rest or crosstrain." If this gap feels too significant, we recommend substituting an easy run of 4–5 miles (6–8 km) on Monday. Also, on the Tuesday of week 6, you can consider doing 8 × 400 instead of 12 × 400. That will save you another 2 miles. With that combination, you bring week 5 up to about 29 miles and bring week 6 down to 38, cutting the difference from 16 to 10 miles—a more manageable number for some runners. The key is to watch your intensities as you start SOS days. At this point you are really fresh and it will be easy to push too hard. Remember, with cumulative fatigue, it will all slowly add up, so what feels good now may be the breaking factor in a couple months!

The icing on the marathon training cake is the easiest section of the program: the taper. After all that hard training, the body is fatigued. There may have even been moments when you wondered if you'd even complete the training. The purpose of this last block is to finally let the body recover from the previous 16 weeks of training, all while maintaining the fitness that was gained. While we don't want you feeling fresh during the majority of training, the opposite is true during these last 10 days before the big race. Even still, you shouldn't completely abandon training, since it is important to maintain a balance between recovery and fitness. This is your time to get a little rest but also hold on to all those positive adaptations your body made up to this point.

Advanced Program

The Advanced Program might be for you if:

- You are a performance-oriented runner
- You have marathon experience
- You have experience running higher mileage

The Advanced Program (Table 4.4, page 120) is best suited for runners who have completed at least one previous marathon. However, it is important to consider your experience. If your past training has involved low weekly mileage plus a high-mileage long run, as suggested by many training programs, you may need to make some adjustments to the Advanced Program. Runners who are used to lower mileage may struggle with the Advanced Program due to its more aggressive structure and higher volume. On the other hand, a runner who has never completed a marathon but is accustomed to 50-plus miles per week will likely thrive using the Advanced Program.

The Advanced Program differs from the Beginner Program in several ways, the most obvious being weekly mileage. From the very first week, the Advanced Program doles out more miles, and it continues to follow that trend throughout. While we coach beginners to hit around 50 miles in their peak weeks, advanced marathoners are instructed to reach just over 60 miles. It is important to note that the increase in mileage doesn't come from an increase in SOS workouts but instead from ramping up the distance of weekday easy runs. Remember that the easy runs provide a strong stimulus for aerobic development through mitochondrial growth and development, muscle-fiber recruitment, and the enhancement of fat use. These benefits are all garnered without the stress that comes along with harder running.

You will also find that SOS workouts begin earlier in the Advanced Program. In the Beginner Program, the runner starts with a base-building period that consists of all easy running, but in the advanced training plan, speed workouts begin the first full week and tempo runs the second full week. In the early implementation of speed in the Advanced Program, Kevin explains, "often, a person using the Advanced Program is running multiple marathons a year. When they do this, they tend to neglect some aspects of training, especially speed." We see this happen at every level, all the way up to the elite ranks. When plans include running several marathons a year, it is easy to fall into the trap of focusing solely on tempo runs and long runs, as a runner is constantly preparing for that next big race. By injecting speed into the Advanced Program early on, the experienced marathon runner can work on one of the most common marathon weaknesses. The other group of advanced marathoners we encounter are those who want to race shorter races in the summer and then a marathon in the fall. While the beginner needs to spend the majority of his or her time increasing overall endurance, this isn't necessary for the advanced runner. By incorporating a slightly longer speed segment and forgoing the high volume of base mileage that the beginner completes, both groups of advanced runners benefit. The speed either helps prepare runners for the shorter races they want to run or helps them work on their weaknesses in the speed department.

To get into speed workouts, follow the sequence provided in Chapter 3. Begin with the 12 × 400 workout, then the 8 × 600s, 6 × 800s, 5 × 1000s, 4 × 1200s, and finally the 3 × 1600 workout. When you get to this point, you will have four weeks speed left. At that point, work back down the pyramid and do the 4 × 1200s, 5 × 1000s, 6 × 800s, finishing the last week of the speed segment with the 12 × 400 workout.

In addition to the earlier implementation of speed workouts, the Advanced Program also differs in its prescription of tempo workouts. While the Beginner Program jumps from a 5-mile tempo run to an 8-mile tempo run, the Advanced version steadily increases in 1-mile bumps: 6, 7, 8, 9, and 10 miles. This is because improvements will come faster for a beginner than they will for a veteran. Consider this: A 6 percent improvement for a 4:00-hour marathoner would mean a 3:45 finishing time. However, a 6 percent improvement for a

2:45 marathoner would yield only a 2:35. While the percentage may be the same, the faster runner will see fewer minutes shaved off the overall time. As a result, the advanced runner needs to spend more time on specific areas of training to maximize benefits.

There are also noticeable differences between plans when it comes to the long run. While the Advanced Program still doesn't bring a runner beyond 16 miles, the structure and buildup are distinct. For instance, a 10-mile run in the Beginner Program is labeled as a long run, but in the Advanced Program it is an easy run. Table 4.1 clearly shows that a 10-mile run for a beginner is more significant than for an advanced runner.

TABLE 4.1 10-MILE RUNS: BEGINNER VERSUS ADVANCED	RUNNER A—BEGINNER	RUNNER B—ADVANCED
Easy pace	9:00 min./mi.	7:30 min./mi.
Duration for 10-mile run	1 hr. 30 mins.	1 hr. 15 mins.
% of weekly mileage	25	18–20

You may be wondering why a long run is done only every other week in the Advanced Program. As with the Beginner Program, we don't want you to do a Sunday long run, a tempo run that totals 16 miles with warm-up and cooldown, and then another Sunday long run all in the span of eight days. It is important to strike a delicate balance among the various elements of training, and too much long running takes away from other important components.

Training Program FAQs

In our training clinics, we encounter many of the same questions regarding marathon preparation, year after year. We all have similar fears, apprehensions, and questions when it comes to taking on a new challenge, such as a marathon. As coaches, we have learned through the years how to best answer those questions, usually sending runners away feeling more confident about being able to fit in all their training and do it successfully. Consider the following most frequently asked questions. For more detailed information on schedule modification, see Chapter 5.

What if I want to switch days around?

We understand that running sometimes has to take a backseat to work and family events. While we hope you can bump marathon training up the priority list for 3–4 months, it is not realistic to expect it to be at the very top. As you may have noticed, SOS days are scheduled for Tuesdays, Thursdays, and Sundays. If you are not able to complete a workout on the day it is prescribed, it is OK to switch days around to accommodate your schedule. If you decide to do this, however, we want to make sure that the switch makes sense. For instance, speed workouts are on Tuesdays in our schedules. If you know that you are always going to struggle getting those workouts in on Tuesdays because of meetings, kids, or other commitments, change all your speed workouts to Mondays. You should also move back other workouts, doing your long runs on Saturdays instead of Sundays, and so forth. This keeps the schedule consistent and merely shifts it back, thereby avoiding any alterations in the training itself. The goal is to avoid putting in back-to-back SOS workouts as much as possible, as the aim is cumulative fatigue, not reaching the point of no return. If you find yourself in this situation, move your SOS days around to allow for an easy day or an off day in between each.

Below are two popular alternatives that we have used to help people fit in all of their training when the standard plan doesn't fit. These both also allow for a touch more recovery. The first combination looks like this:

Monday: Easy
Tuesday: Speed or strength

Wednesday: Off
Thursday: Friday's easy run
Friday: Tempo
Saturday: Easy
Sunday: Long

This combination switches Thursday and Friday, allowing two days of recovery between the intense speed or strength and the demanding tempo run. For some, this may be more important than the recovery between the tempo and the long run.

The second option is a little more involved:

Monday: Speed/strength
Tuesday: Monday's easy run
Wednesday: Off
Thursday: Tempo
Friday: Easy
Saturday: Long
Sunday: Saturday's easy run

This alternative often appeals to runners who want their Sunday to be less run-focused. With this shift, they can get a long run in, but still manage their other commitments. Either one of these combinations is also excellent for the masters runner who wants a little extra time to recover between intense sessions, but still wants to get everything in.

What if I want to run more weekly mileage?

Many runners assume if they want to increase weekly mileage, tacking miles onto the long run is the obvious choice. But tinkering with the long run is the last thing you should do. Kevin contends, "If you're looking to add mileage, increase the easy days to 10 miles or more, rather than increasing long runs dramatically." He also notes that another way to add mileage is simply to run easy on your scheduled off day. Looking at a typical week, here are some suggestions as to where you can easily add mileage:

Monday: Increase run by 1-2 miles (1.5-3 km)

Tuesday: Maximize warm-up and cooldown to 2-3 miles (3-5 km) each

Wednesday: Add a 30-60 minute recovery run

Thursday: Same as Tuesday

Friday: Same as Monday

Saturday: As originally scheduled

Sunday: Do all the above first, then increase the long run, but be mindful to stay within the 25-30 percent of volume and under ~3 hours in length parameters.

What about double runs? We suggest you only add doubles once you are averaging about 12 miles per day. For instance, if you are running 10 miles per run on your easy days, plus workouts and a long run, then you can consider adding a second run to increase mileage. However, if you aren't already getting supplemental training in, such as strength and flexibility, then I would suggest considering adding those instead of extra runs.

Remember, your fitness must respond positively to this. If you start adding mileage and your paces start slowing and you feel like you are on the edge of staying healthy, then back off some of the mileage and see how you respond. Ensuring you are recovering and are structurally capable of handling the training are more important than just logging miles.

What if I want to race during the training program?

While we generally don't favor racing much during marathon training, sometimes it becomes necessary. The beginner often needs to complete a 5K or 10K race to establish a baseline for the SOS workouts. Other times, a longer race is needed to help pinpoint a specific marathon goal time. In either case, the alteration in the schedule involves replacing the midweek tempo run with an easy day that was originally prescribed for the weekend. You will want to pick the week of your midschedule race strategically, and you will need to make adjustments to the Hansons plan prior to that race. For details on savvy schedule modification for mid-program races, see Chapter 5.

Because some scaling back or scratching of SOS days is required, you can see why we don't encourage a lot of racing during training. A midschedule race means adjustments to the planned schedule, and over time that means we aren't training for our goal race. Rather, we are using races to get into shape and filling in other training where we can.

How much should I warm up and cool down?

Traditionally we recommend a 1.5-mile warm-up and cooldown before and after hard workouts. For most beginners, this is 15–20 minutes. More advanced runners looking for an easy way to increase weekly mileage may benefit from increasing both the warm-up and cooldown to 2–3 miles.

What if I want to take a day off because I feel tired?

If this is the case, you should first determine whether you are injured or simply fatigued. If you are injured, you'll want to consult a coach or physician on what course of action to take. But do know that in training, we all experience various aches and pains. In fact, many runners just don't feel that great when they're logging lots of miles and running hard. Feeling somewhat worn-out is a normal and necessary part of the process. If you find you are getting tired, make sure your easy days are truly easy and you aren't cheating your SOS paces down.

If you are tired but still running strong and hitting your desired paces, then that is cumulative fatigue. However, if you are feeling worn down, on the verge of illness, and paces are starting to suffer, then that is the onset of overtraining. In that case, you should reassess your goals and take a look at your paces. Often, the goal pace might be fine, but a runner is simply running too fast on a regular basis, especially with easy days. If so, scale back your paces and even take a few days easy to see if you bounce back. At this stage, it's key to look at how well you are recovering. If you are stressed out from work and getting four hours of sleep per night, then that may be the source of your problem. I encourage looking at all facets of what is happening in your life before assuming that it is the training.

What if I don't have time to do the whole workout?

This can become an increasing problem as the tempo runs get longer and the strength workouts begin because, at this point, training tends to require more of your time. If there just aren't enough hours in the day, do what you can. Remember, something is always better than nothing. If you have a 10-mile tempo run on the schedule but have time for only 6 miles, then do 6 miles. You'll certainly garner greater benefits from a 6-mile tempo than nothing at all. And if all you can get in is a 30-minute easy run, then get it in. Don't stress over what you can't control, but also don't use a chaotic day with a scheduled workout as an excuse to skip exercise entirely. Even if you weren't training for a marathon, this is good for your overall health and well-being. I've done some of my best problem-solving on a 30-minute run sandwiched in between projects and meetings.

JUST FINISH

TABLE 4.2 JUST FINISH PROGRAM

WEEK	MON	TUES	WED	THURS
1	Rest or crosstrain	Easy 2 mi. (3 km)	Rest or crosstrain	Easy 3 mi. (5 km)
2	Rest or crosstrain	Easy 3 mi. (5 km)	Rest or crosstrain	Easy 3 mi. (5 km)
3	Rest or crosstrain	Easy 4 mi. (7 km)	Rest or crosstrain	Easy 4 mi. (7 km)
4	Rest or crosstrain	Easy 5 mi. (8 km)	Rest or crosstrain	Easy 3 mi. (5 km)
5	Rest or crosstrain	Easy 5 mi. (8 km)	Rest or crosstrain	Easy 4 mi. (7 km)
6	Easy 4 mi. (7 km)	Easy 5 mi. (8 km)	Rest or crosstrain	Easy 5 mi. (8 km)
7	Easy 4 mi. (7 km)	Easy 5 mi. (8 km)	Rest or crosstrain	Easy 5 mi. (8 km)
8	Easy 6 mi. (10 km)	Easy 6 mi. (10 km)	Rest or crosstrain	Easy 6 mi. (10 km)
9	Easy 5 mi. (8 km)	Easy 5 mi. (8 km)	Rest or crosstrain	Easy 5 mi. (8 km)
10	Easy 7 mi. (12 km)	Easy 5 mi. (8 km)	Rest or crosstrain	Easy 6 mi. (10 km)

FRI	SAT	SUN	WEEKLY TOTAL
Rest or crosstrain	Easy 3 mi. (5 km)	Easy 4 mi. (7 km)	**12 mi.** (20 km)
Easy 3 mi. (5 km)	Easy 3 mi. (5 km)	Easy 4 mi. (7 km)	**16 mi.** (27 km)
Easy 4 mi. (7 km)	Easy 4 mi. (7 km)	Easy 5 mi. (8 km)	**21 mi.** (36 km)
Easy 3 mi. (5 km)	Easy 5 mi. (8 km)	Easy 4 mi. (7 km)	**20 mi.** (33 km)
Easy 5 mi. (8 km)	Easy 4 mi. (7 km)	Easy 6 mi. (10 km)	**24 mi.** (40 km)
Easy 4 mi. (7 km)	Easy 8 mi. (13 km)	Easy 8 mi. (13 km)	**34 mi.** (56 km)
Easy 4 mi. (7 km)	Easy 6 mi. (10 km)	Long 10 mi. (15 km)	**34 mi.** (55 km)
Easy 5 mi. (8 km)	Easy 6 mi. (10 km)	Long 10 mi. (15 km)	**39 mi.** (63 km)
Easy 6 mi. (10 km)	Easy 5 mi. (8 km)	Long 15 mi. (25 km)	**41 mi.** (67 km)
Easy 5 mi. (8 km)	Easy 8 mi. (13 km)	Long 10 mi. (15 km)	**41 mi.** (66 km)

Continues

JUST FINISH

TABLE 4.2 CONTINUED

WEEK	MON	TUES	WED	THURS
11	Easy 5 mi. (8 km)	Easy 7 mi. (12 km)	Rest or crosstrain	Easy 5 mi. (8 km)
12	Easy 5 mi. (8 km)	Easy 7 mi. (12 km)	Rest or crosstrain	Easy 6 mi. (10 km)
13	Easy 7 mi. (12 km)	Easy 5 mi. (8 km)	Rest or crosstrain	Easy 5 mi. (8 km)
14	Easy 5 mi. (8 km)	Easy 7 mi. (12 km)	Rest or crosstrain	Easy 6 mi. (10 km)
15	Easy 7 mi. (12 km)	Easy 5 mi. (8 km)	Rest or crosstrain	Easy 5 mi. (8 km)
16	Easy 5 mi. (8 km)	Easy 5 mi. (8 km)	Rest or crosstrain	Easy 5 mi. (8 km)
17	Easy 7 mi. (12 km)	Easy 5 mi. (8 km)	Rest or crosstrain	Easy 5 mi. (8 km)
18	Easy 5 mi. (8 km)	Easy 5 mi. (8 km)	Rest	Easy 5 mi. (8 km)

FRI	SAT	SUN	WEEKLY TOTAL
Easy 6 mi. (10 km)	Easy 8 mi. (13 km)	Easy 16 mi. (27 km)	47 mi. (78 km)
Easy 5 mi. (8 km)	Easy 8 mi. (13 km)	Easy 10 mi. (15 km)	41 mi. (66 km)
Easy 6 mi. (10 km)	Easy 6 mi. (10 km)	Long 16 mi. (27 km)	45 mi. (75 km)
Easy 5 mi. (8 km)	Easy 8 mi. (13 km)	Long 10 mi. (15 km)	41 mi. (66 km)
Easy 6 mi. (10 km)	Easy 6 mi. (10 km)	Long 16 mi. (27 km)	45 mi. (75 km)
Easy 5 mi. (8 km)	Easy 8 mi. (13 km)	Long 10 mi. (15 km)	38 mi. (60 km)
Easy 6 mi. (10 km)	Easy 6 mi. (10 km)	Easy 8 mi. (13 km)	37 mi. (61 km)
Easy 4 mi. (7 km)	Easy 3 mi. (5 km)	RACE!	48.2 mi. (78 km)

TABLE 4.3 BEGINNER PROGRAM

WEEK	MON	TUES	WED	THURS
1	–	–	OFF	Easy 3 mi. (5 km)
2	OFF	Easy 2 mi. (3 km)	OFF	Easy 3 mi. (5 km)
3	OFF	Easy 4 mi. (7 km)	OFF	Easy 4 mi. (7 km)
4	OFF	Easy 5 mi. (8 km)	OFF	Easy 3 mi. (5 km)
5	OFF	Easy 5 mi. (8 km)	OFF	Easy 4 mi. (7 km)
6	Easy 4 mi. (7 km)	12 × 400 400 recovery	OFF	5 mi. (8 km)
7	Easy 4 mi. (7 km)	8 × 600 400 recovery	OFF	5 mi. (8 km)
8	Easy 6 mi. (10 km)	SPEED 6 × 800 400 recovery	OFF	TEMPO 5 mi. (8 km)
9	Easy 5 mi. (8 km)	5 × 1K 400 recovery	OFF	8 mi. (13 km)
10	Easy 7 mi. (11 km)	4 × 1200 400 recovery	OFF	8 mi. (13 km)

SPEED WORKOUTS
See pace charts, pp. 68–74

STRENGTH WORKOUTS
See pace charts, pp. 78–81

TEMPO WORKOUTS
See pace chart, p. 86

BEGINNER

FRI	SAT	SUN	WEEKLY TOTAL
OFF	Easy 3 mi. (5 km)	Easy 4 mi. (7 km)	10 mi. (17 км)
Easy 3 mi. (5 km)	Easy 3 mi. (5 km)	Easy 4 mi. (7 km)	15 mi. (25 км)
Easy 4 mi. (7 km)	Easy 4 mi. (7 km)	Easy 5 mi. (8 km)	21 mi. (36 км)
Easy 3 mi. (5 km)	Easy 5 mi. (8 km)	Easy 5 mi. (8 km)	21 mi. (34 км)
Easy 5 mi. (8 km)	Easy 4 mi. (7 km)	Easy 6 mi. (10 km)	24 mi. (40 км)
Easy 4 mi. (7 km)	Easy 8 mi. (13 km)	Easy 8 mi. (13 km)	39 mi. (68 км)
Easy 4 mi. (7 km)	Easy 6 mi. (10 km)	Long 10 mi. (16 km)	38 mi. (64 км)
Easy 5 mi. (8 km)	Easy 6 mi. (10 km)	Long 10 mi. (16 km)	41 mi. (66 км)
Easy 6 mi. (10 km)	Easy 5 mi. (8 km)	Long 15 mi. (24 km)	47 mi. (80 км)
Easy 5 mi. (8 km)	Easy 8 mi. (13 km)	Long 10 mi. (16 km)	46 mi. (71 км)

Continues

Weekly mileage includes a 1-mile (2-km) warm-up and cooldown for Speed, Strength, and Tempo workouts.

BEGINNER

TABLE 4.3 CONTINUED

WEEK	MON	TUES	WED	THURS
11	Easy 5 mi. (8 km)	6 × 1 mi. (2 km) 400 recovery	OFF	8 mi. (13 km)
12	Easy 5 mi. (8 km)	4 × 1.5 mi. (2.5 km) 800 recovery	OFF	9 mi. (14 km)
13	Easy 7 mi. (11 km)	3 × 2 mi. (3 km) 800 recovery	OFF	9 mi. (14 km)
14	Easy 5 mi. (8 km)	2 × 3 mi. (5 km) 1-mi. (2 km) recovery	OFF	9 mi. (14 km)
15	Easy 7 mi. (11 km)	3 × 2 mi. (3 km) 800 recovery	OFF	10 mi. (16 km)
16	Easy 5 mi. (8 km)	4 × 1.5 mi. (2.5 km) 800 recovery	OFF	10 mi. (16 km)
17	Easy 7 mi. (11 km)	6 × 1 mi. (2 km) 400 recovery	OFF	10 mi. (16 km)
18	Easy 5 mi. (8 km)	Easy 5 mi. (8 km)	OFF	Easy 6 mi. (10 km)

(TUES column labeled STRENGTH; THURS column labeled TEMPO)

SPEED WORKOUTS
See pace charts, pp. 68–74

STRENGTH WORKOUTS
See pace charts, pp. 78–81

TEMPO WORKOUTS
See pace chart, p. 86

FRI	SAT	SUN	WEEKLY TOTAL
Easy 5 mi. (8 km)	Easy 8 mi. (13 km)	Long 16 mi. (27 km)	54 mi. (91 KM)
Easy 5 mi. (8 km)	Easy 8 mi. (13 km)	Long 10 mi. (16 km)	49 mi. (80 KM)
Easy 6 mi. (10 km)	Easy 6 mi. (10 km)	Long 16 mi. (27 km)	56 mi. (91 KM)
Easy 5 mi. (8 km)	Easy 8 mi. (13 km)	Long 10 mi. (16 km)	49 mi. (81 KM)
Easy 6 mi. (10 km)	Easy 6 mi. (10 km)	Long 16 mi. (27 km)	57 mi. (93 KM)
Easy 5 mi. (8 km)	Easy 8 mi. (13 km)	Long 10 mi. (16 km)	50 mi. (82 KM)
Easy 6 mi. (10 km)	Easy 6 mi. (10 km)	Easy 8 mi. (13 km)	49 mi. (82 KM)
Easy 5 mi. (8 km)	Easy 3 mi. (5 km)	RACE!	50 mi. (81 KM)

BEGINNER

Weekly mileage includes a 1-mile (2-km) warm-up and cooldown for Speed, Strength, and Tempo workouts.

TABLE 4.4 ADVANCED PROGRAM

WEEK	MON	TUES	WED	THURS
1	—	—	OFF	Easy 6 mi. (10 km)
2	Easy 6 mi. (10 km)	12 × 400 400 recovery	OFF	Easy 6 mi. (10 km)
3	Easy 6 mi. (10 km)	8 × 600 400 recovery	OFF	6 mi. (10 km)
4	Easy 6 mi. (10 km)	6 × 800 400 recovery	OFF	6 mi. (10 km)
5	Easy 6 mi. (10 km)	5 × 1 km 400 recovery	OFF	6 mi. (10 km)
6	Easy 6 mi. (10 km)	4 × 1200 400 recovery	OFF	7 mi. (11 km)
7	Easy 6 mi. (10 km)	400-800-1200-1600-1200-800 400 recovery	OFF	7 mi. (11 km)
8	Easy 6 mi. (10 km)	3 × 1600 600 recovery	OFF	7 mi. (11 km)
9	Easy 8 mi. (13 km)	6 × 800 400 recovery	OFF	8 mi. (13 km)
10	Easy 6 mi. (10 km)	3 × 1600 600 recovery	OFF	8 mi. (13 km)

SPEED
WORKOUTS
See pace charts, pp. 68–74

STRENGTH
WORKOUTS
See pace charts, pp. 78–81

TEMPO
WORKOUTS
See pace chart, p. 86

FRI	SAT	SUN	WEEKLY TOTAL
Easy 6 mi. (10 km)	Easy 6 mi. (10 km)	Easy 8 mi. (13 km)	**26 mi.** (43 km)
Easy 6 mi. (10 km)	Easy 6 mi. (10 km)	Easy 8 mi. (13 km)	**41 mi.** (59 km)
Easy 7 mi. (11 km)	Easy 6 mi. (10 km)	Long 10 mi. (16 km)	**46 mi.** (77 km)
Easy 6 mi. (10 km)	Easy 8 mi. (13 km)	Easy 8 mi. (13 km)	**45 mi.** (75 km)
Easy 7 mi. (11 km)	Easy 6 mi. (10 km)	Long 12 mi. (20 km)	**47 mi.** (80 km)
Easy 6 mi. (10 km)	Easy 10 mi. (16 km)	Easy 8 mi. (13 km)	**47 mi.** (78 km)
Easy 7 mi. (11 km)	Easy 8 mi. (13 km)	Long 14 mi. (23 km)	**54 mi.** (88 km)
Easy 6 mi. (10 km)	Easy 10 mi. (16 km)	Easy 10 mi. (16 km)	**49 mi.** (82 km)
Easy 7 mi. (11 km)	Easy 8 mi. (13 km)	Long 15 mi. (25 km)	**57 mi.** (94 km)
Easy 6 mi. (10 km)	Easy 10 mi. (16 km)	Easy 10 mi. (16 km)	**50 mi.** (84 km)

ADVANCED

Continues

Weekly mileage includes a 1.5-mile (3-km) warm-up and cooldown for Speed, Strength, and Tempo workouts.

ADVANCED

TABLE 4.4 CONTINUED

WEEK	MON	TUES	WED	THURS
11	Easy 8 mi. (13 km)	STRENGTH 6 × 1 mi. (2 km) 400 recovery	OFF	TEMPO 8 mi. (13 km)
12	Easy 6 mi. (10 km)	STRENGTH 4 × 1.5 mi. (2 km) 800 recovery	OFF	TEMPO 9 mi. (14 km)
13	Easy 8 mi. (13 km)	STRENGTH 3 × 2 mi. (3 km) 800 recovery	OFF	TEMPO 9 mi. (14 km)
14	Easy 6 mi. (10 km)	STRENGTH 2 × 3 mi. (5 km) 1-mi. (2 km) recovery	OFF	TEMPO 9 mi. (14 km)
15	Easy 8 mi. (13 km)	STRENGTH 3 × 2 mi. (3 km) 800 recovery	OFF	TEMPO 10 mi. (16 km)
16	Easy 6 mi. (10 km)	STRENGTH 4 × 1.5 mi. (2 km) 800 recovery	OFF	TEMPO 10 mi. (16 km)
17	Easy 8 mi. (13 km)	STRENGTH 6 × 1 mi. (2 km) 400 recovery	OFF	TEMPO 10 mi. (16 km)
18	Easy 6 mi. (10 km)	Easy 5 mi. (8 km)	OFF	Easy 6 mi. (10 km)

SPEED WORKOUTS
See pace charts, pp. 68–74

STRENGTH WORKOUTS
See pace charts, pp. 78–81

TEMPO WORKOUTS
See pace chart, p. 86

FRI	SAT	SUN	WEEKLY TOTAL
Easy 7 mi. (11 km)	Easy 8 mi. (13 km)	Long 16 mi. (27 km)	61 mi. (103 км)
Easy 6 mi. (10 km)	Easy 10 mi. (16 km)	Easy 10 mi. (16 km)	55 mi. (89 км)
Easy 7 mi. (11 km)	Easy 8 mi. (13 km)	Long 16 mi. (27 km)	62 mi. (101 км)
Easy 6 mi. (10 km)	Easy 10 mi. (16 km)	Easy 10 mi. (16 km)	55 mi. (92 км)
Easy 7 mi. (11 km)	Easy 8 mi. (13 km)	Long 16 mi. (27 km)	63 mi. (103 км)
Easy 6 mi. (10 km)	Easy 10 mi. (16 km)	Easy 10 mi. (16 km)	56 mi. (91 км)
Easy 7 mi. (11 km)	Easy 8 mi. (13 km)	Easy 8 mi. (13 km)	55 mi. (92 км)
Easy 6 mi. (10 km)	Easy 3 mi. (8 km)	RACE!	52 mi. (88 км)

ADVANCED

Weekly mileage includes a 1.5-mile (3-km) warm-up and cooldown for Speed, Strength, and Tempo workouts.

5

SCHEDULE MODIFICATIONS

AT HANSONS WE REALIZE that our training programs can't be set in stone. Even the elite runners we coach have hiccups in their training, so we understand that changes may need to be made. Family obligations happen, work schedules change, and unfortunately, injuries and illnesses occur. These circumstances sometimes necessitate a modification in your training regimen. Some folks even want to add mileage to their training, requiring a whole different kind of modification. This discussion of the most common scenarios and the best ways to handle them will help you be ready with a backup plan no matter what the circumstance.

Increasing Weekly Mileage

Our programs fit a wide range of time goals and abilities; however, we still receive some requests for information on how to add to the weekly volume. As we have discussed, the faster that runners want to complete the marathon, the more training they have to put in (to a point). That added training generally comes in the form of an increase in weekly mileage. If you are a first-time marathoner following the Just Finish or Beginner Program, you are probably better off sticking with the recommended mileage for your first 26.2-mile training journey. However, from time to time, we see a special case where a runner is quite experienced in shorter race distances, but just hasn't run a marathon yet. If you are in this camp, we suggest simply starting with the Advanced Program. That'll give you an increase in weekly mileage without throwing too much at you. Even if you have been highly successful in shorter races, running high mileage is an entirely different beast. If you haven't run high weekly volume, give the Advanced Program a shot for your first marathon and then consider slowly adding mileage for your second attempt at the distance, depending on how your body responds.

If you are experienced in the marathon distance and have chosen to follow the Advanced Program, things become a bit more complicated. While the intuitive choice may be to add mileage to the long run, we first suggest running on your rest days to add mileage. If you are looking to ramp up your weekly mileage, we recommend adding an easy 4–8 miles on Wednesday, your rest day, and voilà! You instantly see roughly a 10 percent increase in mileage. For many runners, an easy running day, rather than a rest day placed between the two SOS days, may actually better stimulate recovery and keep you in a routine.

Another approach for adding mileage is through the modification of easy days in the Advanced Program. Since most of the easy days have runs of 6–8 miles, it is reasonable for an experienced marathoner to increase those runs to 8–10 miles. By adding 2 miles to each easy run during the week, you bank an additional 8 miles per week, topping you out in the 70 miles-per-week range. We have used this approach with a number of competitive men and women who run in the low- and sub-3:00-hour range, and have seen excellent results and personal barriers broken with this simple modification.

Although we have instructed you not to tinker with the long runs, we do have one exception that serves as another method through which you can add mileage to the Advanced Program. We don't recommend throwing in a 20- to 22-miler, but we occasionally recommend increasing the "shorter" long runs. So instead of doing a long run every other week, run one weekly.

This will quickly add mileage over the course of training. Even so, Kevin and Keith warn to stay away from the 20-mile long run unless you're approaching 90–100 miles per week.

For the ambitious few who have slowly increased their mileage and are looking to safely hit that 90–100 miles-per-week range, we again suggest adding miles to easy days, making those days at least 10 miles each. If you run all seven days per week, with four easy days, that will total 40 miles per week, or 40–50 percent of your goal. In this scenario, strength workouts total 11 miles and we usually recommend adding a 3-mile warm-up and cooldown before and after to log a few extra miles. Including the warm-up and cooldown, tempo runs will peak at around 14 total miles and we suggest increasing the Saturday run to 12 miles. Then, when you add an 18–20-mile long run, you've got about 95–97 miles on your legs for the week.

Runners will also often ask us about running twice a day. As with the long run, our recommendation depends on the person. For most people, it's hard enough to find time to run once a day, let alone twice. If you are looking to add up to 10 miles per week, then it's usually easier to just add Wednesday as an easy run. Then you are left with only a few miles to account for, and it's simpler to add a mile to a run a couple times during the week. For those running 70–80 miles per week, an 8- to 10-mile run will take anywhere from an hour to 80 minutes (e.g., 10 miles at 8:00 minutes per mile). For people who are running that sort of mileage and looking to finish in 2:30–3:10 in the marathon, a 10-mile run is not a major run, but rather a regular run. Even in this scenario, a second run may still not make a lot of sense. In this case, easy runs of 8–10 miles added to the SOS will already put you well into the 70–80 miles-per-week range. Once a person approaches the 100-miles-per-week range, however, two runs per day should be considered. At that point you are talking about 14–15 miles or more per day. It may not seem like much compared with 10 miles of single runs, but at this level those 4–5 extra miles put in during a second run can elicit real physiological adaptations.

In Appendix A, we discuss the plan followed by the elite athletes in the Hansons-Brooks Distance Project. Here you can garner some ideas on how higher weekly volume can be broken up. To reach the coveted 100-mile mark, you can either increase your easy runs from 10 miles to 12 miles, which will give you an extra 6 miles per week, or you can add a second 4-mile run a couple of days a week. All of this added mileage is done without messing with the volume or intensity of the core SOS workouts, demonstrating what huge gains added easy mileage can spur on its own. As coaches, we have seen the structure work successfully for men running in the mid-2:20s and women running sub-3:00-hour marathons.

One final note: When it comes to adding mileage, remember that if you aren't hitting workouts, then you should probably back everything down to the original volumes.

Adjusting for Races

One of the most common reasons runners require a change in their training program is to accommodate races. While we generally suggest including other races sparingly leading up to a marathon, in certain instances such competitions are advantageous. In particular, we have discussed the benefits of a beginner racing a 5K or 10K to help establish a baseline for the more marathon-specific training. But in order for this race to be useful, you must be strategic in scheduling it. For those using the Beginner Program, the first and best opportunity is at the end of week 8. The first five weeks are spent increasing base mileage to prepare you to handle harder-intensity running, which is followed by the speed segment of training, along with increasing mileage. Since it takes about three weeks to adjust to new training stressors, it makes sense to schedule a race at that point.

Additionally, you will notice that by the second week of the speed segment, the first 10-mile run appears. In order to add a race, you have to forfeit something, and in this case, the first longer run is an easy element to lose.

You will be running an 8-miler the week before and a 10-miler the week after, so you won't miss out on anything that can't be made up later if you schedule a race that particular weekend. If you wait until the fourth week of the speed training, however, you'll be forced to miss your first 8-mile tempo run, which is a significant jump from the 5-mile tempo run the week before. What's more, you'd also have to run a 15-mile long run the following week without a "stepping-stone" long run the week prior. By doing a race three weeks into speed training, your body is prepared for higher intensity running and the loss of important workouts is minimized.

The training grid (Table 5.1) demonstrates more specifically how you might shift around your workouts to best accommodate that race. You'll notice that during the week, Thursday's scheduled tempo run is replaced by Saturday's easy run, while the Friday run remains the same. Saturday is then race day, which replaces the tempo run. This is a strategic replacement, as both a race and a tempo run stimulate the anaerobic threshold. Hence, the Sunday run is replaced by another easy run that is longer in duration. Beyond that week the schedule picks back up right where it left off.

For those using the Advanced Program, at the end of week 4 and week 6 are the best times to insert a 5K or 10K. Here, the first weeks are spent focusing on speed and tempo runs, while gradually building your Sunday long runs. For week 4, the long run that would be missed due to a weekend race would not be a new distance, making it easier to take it out of the schedule. A race scheduled at the end of the sixth week is also a good idea; however you should tweak your workouts that week for best results. I suggest skipping the tempo run on Thursday, since you will then have to turn around and run essentially another hard workout on Saturday with the race. Instead, put in a longer easy run for Thursday, followed by an easy run on Friday, ending with the race over the weekend. Finally, your Sunday long run can be cut a bit shorter in comparison with what you did the week before and will do the following week. If you feel comfortable enough to

TABLE 5.1 WEEKS 7 AND 8: BEGINNER PROGRAM

WEEK	MON		TUES	WED		THURS
7	Easy 4 miles (7 km)	SPEED	8 × 600 400 recovery	OFF		Easy 6 miles (10 km)
8	Easy 6 miles (10 km)		6 × 800 400 recovery	OFF	TEMPO	5 miles (8 km)

run the mileage, do so. However, if you feel tired or banged up from the race, it is OK to cut it back by 20 percent.

It is important not to race too often, regardless of which program you are using. Races cause adjustments in tempo runs, long runs, and sometimes both. While the impact is smaller early in the training, it becomes a larger issue the closer the marathon gets. With all that said, sometimes runners want to run a longer race several weeks before the marathon to test their fitness and get in the racing state of mind. In Michigan in late August, this means the Bobby Crim 10-mile race. For those running a fall marathon, this particular race fits nicely into training since it is 4–6 weeks before most of Michigan's local marathons. Additionally, when you add the warm-up and cooldown to the 10-mile distance, the mileage that day meets or surpasses the long-run distance for that week, making it a good substitute. On the other hand, there is a half-marathon in the Michigan area several weeks later, which we strongly advise against. Whereas the timing of the 10-mile race makes sense, the half-marathon is much too close and will only serve to fatigue the runner and throw off training. These two examples highlight the bottom line on adding a race to your training: The race should fit into the overall plan and supplement your training rather than taking away from your ultimate goal, which is your best possible performance on marathon day.

FRI	SAT	SUN	WEEKLY TOTAL
Easy 4 miles (7 km)	RACE (5K or 10K)	Easy 8 miles (13 km)	32–35 mi. (50–55 KM)
Easy 5 miles (8 km)	Easy 6 miles (10 km)	Easy 8 miles (13 km)	39 mi. (57 km)

SPEED WORKOUTS

TEMPO WORKOUTS

Adjusting for Conflicts

Prior to marathon training, many runners are fairly haphazard in their approach to running, putting in varying amounts of volume and intensity depending on mood, weather, and the like. While any exercise is obviously good for your body, marathon training requires more focus and strategy. Herein lies one of the greatest challenges to marathon training: scheduling conflicts. For example, your child's T-ball games are on Thursdays, the same day you are supposed to do your tempo workouts. Or maybe you have to work every Sunday, which is also the scheduled long-run day. As coaches, we find ourselves reassuring runners about these issues every marathon cycle. By giving you three simple guidelines for working around life's obligations, we offer you the tools to tend to your responsibilities without letting your running get off track.

GUIDELINE 1: MAINTAIN REGULARITY IN TRAINING

If you decide to switch your workouts around, stay as consistent as possible. For instance, if you trade Thursday's workout for Friday's one week, make sure you do it every week. The key is to avoid constantly swapping different days every week. If you move your strength workout to Friday one week, but then do another strength workout the following Tuesday, you've done two strength workouts within a five-day period. Not only does this upset the training balance, but it can also lead to injury and overtraining.

If you know something is going to regularly conflict on a certain day of the week, make sure the changes are uniform across weeks and months. If you work all day Sunday, switch your long runs to Saturdays throughout the entire training cycle. Routine is the key here. The more you can maintain it, the better.

GUIDELINE 2: ENSURE REST DAYS AND EASY DAYS REMAIN IN PLACE

Put simply, you should always take either an easy day or a rest day in between SOS workouts. This allows for proper recovery. If you miss your speed workout on Tuesday and complete it on Wednesday instead, and then go right into your tempo run on Thursday, you're asking for an injury. In this situation, the best bet is to move the tempo run to Friday, leaving an easy run on Saturday, and a long run on Sunday. This proves that you can adjust for certain obligations and disruptions without upsetting the entire balance of training.

GUIDELINE 3: REMEMBER SOMETHING IS ALWAYS BETTER THAN NOTHING

Consider the previous example, where an SOS workout was missed on Tuesday. What's a runner to do if there is no other possible day to reschedule the workout later in the week? One option is to just move on. That's right: Cut your losses and move on to the next SOS workout. In some circumstances, there may be no way around this scenario. If you don't have time to get in the full workout, however, consider sneaking in a quick run, or abbreviate the workout and get in what you can. Even a 25-minute run is better than forgoing a workout altogether.

Adjusting for Added Recovery

We outline some excellent recovery strategies in Chapter 9. As a first step toward adding more recovery, we suggest trying these out. But there are also adjustments that can be made to your schedule to allow for more recovery. For example, the stretch from Tuesday to Thursday can be intimidating. Rather than skipping workouts altogether, which can be tempting, we suggest swapping Thursday and Friday. Therefore, Thursday's tempo would now be on Friday and Friday's easy run would be on Thursday. This allows two full days of recovery between the two highest-intensity days of the week.

Adjusting for Illness or Injury

Illness and injury are the most frustrating reasons you may need to adjust your marathon training. Over the months you spend preparing for the 26.2-mile distance, you are likely, at the very least, to catch a bug. The chance of injury, on the other hand, is largely avoided through smart training, but it is not entirely eliminated. Even when you're doing everything right, you can trip on a curb and take a spill or roll an ankle on uneven terrain.

First, you must decide if you truly need a day or two off, or if you can modify the workout instead. If pain is your issue, the following are good rules of thumb in making this determination:

- From zero to 10, the pain should be no more than a 3.
- The pain should not be severe enough to cause a limp during or following the run.
- If you need medication to run or to numb pain, then you should not be running.

With illness, the guidelines are fuzzier. Our general rule of thumb is that if you have a fever, do not run and instead focus on recovery. Running through a fever will ultimately set you back even further by delaying your recovery. But if you simply have a cold with a runny nose, then you are probably OK to push through or modify what you do for the day.

Below is a quick guide to help you modify the day's workout and minimize damage or loss of fitness. Choose the modification that suits your situation and will make things better, not worse.

1. Full workout, just as prescribed
2. Full workout, but translated to its equivalent in effort-based terms (e.g., instead of 10 × 400 meters with 400-meters rest, do 10 × 2 minutes on/3 minutes off)
3. Full scheduled volume for the day, but modified workout (either slower paces or reduced hard running volume)
4. Full scheduled volume for the day, but with no workout, just easy mileage
5. Easy run, with less volume than prescribed
6. Crosstraining plus core work/resistance
7. Core work/resistance
8. Rest

Sometimes, however, we are faced with serious layoffs from training and the schedule may need to be adjusted (and worst-case scenario, goals abandoned). Here is how to navigate these layoffs, depending on their length.

You missed 1–2 days. Maybe you tweaked your knee or were sick in bed for a couple days. If you come out unscathed after a day or two, training can resume normally without scaling back mileage or intensity. You just lose a couple days of running; no harm done. For example, if you took a wrong step at the end of your long run on Sunday and twisted your ankle, causing you to miss training on Monday and Tuesday, simply jump back in on Wednesday. If you are feeling 100 percent, complete Tuesday's SOS workout on Wednesday and move the Thursday tempo to Friday. This allows you to still fit in all of the week's SOS workouts, but also adheres to the rule of scheduling an easy or rest day between hard runs. However, if you aren't able to reschedule your SOS days to fit within those parameters, then just forge ahead with your tempo run on Thursday and let go of the missed SOS workout. While a number of missed workouts can spell doom for your marathon goals, a single· lost workout will never be your demise.

If you are following the Just Finish Program, missing 1 or 2 days will cause minimal (if any) setback. If you miss 1 day, just jump back into the schedule as if nothing happened. For 2 days missed, scale that first run back by 1–2 miles and then proceed as the schedule dictates.

You missed 3–6 days. Physiological regression will be minimal, even if no running at all takes place within this time frame. Usually, a person missing this many days has something more than a 24-hour flu or a simple ache or pain. But if you are feeling healthy enough to get in a couple short, easy jogs while you recuperate, by all means do it. However, if you're truly laid up, rest assured that the consequences of a few days off won't affect your end goal. After 3–4 days of missed training, come back slowly by running easy for 2–3 days, then pick the schedule back up and follow it as usual. If you're following the Just Finish Program, scale your first three runs back by 25–30 percent, and then continue as originally scheduled. If 5–6 days are missed, run easy for 3–4 days, and then revert back to the previous week's training regimen. After that week, jump ahead and catch back up with the training schedule. For instance, if you miss week 3, run easy through week 4, and then return to week 3's plan during the fifth week. After that, jump to week 6 and follow the training as it was originally prescribed. For the Just Finish Program followers, the same guidelines apply.

You missed 7–10 days. At this point the body starts to lose some of those hard-earned physiological gains you have made. You've probably heard the saying, "you lose it twice as fast as you gain it." It always seems that it takes a lot more time and effort to gain fitness than it does to lose it. No running for a week and a half definitely necessitates serious schedule modification, particularly for those following the Advanced and Beginner Programs; however, that modification depends upon at what point in the plan the .missed block occurs. If it occurs before the strength portion of the training program, then the runner won't have to make any major adjustments to race goals. However, if the setback happens after the strength workouts begin, the runner will probably need to adjust race-time goals for the following reasons: (1) There may not be time to get in all the prescribed training, and (2) the desired physiological adaptations might not have the necessary time to occur. Keep in mind that if you can still manage to do some short, easy runs during this period and have the go-ahead from your doctor, the time it takes to return to normal training will be significantly less. In either case, you don't need to abandon your plans to run the marathon, although adjustments are necessary.

Upon your return to training, you should run easy for the same number of days that were missed. If a week was lost, then run easy for a week. After that, go back to the last training week that you were able to complete and repeat it, then run the week that was originally missed, and from there pick the schedule back up. So, with a week missed, it takes three weeks to get back on track. If you were able to run easy during your time off, subtract a week from that time frame. While this advice applies throughout the training program, once strength workouts have begun, you may do the math and realize, "Wow! I don't have enough time." Unfortunately, it happens. While many people can still rebound quickly enough to run the race, the goal time will likely be compromised. Once you get into that final 4–6 weeks of training, the pros and cons of racing should be weighed. If you are really looking to run that Boston qualifier and you miss 10 days of running with five weeks to go, you may choose to look at other race options to buy yourself a bit of time. If you are comfortable with potentially missing the mark, however, then go for it. For those following the Just Finish Program, take your last completed week and run 60 percent of that week's mileage upon returning to running. Then, repeat your last completed scheduled week—so the week you ran at 60 percent will now be repeated, but at 100 percent effort. After that, jump back to where you were at on the schedule.

You missed 11+ days. If you are forced to miss this much time, you are faced with a serious decision, regardless of which program you followed. After two weeks of lost training, the decreases in physiological gains are quite significant—as much as 3–5 percent. While this might not seem like much, consider this: For a runner attempting a 3:00-hour marathon, a 4 percent loss means a gain of seven minutes to the overall finishing time. The slower the marathon time, the more time gained. Even worse, after 21 days away from running, 10 percent or more fitness is forfeited. This means that VO_2max and blood volume can decrease by up to 10 percent, anaerobic threshold decreases significantly, and muscle glycogen decreases by as much as 30 percent. These are all important to marathon performance and if you miss two weeks of running, it may take more than two weeks to even get back to your pre-injury level, setting you far off course. In particular, if this happens during the strength portion of the program, there simply may not be enough time to regain your fitness levels and get you ready for the goal race.

While you won't run your best, advanced runners in this situation may be able to sneak in shorter training segments and still complete the race, albeit falling short of the original time goals. However, beginners and first-time marathon runners should be cautious when it comes to losing substantial amounts of training time and forging ahead to the goal race. For runners in this situation, consider choosing a new race or at least revising time goals. In all of our years coaching, we've seen too many people rush back from injury to make a race deadline, often leading them to forgo proper recovery and have a poor race experience.

If you are set on running the originally scheduled race, be sure to step back and understand what the time off from running means for you physiologically. If you've taken two weeks off, adjust your race goal by 3 to 5 percent. If you've missed closer to three weeks, adjust your expected performance by

7 to 10 percent. For example, if Runner A missed two weeks of training and was shooting for a 3:30 marathon, the goal should be adjusted between 6.3 minutes (210 × 0.03) to 10.5 minutes (210 × 0.05). The new time goal would then be 3:36–3:41. If you take more than four weeks off, we suggest choosing a new race altogether.

Downtime Discretion

Although we have just presented a number of ways to modify your training schedule, we contend that it is best to avoid taking unscheduled days away from training if at all possible. This applies even when your legs are tired and sore, since soreness and injury are not inextricably linked. There will be times during marathon training when your legs are achy, fatigued, and nonspecifically sore; it just comes with the territory. Many of the adaptations that happen during training occur as a result of running on the days you just don't feel like running.

If you have an injury, however, your response should be different. For less severe injuries, make sure that you are not only taking time off, but also using that time to identify the root cause of the problem. Otherwise you may continue to run into the same issue upon returning to training. For example, if you are experiencing shin splints, figure out what you need to do to reduce the pain, like getting new shoes or implementing a strength routine. If your body will allow it, reduce the volume and intensity but continue running short and easy through the healing process. While training may need to be reduced, it doesn't necessarily have to stop completely to allow for recovery—if the cause of the injury is identified and treated, that is. When you can maintain some fitness, downtime is significantly minimized and regular training can be resumed much sooner.

PART III

THE STRATEGY

6

SELECTING RACE GOALS

ONE OF OUR FIRST OBJECTIVES with runners new to the Hansons' training clinics is to assist them in choosing a marathon goal. Vague goals can lead to a less-than-satisfying overall marathon experience. The problem with many marathon-training plans that merely help a runner finish a race is that they don't adequately ease runners into marathon mileage, which can make training and racing unpleasant and even painful. Even with our Just Finish Program, we want to push you beyond what is comfortable. Our goal isn't to just get you through a program with low-volume running during the week and then throw you into a grueling weekly long run that is 50 percent or more of your weekly total. Rather, the Just Finish plan is a platform to provide you with a first-time experience to Hansons-style training from which you can build into more complex training.

Borrowing from the business world, we suggest setting SMART goals: specific, measurable, attainable, realistic, and timely. A specific goal is one that is defined and clear-cut, so rather than stating you want to finish a marathon, you should identify a very specific goal. By setting a measurable goal, such as 3:25, for instance, you give yourself a definite objective. You also want to be sure that goal is attainable. While a 3:25 marathon may be within reach for someone who previously ran a 3:40, it may not be for someone who holds a 5:25 personal record (PR). Similarly, a realistic goal is one that considers your physical abilities and scheduling constraints. If you are only going to have time to train four days a week, it is unlikely you'll be able to achieve a 2:25 marathon. Lastly, a timely goal is one that is contained within a specific time frame. This one is easy because you automatically have the period between the start of the training plan and the moment the starting gun fires at your chosen race. By following these criteria, you are more likely to achieve your predetermined objectives going into a race.

In a perfect world, we'd encourage runners to set smaller goals before considering the marathon distance. When runners slowly move up the race ladder from a 5K to a 10K to a half-marathon, and then, finally, the marathon, they build their aerobic capacities and tolerance to increased training volumes. What's more, the shorter races provide a solid baseline for marathon training, giving feedback for what a reasonable marathon goal time might be for that individual. Bear in mind that our Beginner and Advanced Programs are tailored to help you reach specific goals, not just to run 26.2 miles. If you are looking to simply cross the finish line by any means necessary, these programs may be more focused and structured than you desire. For Just Finish runners, it is not necessary to start the program with a time goal in order to complete that schedule. Many runners approach the program with the basic goal of finishing a marathon, time aside. However, it is not uncommon for those runners to set personal goals, such as to break five hours, or to run the entire race without stopping. Personal goals such as these can be highly motivating. Therefore, although setting a time goal is not mandatory, I certainly don't discourage coming up with your own very specific goals along the way.

For Beginner and Advanced Program followers, nailing down a specific time goal allows you to identify how you should train to achieve that mark. Rather than training you to merely make it across that line, we want to give you the tools to execute the marathon distance successfully, leaving your love for running and hunger for competition intact. Those goals give you a starting point for training by guiding your workouts and providing a tangible target to shoot for throughout marathon preparation.

Time goals can be determined in various ways. Most commonly, runners seek a qualifying time for a certain race, such as a Boston qualifier, or a time that will gain access to a desirable start line corral at another major marathon. This is the easiest type of goal to pinpoint because the standard is already set. For runners who have previously completed the marathon distance, a new PR is another popular time to tackle. In particular, we hear from many runners who want to break the big barriers, such as the 5:00-, 4:00-, and 3:00-hour marks. While we encourage you to set the bar high, make sure your goal is manageable and keeps you engaged in your training. There are several guidelines to consider as you zero in on a SMART marathon goal.

Goal-Setting Guidance

Current training and past training. Your goals should be contingent on your current foundation of training. For instance, someone who has been injured for the past six months will set different goals than a runner who has been consistently running 50 miles per week. In the same way, the goals of a beginner will vary dramatically from the goals of a seasoned marathoner.

Current personal best. If you have previously run a marathon on relatively low mileage, even a slight uptick in miles will often lead to great jumps in your personal best. However, if you are a 2:30 marathoner who has already been running 80–100 miles a week, improvements will be less significant. Consider this: A 5 percent improvement for a 4:00-hour marathoner is about 12 minutes, which would get that runner under the 3:50 mark. However, the same percentage of improvement for a 2:30 marathoner is about 7:30 minutes, which would bring them from being competitive on a regional level to a borderline national-class runner. Obviously, that 5 percent improvement means something different depending on one's pace.

Training and availability. The time you devote to training has a huge effect on the quality and volume of the training, and thus, the final result. When choosing a goal, look at how much time you'll have to train. Time determines not only how hard and long you can train on a day-to-day basis, but also how consistent you can be over a long period. For example, a runner can compete fairly well in local 5Ks by logging 30–40 miles per week, perhaps running 3–4 days with a long run of 1 hour. While this works for shorter distances, this person would likely struggle to get in adequate training for a half-marathon or marathon on that same timetable. Could this runner complete a marathon running 40 miles a week? Most certainly. Would it allow for his or her best effort at that distance? Simply put, no.

Training window. The length of time you have until the goal race will offer some guidance in goal-setting. If you are a newer runner or new to the marathon distance, plan for a longer buildup period before you attempt 26.2 miles. However, if you are a veteran who trains consistently, then the marathon-specific training can be much shorter because you have a well-established mileage base. Some runners prefer a slower buildup, while others chose a short, intense segment of training.

External factors. When setting your marathon goal, consider that outside factors, such as terrain, temperature, and race size all have the potential to affect your performance. If you are accustomed to training in cool, dry conditions, but your chosen goal race is likely to be hot and humid, adjust your final time goal. You may also predict a slightly faster time on a flat course and a somewhat slower time on a course with an abundance of hills. Additionally, if you are running a large marathon and are stuck behind a big crowd in one of the last corrals, you may want to tack on a few extra minutes. While your chip won't begin timing until you cross the start line, your time may be affected by a slower mass of runners in front of you.

Race-Equivalency Chart

A race-equivalency chart (Table 6.1) is a particularly handy tool for a runner looking to pinpoint a realistic time goal based on current ability. These charts offer you the chance to take a recent race time from another distance and see what an equal performance would be for an alternate distance. Instead of simply multiplying your mile pace at a shorter distance by 26.2, it offers an "equal performance" prediction. For instance, according to the chart, if you ran a 23:00-minute 5K, you should be able to run a 3:44:13 marathon. Since pace naturally slows with distance, the chart suggests what you'd probably be capable of in an equal performance at a longer distance.

If you don't have a race time logged, another option is to complete a "field test" by going to your local track and doing a time trial. To do this, complete a short warm-up as you would before any SOS workout. Then run 1 mile as fast as you can at a steady, hard pace. Following your cooldown, bring your time back to the race equivalency chart and check what might be a reasonable time goal for the marathon. The longer the race or time trial, the more accurate the marathon prediction on the chart will be. Unsurprisingly, a half-marathon will be a better determinant than a 1-mile time trial. The best way to figure out an appropriate goal is to plug in several times from varying distances and see the range that they put you in. I have known a few runners who couldn't use shorter race distances as predictors because they could hold very close to their best 5K pace all the way up to the half-marathon distance. Every runner is different, so if you have several times available from different distances, you will be able to more accurately predict a finishing time in the marathon.

Regardless of the goal time, be sure to select it before you begin the strength segment of the training program, which is when the majority of the

TABLE 6.1 RACE-EQUIVALENCY CHART

MILE	2 MILE	5K	10K	15K
12:59	27:43	45:00	1:33:29	2:24:51
12:16	26:10	42:30	1:28:17	2:16:49
11:32	24:38	40:00	1:23:06	2:08:46
11:24	24:19	39:30	1:22:03	2:07:09
11:15	24:01	39:00	1:21:01	2:05:33
11:06	23:42	38:30	1:19:59	2:03:56
10:58	23:24	38:00	1:18:56	2:02:19
10:49	23:06	37:30	1:17:54	2:00:43
10:40	22:47	37:00	1:16:52	1:59:06
10:32	22:29	36:30	1:15:49	1:57:30
10:23	22:10	36:00	1:14:47	1:55:53
10:14	21:52	35:30	1:13:45	1:54:17
10:06	21:33	35:00	1:12:42	1:52:40
9:57	21:15	34:30	1:11:40	1:51:03
9:48	20:56	34:00	1:10:38	1:49:27
9:40	20:38	33:30	1:09:35	1:47:50
9:31	20:19	33:00	1:08:33	1:46:14
9:22	20:01	32:30	1:07:31	1:44:37
9:14	19:42	32:00	1:06:28	1:43:01
9:05	19:24	31:30	1:05:26	1:41:24
8:56	19:05	31:00	1:04:24	1:39:47
8:48	18:47	30:30	1:03:21	1:38:11
8:39	18:28	30:00	1:02:19	1:36:34
8:30	18:10	29:30	1:01:17	1:34:58
8:22	17:51	29:00	1:00:15	1:33:21
8:13	17:33	28:30	59:12	1:31:45
8:04	17:14	28:00	58:10	1:30:08
7:56	16:56	27:30	57:08	1:28:31
7:47	16:37	27:00	56:05	1:26:55
7:39	16:19	26:30	55:03	1:25:18
7:30	16:00	26:00	54:01	1:23:42
7:21	15:42	25:30	52:58	1:22:05

Use one race distance to see what an equal performance would be for another distance. Do not confuse with a pace chart, which indicates paces associated with various finishing times.

10 MILE	HALF-MARATHON	25K	MARATHON
2:36:38	3:28:01	4:10:24	7:18:42
2:27:56	3:16:27	3:56:29	6:54:19
2:19:14	3:04:54	3:42:35	6:29:57
2:17:29	3:02:35	3:39:48	6:25:04
2:15:45	3:00:16	3:37:01	6:20:12
2:14:00	2:57:58	3:34:14	6:15:20
2:12:16	2:55:39	3:31:27	6:10:27
2:10:32	2:53:20	3:28:40	6:05:35
2:08:47	2:51:02	3:25:53	6:00:42
2:07:03	2:48:43	3:23:06	5:55:50
2:05:18	2:46:24	3:20:19	5:50:57
2:03:34	2:44:06	3:17:32	5:46:05
2:01:49	2:41:47	3:14:45	5:41:12
2:00:05	2:39:28	3:11:58	5:36:20
1:58:21	2:37:10	3:09:11	5:31:27
1:56:36	2:34:51	3:06:25	5:26:35
1:54:52	2:32:32	3:03:38	5:21:42
1:53:07	2:30:14	3:00:51	5:16:50
1:51:23	2:27:55	2:58:04	5:11:58
1:49:38	2:25:36	2:55:17	5:07:05
1:47:54	2:23:18	2:52:30	5:02:13
1:46:10	2:20:59	2:49:43	4:57:20
1:44:25	2:18:40	2:46:56	4:52:28
1:42:41	2:16:22	2:44:09	4:47:35
1:40:56	2:14:03	2:41:22	4:42:43
1:39:12	2:11:44	2:38:35	4:37:50
1:37:28	2:09:26	2:35:48	4:32:58
1:35:43	2:07:07	2:33:01	4:28:05
1:33:59	2:04:48	2:30:14	4:23:13
1:32:14	2:02:30	2:27:27	4:18:20
1:30:30	2:00:11	2:24:41	4:13:28
1:28:45	1:57:52	2:21:54	4:08:36

Continues

TABLE 6.1 CONTINUED

MILE	2 MILE	5K	10K	15K
7:13	15:24	25:00	51:56	1:20:29
7:04	15:05	24:30	50:54	1:18:52
6:55	14:47	24:00	49:51	1:17:15
6:47	14:28	23:30	48:49	1:15:39
6:38	14:10	23:00	47:47	1:14:02
6:29	13:51	22:30	46:44	1:12:26
6:21	13:33	22:00	45:42	1:10:49
6:12	13:14	21:30	44:40	1:09:13
6:03	12:56	21:00	43:37	1:07:36
5:55	12:37	20:30	42:35	1:05:59
5:46	12:19	20:00	41:33	1:04:23
5:37	12:00	19:30	40:30	1:02:46
5:29	11:42	19:00	39:28	1:01:10
5:20	11:23	18:30	38:26	59:33
5:11	11:05	18:00	37:24	57:57
5:03	10:46	17:30	36:21	56:20
4:58	10:37	17:15	35:50	55:32
4:54	10:28	17:00	35:19	54:43
4:50	10:19	16:45	34:48	53:55
4:45	10:09	16:30	34:17	53:07
4:41	10:00	16:15	33:45	52:19
4:37	9:51	16:00	33:14	51:30
4:32	9:42	15:45	32:43	50:42
4:28	9:32	15:30	32:12	49:54
4:24	9:23	15:15	31:41	49:05
4:19	9:14	15:00	31:10	48:17
4:15	9:05	14:45	30:38	47:29
4:11	8:55	14:30	30:07	46:41
4:06	8:46	14:15	29:36	45:52
4:02	8:37	14:00	29:05	45:04
3:58	8:28	13:45	28:34	44:16
3:53	8:18	13:30	28:03	43:27

Use one race distance to see what an equal performance would be for another distance. Do not confuse with a pace chart, which indicates paces associated with various finishing times.

10 MILE	HALF-MARATHON	25K	MARATHON
1:27:01	1:55:34	2:19:07	4:03:43
1:25:17	1:53:15	2:16:20	3:58:51
1:23:32	1:50:56	2:13:33	3:53:58
1:21:48	1:48:38	2:10:46	3:49:06
1:20:03	1:46:19	2:07:59	3:44:13
1:18:19	1:44:00	2:05:12	3:39:21
1:16:34	1:41:42	2:02:25	3:34:28
1:14:50	1:39:23	1:59:38	3:29:36
1:13:06	1:37:04	1:56:51	3:24:43
1:11:21	1:34:46	1:54:04	3:19:51
1:09:37	1:32:27	1:51:17	3:14:58
1:07:52	1:30:08	1:48:30	3:10:06
1:06:08	1:27:50	1:45:43	3:05:14
1:04:24	1:25:31	1:42:57	3:00:21
1:02:39	1:23:12	1:40:10	2:55:29
1:00:55	1:20:54	1:37:23	2:50:36
1:00:02	1:19:44	1:35:59	2:48:10
59:10	1:18:35	1:34:36	2:45:44
58:18	1:17:26	1:33:12	2:43:17
57:26	1:16:16	1:31:49	2:40:51
56:34	1:15:07	1:30:25	2:38:25
55:41	1:13:58	1:29:02	2:35:59
54:49	1:12:48	1:27:38	2:33:33
53:57	1:11:39	1:26:15	2:31:06
53:05	1:10:30	1:24:51	2:28:40
52:13	1:09:20	1:23:18	2:26:14
51:20	1:08:11	1:22:05	2:23:48
50:28	1:07:02	1:20:41	2:21:21
49:36	1:05:52	1:19:18	2:18:55
48:44	1:04:43	1:17:54	2:16:29
47:52	1:03:33	1:16:31	2:14:03
46:59	1:02:24	1:15:07	2:11:36

ASK THE COACH

How much can I expect to improve from one marathon to another?

That depends a lot on where you start from. Regardless of age, a good rule of thumb is that the less experience you have with a distance, the bigger improvements you can make. For instance, I can coach a new runner who ran 5:00 hours in his first marathon attempt to 4:00 hours in his next attempt (provided the time allows for another complete training cycle). That's a 20 percent improvement! On the other end of the spectrum, to take a seasoned 2:15 marathoner to 2:14 takes more planning and attention to detail than our 5:00-hour runner, and yields only about a 1 percent improvement. By simply getting a 5:00-hour marathoner to run a little more, I can see big improvements. Whereas with the 2:15 runner, we must pay far more attention to details, such as nutrition, stretching, and strength training, in order to eke out even the smallest of improvements.

Understanding where you are with training and past performances are the keys to figuring out how much you can improve from one training segment to the next.

marathon-specific training is completed. That time goal provides a tangible number on which to base those SOS workouts.

Adjusting Goals

While race-equivalency charts are helpful, some runners, especially those new to the marathon distance, find they need to adjust their goal time once they get into training. If you overestimated what you'd be capable of on marathon day, you'll know for certain once you get into longer tempo runs and strength runs. If you're struggling on an 8-mile tempo run at goal pace, it is safe to assume that the pace will be too tough to hold for another 18 miles on race day. In this case, it is best to adjust your goal time to a slightly slower

ASK THE COACH

I'm 56. Can I still PR?

Essentially, how much you can improve depends more on your experience with the event than on your age. You will typically see the biggest percent improvement from your first to second marathon, while your fifth to sixth marathon, for example, typically yields a much smaller percent improvement. Age is less of a factor in this than you might expect. However, if you are an experienced marathoner in the masters category, you'll eventually have to face Father Time. This is not to say you'll see a dramatic drop-off in performance, but rather, your training regimen may need to change in order to maintain your level of performance. While it is highly individual, undoubtedly, at some point, performance levels off and then gradually declines for all veteran runners.

finishing performance in order to ensure that you have confidence going into the race.

At the other end of the spectrum, some runners want to set the bar higher once they begin SOS workouts. Perhaps you originally thought a 3:30 marathon was reasonable and now you think 3:15 would be more appropriate. This situation can be tricky. While we like to encourage runners to pursue their greatest potential, we also don't want to set them up for failure. If you become overzealous in your training, you risk overtraining and injury, which means you might not even get to the starting line, much less the finish. Ask yourself if, when you first began training, you would have been happy with your original time goal. If the answer is "yes," then why jeopardize training by entering into uncharted territory? Especially with race day nearing, ramping up training can spell disaster for a runner. Always remember: You'll run a better marathon slightly undertrained than you will overtrained. In fact, many times the greatest battle is just getting to the starting line healthy and fresh.

Other Types of Goals

In addition to your overall time goal, you may have other small goals you want to reach along the way. For instance, many of the runners who attempt the program have never run 30, 40, or 50 miles per week; maybe your first incremental goals are simply to hit those marks. Reaching a weekly mileage goal can be a huge motivating factor, especially when you are fatigued and questioning why you're doing this in the first place. Not only can this rejuvenate your spirit for running and keep you moving forward, it demonstrates that tangible progress is being made. You can also set goals related to supplemental training (discussed in detail in Chapter 7). Many runners find motivation in setting targets for their crosstraining, stretching, and resistance training routines, as well as prioritization. These goals may be as general as "I'm going to stretch after every workout." The higher you have set your ultimate time goal, the more important these variables become.

In the same way you should use the SMART goals strategy for your race-day goal, you should also utilize it to set these smaller goals along the way. Be sure these goals are specific, measurable, attainable, realistic, and timely. Goals of any sort narrow your focus and give meaning to your training. Without them, runners are left to their own devices, training haphazardly and setting themselves up for failure. Give your goals some serious consideration and begin by setting the small goals that will help you achieve that ultimate time goal.

7

SUPPLEMENTAL TRAINING

AS YOU HAVE PROBABLY GATHERED, to run your best marathon you must prepare by doing a whole lot of running. Nevertheless, there are other activities that you can do in smaller quantities to boost optimal performance and prevent injury. These include crosstraining, flexibility, and strength work. Since you want these activities to support your training, rather than hinder it, you have to be careful what supplemental training you include and when. Marathon preparation is hard enough. This is not the time to begin a Tae Kwon Do class or power-lifting regimen. Implementing a minimal amount of crosstraining, along with a bit of flexibility and strength, however, may better your marathon performance. Not only do these types of exercises allow you to work on certain weaknesses that may be limiting your running potential, but they also provide variety to your training, making you a better overall athlete. Just remember that this is supplementing training, not replacing it.

Crosstraining

While crosstraining attracts a lot of attention in sports media and is a staple of some training plans, the Hansons Marathon Method limits its inclusion. The reasoning is quite simple: The most direct path to becoming a better runner is through running. This notion follows a basic principle of physiology, known as "the rule of specificity." The idea is that your body adapts specifically to the stress that it is placed under. Although a 30-minute swim is great for general fitness, it doesn't translate directly into good running performance.

We always tell runners in our training programs to consider their previous experience with a crosstraining activity and to stay away from new exercises until after the marathon. While you may be feeling fitter than ever during training, be sure to temper that zeal for exercise. You are already under enough physical stress leading up to the marathon; adding a new activity to the mix just increases risk of injury and threatens to derail your focus. Runners most commonly want to add in crosstraining on Wednesdays, their day off of running. While biking or doing Pilates is great for your health in almost every other circumstance, those activities may serve only to curb recovery from running, making them less productive and potentially destructive. If you always ride your bike to work and have been for years, by all means, continue your routine within reason. In this case, your body has already adapted to that exercise. If it is a long ride, however, consider taking the bus on SOS workout days. If you were a Pilates junkie before marathon training, you should cut your practice down, but not necessarily out. Remember: *Don't start anything new until after 26.2.*

The other guide to deciding whether or not to crosstrain is your body itself. If you are having trouble recovering from running workouts, you shouldn't be piling on supplemental training. And if you think you may be overtraining, replacing running with a crosstraining activity isn't the answer either. If that is the case, you would benefit more from a day off so you can return to running feeling fresh the following day. If you are following the schedule and still feel you need something else beyond the recommended running, we suggest shifting your focus away from crosstraining and toward other details like flexibility and strength training. We'll discuss both in detail later in this chapter.

We occasionally encounter runners who claim that they simply can't handle higher mileage and therefore need to crosstrain to replace mileage. Before automatically sending them to the elliptical, I take a hard look at the paces they are running, the shoes they are wearing, the races they are doing, and anything else that could potentially be sabotaging their running. Most of the time, it is a training issue; however, once in a while, a person just can't seem to adapt to running mileage no matter what changes are made. If you find yourself in this boat, step back and weigh the pros and cons of your marathon goal. If you find that you truly can't handle the mileage, then a marathon may not be your event and that's OK. Over the years, however, we have encountered far more runners who struggle to remain healthy on low-mileage/high long-run programs than they do on the moderate weekly mileage/long-run volumes offered by the Hansons Marathon Method.

Despite our cautious approach to crosstraining, we do believe it can play a small but significant role in marathon preparation. The most obvious reason to include alternate exercises is for injury rehabilitation. If you find yourself with an injury, supplemental exercises can actually get you back on your feet faster by providing a reduced weight-bearing activity, allowing for increased blood flow to the injured area to promote tissue repair. Additionally, they help maintain cardiovascular fitness, thereby making your return to running fairly seamless. Indeed, sitting on the couch waiting for something to heal isn't the answer.

The key to crosstraining during injury is to find an activity that mimics running as closely as possible, such as an elliptical trainer or a stationary bike. While options like the rowing machine may be a great cardiovascular exercise, the emphasis is placed on the upper body and won't help the running muscles. It should be noted that the protocol can vary based on the specific injury. If you have a broken foot, for instance, biking will only aggravate the ailment further. Be cognizant of whether the activity affects the area and steer clear of anything that causes pain.

Another instance in which we might recommend crosstraining is during periods of planned downtime away from running. For example, after every marathon, runners in our Elite Program automatically take two weeks off of running. The 26.2 miles of pounding beats a runner up, especially after the first attempt at the distance. A two-week hiatus can give runners time to restore damaged muscles, rejuvenate the spirit, and plan the next move. Crosstraining offers the opportunity to enhance that recovery by providing a way to continue burning calories and avoid losing all of the fitness gained during marathon training.

The final reason we prescribe crosstraining is to provide a beginning runner a means through which to ease into the sport. For those who have never run or aren't already active, there is a limit to how many days they can safely run, at least at the onset of training. When starting out, they may only be able to run for 15 minutes at a time, two or three days a week. In this situation, it is important to fill the other days with workouts on the elliptical, or a bike, or even a walk. As general fitness improves, these crosstraining days can gradually be replaced with running. For most true beginners, it can take several months to transition into running five or six days per week. However, the key in this situation is that the new runner is using crosstraining as a bridge from just starting out to becoming strong enough or fit enough to handle more days of running in a week.

Flexibility and Stretching

Flexibility has long been a hot-button topic in the running community. I remember standing among my high school track team in a circle while the team captains barked out things like "Hurdler stretch!" and "Switch legs!" before jogging from the gym up to the track to work out. For a long time it seemed like nobody really knew what was good for us. Indeed, the term flexibility itself is vague. What does it mean exactly? It is simply a general label that covers a number of different ideas. In this section, we will endeavor to parse this term for you and give you guidance to move forward.

Stretching has been inextricably linked to the sport of running since the jogging craze of the 1970s, but the topic is more complex than you might think and can impact your running in a number of ways. By itself, flexibility refers to the maximal static range of motion (ROM) for a particular joint. The more flexible a person is throughout his or her joint ROM, the more easily the muscles surrounding that joint can be stretched. While this makes for a more elastic muscle that's less prone to injury, it also means the muscle can't create as much power. Imagine a Stretch Armstrong doll; the more you pull his arm, the wimpier-looking he gets. In the same way, the farther you stretch a muscle, the less elastic power it will have to fire. This is where active ROM becomes important. This type of flexibility, called dynamic stretching, is conducted through a set of active movements that target the running joints and muscles. To properly implement a flexibility routine, you must understand the difference between static and dynamic stretching and where they do (and do not) belong in your training. While there has been conflicting research over the years, the latest and most convincing evidence suggests that there is a time and a place for both active (dynamic) and static stretching. For both performance and injury prevention, it is important to do the right type of stretching at the right times.

DYNAMIC STRETCHING

This form of flexibility training involves rhythmic movement throughout a person's full range of motion. These motions are deliberate and controlled. One type of active stretching, often referred to as "ballistic stretching," is fast-paced, bouncy, and takes the joint beyond the natural range of motion. This can be fairly dangerous and put you at risk for injury, so we generally suggest avoiding ballistic movements. Dynamic stretching, on the other hand, focuses on proper form and motions that help to actively increase range of motion within reasonable parameters. Dynamic stretching benefits a runner in a number of ways. First and foremost, the dynamic movements reduce muscle stiffness, which decreases the risk of muscular injury. They also help prepare your body to run faster by loosening you up without stretching your muscles to the point of reducing their power. In fact, dynamic stretching can actually stimulate fast-twitch and intermediate fibers that are often neglected during traditional run training. The other advantage of this type of stretching is its influence on training the brain and the muscles to work in concert by engaging the muscle fibers and the nervous system simultaneously.

Dynamic stretching should be done before your main run. It is effective in two key ways. First, it makes an excellent transition phase from complete rest to running. For example, because I wake up early and have a 30-minute drive to meet my team for 8 a.m. runs, I always take a few minutes before the run for dynamic stretching. I feel looser and can start out a run significantly faster than I could otherwise. Second, dynamic stretching is a great way to improve running form and economy, by focusing on running-specific movements.

To implement, warm up 1–3 miles and then perform some of the exercises below, choosing the exercises you like best. Perform them in any order you please. The first six, which we call "dynamic warm-up level 1" (DWU1), are perfect for a quick daily pre-run routine for easy or long runs. This should take no more than 10 minutes. For a pre-SOS workout, add exercises 7–12 (dynamic warm-up level 2, or DWU2) to the mix. This routine should take no more than 20 minutes.

DYNAMIC WARM-UP LEVEL 1 (DWU1)

DWU1

1 Arm Swings

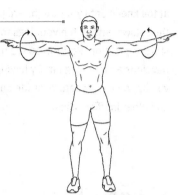

Standing tall with feet shoulder-width apart, swing your arms in a circular, clockwise motion, mimicking propeller blades on each side of your body. Avoid crossing your arms over your chest. Keep your back straight and knees slightly bent. After 6–10 repetitions, swing the arms from the sides across your chest in a back-and-forth motion for another 6–10 repetitions. These exercises help relax the major upper-body muscles, making your upper body more efficient during running. This is particularly advantageous because runners tend to carry tension in their arms and shoulders, which affects the rest of the stride.

2 Side Bends

With the same posture as Arm Swings but with hands on your hips, lean smoothly from left to right, being careful not to lean backward or forward. Repeat 16–20 times. These bends assist in keeping the spine mobile.

3 Hip Circles

With hands on your hips, make hip circles, as though you are using a Hula-Hoop. Perform in a clockwise motion for 10–12 rotations and then reverse direction for another 10–12 rotations. By opening up your hips, this exercise allows for a better range of motion in your stride.

4 Half-Squat

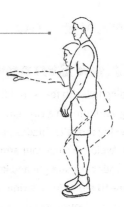

With hands on hips or straight in front of you, bend at the knees until your thighs are parallel to the floor, then slowly straighten your legs to return to the starting position. Perform 10–12 times. The Half-Squat develops a higher leg lift. By having a higher leg lift, you improve your natural stride and avoid shuffling and other inefficiencies.

5 Leg Kicks

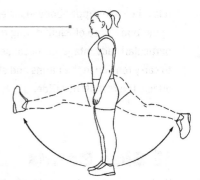

Stand with your left side next to a wall or fence, placing your weight on your right (outside) leg and left hand on the wall/fence. Swing your left leg forward and backward in a pendulum motion for 10–12 repetitions. Reverse position and do the same with the right leg.

6 Leg Swings

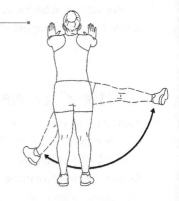

Stand facing a wall/fence with both hands on the wall/fence, placing your weight on your left leg. Swing your right leg across the front of your body. Swing it as far left as you can move comfortably and then back to the right as far as you can move comfortably. Do 10–12 times and switch legs.

DYNAMIC WARM-UP LEVEL 2 (DWU2)

1 Slow Skipping

Skip slowly for 30–50 meters (10–15 seconds). Turn around and skip back to your starting position.

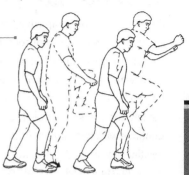

2 High Knees

Jog slowly and focus on lifting your knees toward your chest in a marching fashion. Pay attention to driving the knee toward the chest, and also maintain proper arm carriage and pump rhythmically with the opposite knee. (Proper arm carriage means elbows bent and moving back and forth as if on a pendulum at the shoulder.) The up-and-down actions should be quick, but your movement forward should be steady and controlled. Travel 30–50 meters, then return to start.

3 Butt Kicks

In this reverse motion of High Knees, pull your heels back rapidly toward your rear end. Again, the motions should be quick, but your linear movement steady. Travel 30–50 meters, turn, and continue back to your starting position.

4 Cariocas

Also known as the "grapevine," this is the trickiest of the exercises in terms of coordination. With arms perpendicular to your torso or bent at your sides, stand with feet shoulder-width apart. Moving to the left, pull your right foot behind the left. Sidestep to the left, then cross the right leg in front of the left. Continue with this motion. Basically the legs are twisting around each other while the torso stays still on the twisting pelvis. Travel 30–50 meters, turn, and continue these steps back to your starting position.

5 Bounders

These are a similar motion to High Knees, except instead of driving the knees high into the chest, focus on pushing off with your trailing leg and driving forward. It is a cross between Slow Skipping and High Knees. Travel 30–50 meters, turn, and continue back to your starting position.

6 Sprints

To close out the routine, do 4–6 repetitions of a 75–100-meter sprint at near-maximal effort. Always do your fast running with the wind, so jog back against the wind to start a new sprint. The sprints shouldn't last more than 15 seconds, so slower runners should begin with 75-meter sprints.

By actively engaging the muscles and getting the neuromuscular connections firing, you are (1) preparing your body to run fast, (2) working on specific running motions that will aid in proper form development, and (3) developing a neuromuscular connection to fast and intermediate muscle fibers that will serve as a major advantage late in the marathon when your slow-twitch fibers are fried. If you are looking to improve performance without sacrificing a lot of time, then we strongly suggest adding a dynamic routine to your training toolbox.

STATIC STRETCHING

When most people talk about stretching, they are referring to static flexibility. Unlike dynamic stretching, static stretching is done standing or sitting still, rather than using an active motion. For years, runners have performed static stretching routines before workouts and races. Ironically, this is probably the worst time for this type of movement as it reduces your muscles' ability to produce force because it stretches the muscles too much. The muscles lose their elasticity as they are stretched, making them less powerful and also putting you at risk for a muscle tear. Even so, there is a place for static stretching in your training toolbox; you just have to know when and how to use it.

When is the best time for static stretching? The answer depends on what you hope to achieve from the stretch. There has been much research to support the use of static stretching after workouts as a means of injury prevention. For instance, calf tightness has been shown to be associated with pronation of the rear foot, which causes the tibia and fibula (lower leg bones) to internally rotate, a pain that is commonly referred to as shin splints. More specifically, this kind of inflexibility can lead to tendonitis, stress fractures, Achilles tendon injuries, and knee issues. Poor flexibility also tends to cause the front of the pelvis to tilt forward, creating excessive curvature in the lower back. The result of all this is a tightening of the lower back muscles, which predisposes the runner to back injuries. However, we have to be careful of what our definition of "after workouts" means. Immediately following an easy run, doing the following light static stretching routine (LS) is fine. It promotes muscle health and helps make you feel better. But if you are trying to improve your tissue length, then save the static stretching for several hours after an intense workout. We'll discuss this second scenario on page 167.

LIGHT STATIC STRETCHING (LS) AFTER A WORKOUT

The following nine stretches should be performed post-run, holding for 20 seconds; perform 1–3 repetitions each. Do not stretch to the point of pain or until the muscle shakes; rather, keep each movement slow and controlled. These stretches should be incorporated into your daily routine and will take about 10–15 minutes. If you are in a rush, the routine can be done later in the day, but never prior to a run.

1 Low Back

Lie flat on your back. Draw both legs toward your chest. For a stretch, place hands behind knees and pull knees close to chest. This stretch will isolate the long back muscles running from the pelvis to the shoulder blades.

2 Shoulder

Stand upright with feet shoulder-width apart. Extend your right arm so that it is perpendicular to the torso. Place your left hand on your right elbow or slightly above it, then gently pull the right arm across your chest toward your left side. Repeat with the left arm. We tend to carry tension in our shoulders. Many runners pull their shoulders up when they get tired, creating poor form and wasting energy. This move reduces that effect.

3 Chest

Standing upright facing an open doorway, place feet shoulder-width apart. One foot should be slightly in front of the other for balance. With your arms extended straight out to the sides (you should look like a T), place your arms against the wall on either side of the doorway, palms touching the wall. Lean forward until you feel a gentle stretch in the pectoral muscles and biceps. Many runners tend to have very tight chest muscles that cause them to hunch their upper back. This stretch fights poor posture and form that can lead to inefficient running.

4 Calves

Stand a foot or two away from a wall, leaning forward so your hands are bracing you against the wall. With the left foot stationary, slide the right foot back another 12 inches. Your heels should stay on the floor. As your chest gets closer to the wall, slightly bend the right leg to stretch the calf muscle. Repeat for the left leg. Added flexibility in the calf muscles helps you to avoid potential pronation and tendon problems.

5 Gluteal

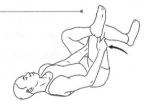

Lie on your back on a soft, flat surface. Bend your left leg so that the knee is pointing upward but the foot is still flat on the floor. Next, fold the right leg so that the ankle of that leg is resting on the left knee. Your right leg should be perpendicular to your left leg. Interlock your hands within the fold of the left leg, pulling the left knee toward your chest as far as you comfortably can. Repeat on the opposite side.

6 Groin

Stand upright with your feet wider than shoulder-width apart. Lower the right hip in squat, bending the right leg and extending your left leg to the side. If needed for balance, place your hands on your right knee. You should feel a stretch along the inside of the left leg. Switch sides and repeat.

7 Hamstrings

Sit on a flat, soft surface. Bend the left knee so that the bottom of the left foot is touching the inside of the right thigh. The right leg should be straight out from the body with a slight bend at the knee. Slowly bend from the waist so that the stretch is truly focused on the hamstring muscle group and not the upper back. Repeat with the right leg.

8 Hip Flexors/Quads

Step forward with your right leg as if performing a lunge; your left leg should be extended behind you, left knee touching the floor. Your right knee should be directly above your right ankle. Keeping the torso straight, push your hips forward so that your right knee is past your right ankle and your left knee is behind your hips. You should feel the stretch in your left hip flexors and quadriceps. Repeat on the other side.

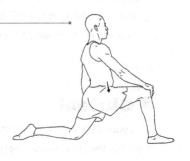

9 Hips

Sit on the floor with your right leg extended, left leg crossed over right. Your left foot will be on the outside of your right leg. Next, place your right arm so that the elbow is on the outside (right side) of the left knee, or simply grip your left knee with your right hand. Your left arm should be a brace near the hip. Twist to the left. Repeat on the opposite side.

The purpose behind stretches 5–9 is identical. The muscles in the pelvis are used for stability, but they can also limit range of motion. If these muscles are tight, the natural stride length is diminished, leading to a decrease in running economy. By keeping these muscles flexible and allowing free range of motion, you maximize your natural stride length.

If your goal is to actually lengthen the tissue, then these stretches should be held for a longer period, which does involve some pain. When we are lengthening the tissues, we are basically pulling apart a knotted mess of muscle fibers. While increasing tissue length is uncomfortable, the good news is that you do not do this type of stretching for all muscles. Most people need this only for their Achilles, hip flexors, and maybe hamstrings.

Hold these stretches for 3–5 minutes, to a point of slight discomfort. Remember, change takes time; even if you do these every day, it will be about 12 weeks before you see noticeable improvement.

Strength Training

Strength (resistance) training is another form of supplemental work some runners choose to utilize. Increased strength contributes to better running in a number of ways. First and foremost, it helps to improve form, especially as you become fatigued. Recently we did a VO_2max test on an athlete and watched her form as she progressed through the test. During the last stages, her posture notably deteriorated, especially in her lower back. This caused her shoulders to round and her stride to shorten significantly. In a follow-up test 14 weeks later, she performed the same test; however, in the interim she followed our basic plan and incorporated some of the strength training discussed below. The results were amazing! She was able to go about 6 minutes longer on the test and maintained good form throughout. Two weeks later, she PR'd at her marathon by more than 8 minutes.

Strength training can also assist in preventing injuries through the protective effects of stronger muscles. Finally, strength training helps to fight fatigue by training the body to be able to draw from fast-twitch fibers late in an endurance event.

A number of different exercises belong under the strength-training umbrella, including the dynamic drills described in the previous section, core-muscle training, and free weights. I often hear that runners avoid strength training because they are worried about putting on bulk and gaining weight. While the theory is correct, in reality it is fairly difficult to add any significant muscle mass onto your body weight. If the right exercises are done in the correct volumes, the average runner won't have to worry about putting on extra pounds. In other words, spending 30 minutes a day 2–3 days per week doing basic strength training is not going to turn you into a linebacker. Just a stronger, better runner.

There are many options for adding strength training to a running program. Our basic philosophy involves three main ideas: (1) It should complement the running regimen; strength work should never replace running. (2) It should improve weaknesses, muscle imbalances, and running form; in essence, strength training should help to improve running performance. (3) It should be short and simple.

Within strength training, there are levels. Just as we wouldn't throw brand-new runners into an interval workout their first day, we would not ask someone new to strength training to do Olympic lifts right out of the gate. Rather, we start with basic body-weight and movement exercises

(BWM). If you incorporate the dynamic stretching component along with the BWM routine below, then you are well on your way to becoming stronger. Start with these two components for several weeks. Once you feel you have mastered these, you can consider adding resistance strength training (RT). Implementation is pretty flexible. If you run in the morning, you can do these right after an easy run or wait and do them during a break at work or in the evening as you watch TV. If you run at night, follow the same logic, stretching right after an easy run, or waiting until the next morning, perhaps while your coffee brews!

STRENGTH: BODY-WEIGHT AND MOVEMENT EXERCISES (BWM)

1 Crunch

Lie on your back, knees bent, and feet flat on the floor. Contract your abdominal muscles to pull your trunk up. Many people use momentum to carry themselves up or use their legs to push off and roll upward, neither of which provides the desired strength work. Instead focus on small movements from abdominal contractions. Movement during the Crunch may be only a few inches. Start with 3 sets of 10, progressing to 3 sets of 25 over the course of several weeks. At that point, increase either the number of sets or the number of reps per set. Strong abdominals are essential in maintaining running form and posture, and make it easier to tuck the pelvis underneath your body, improving stride through better body positioning.

Variation: You may also do Crunches on a ball. With knees bent at 90 degrees and back supported by the ball, contract your abdominal muscles to pull your trunk up.

2 Back Extension

Lie facedown on the floor, with the majority of your weight on your stomach. Extend both legs out about shoulder-width apart, and extend both arms straight out in front of you. (Alternately, fold your hands and rest them on the small of your back.) Contract the lower back muscles and square off your shoulders so that your entire back is straightened. Hold for 2–3 seconds and release. Repeat 12–15 times. During running, the back absorbs a lot of force upon each footstrike; the stronger it is, the better it will handle this shock.

Variation: This may also be done on an exercise ball with your toes on the floor for balance.

BWM

3 Superman

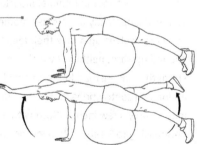

The Superman is similar to the Back Extension, but instead of simply contracting the back muscles in a stationary position, you lift one arm and the opposite leg. Lying facedown, lift your left arm and right leg at the same time. This strengthens the arms, glutes, and back in one shot. Hold each contraction for 1–2 seconds before releasing. Repeat 12–15 times on each side. Having a strong upper back means less shoulder slouching and promotes proper posture and upper-body running motion.

Variation: This may also be done on an exercise ball.

4 Squat

Stand with feet shoulder-width apart, hands at your sides. Flex your hips and knees as if sitting in a chair. The goal is to get your rear end as close to the floor as you are able, in a deep squat, in order to engage your glutes and hamstrings. If you can't go past a 90-degree angle in your hips, then go as far as you can. Over time, as you continue practicing, you will be able to deepen your squat.

5 Bridge

Lie on the floor with both legs bent and feet flat on the floor. Ideally your arms will be crossed over your chest, but you can extend them to the side if needed for stability. Rise up by contracting the glutes, back, and hamstring muscles. The only points of contact with the floor should be the shoulders and the feet. Hold each contraction for 1–3 seconds and perform 12–15 repetitions. As this becomes easier, you can move to a one-legged version, with one leg bent and the other leg straight and raised off the floor. This is intended to strengthen the glutes and hamstrings, which are often weaker than the quads due to running. It also stretches the notoriously tight hip flexors.

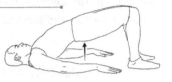

BWM

6 Side Plank

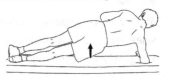

While the traditional plank focuses on the front abdominals, the side plank focuses on the obliques, or side abdominals. Lie on your right side. Then bend your right arm so that the humerus bone, or the bone between the shoulder and elbow, is the "post" and your forearm is perpendicular to the rest of your body. Your right foot should rest on the floor with your left foot on top of it. Don't sag in the midsection or bend at the waist. Hold the position for 10–20 seconds then repeat on the left side. Increase the duration as you get stronger. This exercise helps to balance strength between the front and side abdominal muscles.

Together, these strength exercises offer an all-encompassing introduction to resistance training. Consider adding them to your running regimen and you'll surely notice a difference in a matter of weeks. While running can take up much of your time, strength training is a quick and easy way to potentially boost performance and ward off injuries.

Once you have adapted to the BWM exercises, consider upping your game by adding weight. Weight can be in the form of dumbbells, tubes or bands, medicine balls, machines, free weights, or machines. Use what you are comfortable with. No matter which you choose, your muscles will get stronger. Once mastered, consider adding resistance training (RT), as described in the next section.

STRENGTH: RESISTANCE TRAINING (RT)

These exercises should be done in 1–3 sets of 10–12 reps. At first, you may need to do only one set; add another as you feel stronger. At the end of the last few repetitions, you should feel like you can't do another rep with proper form. This is important as these last fatigued reps promote the greatest amounts of adaptation. Use a weight that feels heavy, but not so heavy that you can't do at least 10 reps. Remember all movements should be controlled, and recovery should be about 60 seconds between each set.

UPPER BODY

❶ Chest Press

Lie on your back on a bench or floor, arms extended to the sides with dumbbell in each hand. Bend legs so that feet are flat on the floor. Push dumbbells up and away from your chest so that arms are extended and perpendicular to your body. Lower in the same manner until weights are slightly below shoulder line.

❷ Lat Pull-Down

Sit on a bench or chair with back support, with feet flat on the floor. Hold dumbbells with arms raised and elbows bent at a 90-degree angle. Weights should be about ear height on either side. Press weights up until arms are extended; be careful not to lean so far back that you feel the chair back. Lower weights back to starting position.

❸ Kneeling Row

Holding a weight in your right hand, stand on the right side of a bench. Place your left hand and left knee on the bench so that your back is parallel to the bench. With right arm extended toward the floor, pull weight toward chest until weight is at chest level. Slowly extend arm back to starting position. Perform all reps on one side before doing the opposite side.

LOWER BODY

❹ Dumbbell Deadlift

Stand with feet shoulder-width apart, a dumbbell to the outside of each foot. Squat and pick up dumbbells (one in each hand). Your rear end should be low to the floor and your chest should be up; this is your starting position. Lift by extending legs first and then your back. Gently lower your back, then your legs, to starting position.

❺ Walking Lunges

Start with dumbbells in each hand and take a large step forward with the right leg. There should be roughly a 90-degree angle in your knee. Rise by extending the right leg, allowing the left leg to "swing" forward to the original starting point. Repeat for the left leg. Do 10–12 reps for each leg.

RT

6 Side Lunges

Stand with feet shoulder-width apart, holding a dumbbell centered at chest height and close to body. Knees should be slightly bent. With left leg anchored, step wide to the right so that the right knee is bent at a 90-degree angle. Step back up by extending the right leg and returning to the starting position. Alternate sides until you have completed 12 lunges for each side.

ASK THE COACH

Is it safe to progress with strength work while I'm training?

First, it is best to become proficient with the movement-based work, spending two weeks minimum at that stage. Then add in RT work once a week (while continuing BWM work for 1–2 days per week) on an easy or off day. After three weeks, do RT twice per week while continuing your BWM work alongside. The movement-based work can even be used as a warm-up preceding the heavier lifting.

If you have less than 10 weeks before your race, then we do not suggest going beyond the movement-based work. Pick up the heavier work when you return to running after your marathon.

If desired, you can eventually move up yet another level to doing more explosive Olympic-style lifting. However, proper form is imperative. Seek out a qualified personal trainer who can show you the correct technique for such lifts.

RT

This chapter gives you a lot of information to consume. But what does it all look like in practice? Refer to Appendix B for examples of what your overall training program might look like if you add stretching, flexibility, and strength training into the mix.

8

MARATHON NUTRITION AND HYDRATION

AS YOU EMBARK ON MARATHON training, it is worth having a sound understanding of the basic nutrition and hydration principles that will play a role in your success. As the saying goes, you'll only get out of your body what you put into it. Stated simply, when you fill the tank with the right kinds of fuel, both training and racing are supported. Never underestimate the fundamental importance of fuel and hydration choices. We are not registered dietitians, so our advice here comes directly from many years of coaching and competing. While we provide general recommendations, be sure to seek medical advice or consult a sports nutritionist for more specific guidance.

Marathon Nutrition

Hard training requires that you consider three important aspects of nutrition: consuming enough calories, consuming the right calories, and consuming calories at the right times. Once you have these three things figured out, you'll be well on your way to building an optimal base of fuel for training and racing.

CONSUMING ENOUGH CALORIES

Marathon training is a major undertaking, and your caloric needs will be different than they are during periods of inactivity or casual exercise. By taking in the right amount of calories, you'll maintain a healthy weight and support your training. Large calorie deficits can sabotage training and performance, leading to issues with overtraining, illness, and injury. Athletes who are afraid of eating too much tend to also be the ones who end up feeling burned out or injured, oftentimes as early as six weeks into hard training.

If you are looking to lose a bit of weight during marathon training, now is not the time to start a calorie-cutting diet. Generally speaking, we have found that hard training alone tends to lend itself to slight weight losses over the long term, without any major dietary shifts. Remember that in order to do that training in the first place, your body needs the proper fuel to stay up and running. Consequently, skipped meals and severe calorie restrictions (reducing your intake by 1,000 calories or more) will greatly impede your training and should be avoided. Not only are such diets unhealthy, they'll also keep you from running your best on a daily basis and will diminish race performance.

CALCULATING CALORIC NEEDS

Here are two quick formulas that give you an idea of how many calories you need on a daily basis. They are simple to use and accurate enough to give you a general range indicating what is appropriate for you based on body weight and level of exercise.

1. Light to moderately active (45–60 minutes of moderate activity, most days of the week)

   Body weight × 16–20 calories per pound = daily calories

2. Very active (60–120 minutes of moderate exercise, most days of the week)

Body weight × 21–25 calories per pound = daily calories

For example, here is a caloric range for a 150-pound runner who engages in 60 minutes of easy running per day:

150 lb. × 16 calories per pound = 2,400 calories
150 lb. × 20 calories per pound = 3,000 calories

This runner should consume between 2,400 and 3,000 calories per day. We provide these two formulas with the expectation that you will use both of them over the course of training. Obviously, you will need to consume more calories on your long-run day than you will on a short, easy day. Let the length of your run be your guide in choosing the equation that will compute the number of calories you should consume on that particular day. Over time, you'll internalize approximately how many calories you should take in so you won't need to continue referring to the equations. In any case, don't obsess over these numbers; they are simply meant to give you a general idea of the number of calories you should be consuming.

Having worked with runners of various ages and levels of experience, we find that most people tend to overestimate how many calories they need. Generally speaking, males should use the middle to higher end of the ranges, while women should refer to the middle to lower end. Age makes a difference too. We often hear this question from aging runners: "Since I'm older, should I be consuming fewer calories?" Again, generally speaking, men will typically need to cut their caloric consumption by 10 calories for every year of age past 20 and women should do so by seven calories per year. That said, these recommendations are based on what happens physiologically throughout the aging process in the context of a population that

TABLE 8.1 SERVINGS BY CALORIE LEVELS

	1,800 CALORIES	2,000 CALORIES	2,200 CALORIES
Grains	11 oz.	12 oz.	13 oz.
Fruits	2 cups	3 cups	3 cups
Vegetables	2 cups	2 cups	2 cups
Milk/yogurt	2 cups	2 cups	2 cups
Protein	6 oz.	6 oz.	8 oz.
Fats	4 tsp.	4 tsp.	5 tsp.

Adapted with permission from Monique Ryan, *Sports Nutrition for Endurance Athletes*, 3rd ed. (Boulder, CO: VeloPress, 2012).

tends to become increasingly sedentary with age. If you have maintained high activity levels throughout your life, caloric modification can be minor.

Table 8.1 gives you a general idea of how your caloric expenditure should be broken down into a healthy, runner-friendly diet. It will give you a good idea of how much you should be eating from the major food groups on a daily basis. As you get into training, extra calories come from sports drinks, bars, or gels that you are consuming before, during, and after major workouts.

CONSUMING THE RIGHT CALORIES

Now you know the approximate number of calories you need to consume during training, but you may still be wondering what types of foods are important to endurance performance. As you may have guessed, all calories are not created equal. While the number may be the same, the residual effects of eating 700 calories at a fast-food joint will vary considerably from consuming 700 calories from a home-cooked meal sourced from a local farmers' market. As you probably know, our bodies draw from three separate sources of energy: carbohydrates, fats, and protein. All are important for

2,400 CALORIES	2,600 CALORIES	2,800 CALORIES	3,000 CALORIES
14.5 oz.	15.5 oz.	16 oz.	17 oz.
3 cups	3 cups	3 cups	4 cups
3 cups	3 cups	3 cups	3 cups
2 cups	2 cups	2 cups (milk) 1 cup (yogurt)	2 cups (milk) 1 cup (yogurt)
8 oz.	9 oz.	10 oz.	10 oz.
5 tsp.	6 tsp.	7 tsp.	7 tsp.

different reasons and, in the right amounts, will keep you properly fueled for everyday excellence.

Carbohydrates

When it comes to marathon nutrition, carbohydrates dominate the discussion, as they should your diet, at least 50 percent of it. The more you train, the higher the number should be. The average runner using this program probably falls into the 50–60 percent range, whereas more competitive runners may be near 70 percent. Over the past few years, however, carbs have received a bad rap from the media, as more than a few folks have tried to cash in on our country's obsession with dieting. It turns out, however, that the conversation is somewhat misguided. To be sure, there is no denying that we are in the midst of an obesity epidemic, placing a major burden on people's health, as well as our nation's economy. It is also true that simple carbohydrates have largely contributed to this problem. But here's the caveat: There are two different types of carbohydrates, simple and complex, and only one of them is detrimental to a person's health when consumed in excess. Simple carbohydrates come from refined grains, soda, candy, and other processed foods, while complex carbohydrates are contained in vegetables and whole grains, such as oatmeal and brown rice. Both types of carbohydrates should play a role in the diet of an endurance athlete and will directly impact performance, but your main emphasis should be on fruits, vegetables, and whole grains. By focusing on complex carbohydrates, you will get the energy you need, as well as a number of important vitamins and minerals.

Carbohydrates are a necessary part of an endurance athlete's diet for a number of reasons. From the perspective of performance, carbohydrates are utilized much faster than fat and protein. That is why at increased intensities, carbohydrates become the sole fuel source by allowing our bodies to continue producing energy through anaerobic means once we have reached our VO_2max. Meanwhile, fat is used only at lower intensities because it can't keep up with high-energy demands, and protein is relied upon when carbohydrate stores are exhausted. Carbohydrates also aid in water absorption, so when you're taking in fluids during a long run, the carbohydrates will actually help the stomach empty faster, allowing the body to more efficiently utilize water. This means that fluids and carbohydrates reach their final destinations more quickly, and the faster they get there, the less likely you are to run out of energy and hit the wall.

Carbohydrates are also the primary fuel source for your brain and central nervous system. That foggy feeling or inability to focus late in a race generally stems from rapidly depleting glycogen (carbohydrate) stores. What's more, carbohydrates play a role in metabolism. You may have heard the saying "Fat burns in the flame of carbohydrates." Basically, by limiting your intake of carbohydrates, you may also limit your ability to burn fat. While not proven, the theory holds that the processes that carbohydrates and fats go through to provide energy result in certain by-products that are necessary for fat to be metabolized. Based on research I have seen, the major processes will still occur, but without carbohydrates, the process is about 20 percent less efficient. The point is that one nutrient can't replace another, and since carbohydrates are the limited source, carbohydrates are most likely to break the cycle: Limiting carbohydrates limits the body's entire fueling process. Finally, your body can't store many carbohydrates, so it's important that you replenish them on a daily basis. They account for a large portion of your recommended dietary intake because without carbohydrates, you wouldn't be able to train consistently, much less run a good marathon.

Carbohydrate stores play a significant role in your running performance. Consider the fact that among the liver, muscles, and bloodstream, your body can store only around 2,000 calories worth of carbohydrates. Your body utilizes those carbohydrate stores when exercising at even moderate intensities, but it begins to burn through them more rapidly as intensity increases. Refer back to Figure 2.2 and you'll see that at 60 percent intensity, the average person is burning fat and carbohydrates about 50/50. Since we have extremely limited carbohydrate stores and marathon pace is somewhere between 60 and 80 percent of maximal capabilities, you can see that if we are burning 100 calories per mile, then at least 50 calories per mile are coming from carbohydrates. To make matters more complicated, the body first burns through the carbohydrate (glycogen) stores in the muscles. Altogether, the muscles store about 1,500 calories, but only the muscles that are being used will actually burn that glycogen; unfortunately, our body doesn't allow one muscle to borrow glycogen from another muscle. For instance, the quadriceps won't be able to access glycogen from the trapezius muscles. So, even though running requires the quads to work harder, thus depleting the associated glycogen stores, they can't simply borrow unused glycogen from the lesser-working traps. Although you may have 1,500 calories worth of glycogen stored in your muscles, you won't be able to access all of it, decreasing the amount of usable glycogen even further.

On top of all this, the glycogen stored in the liver is reserved for your brain and central nervous system. The amount in the blood is even lower than what the liver has to offer, so don't count on that taking you very far.

In fact, when you've hit the wall in a marathon, you're at the point where you've become reliant on your blood sugar to assist the running muscles, so you're running on an empty tank. Plainly put, proper carbohydrate consumption provides the foundation of your nutritional training plan. Without those building blocks, your body will not tolerate any volume of mileage or level of intensity.

Fats

Fats are a necessary part of a balanced diet, especially when you consider the large quantity of fat that our bodies store. If you limit your fat intake, either you're not eating enough food in general or you're forced to eat other nutrients all day long in order to feel satiated. Since fat has about twice as many calories per gram as carbohydrates, a little bit of fat will go a long way in keeping you feeling full. Fat is also involved with the structure of cell membranes and spinal cord tissue, which can directly affect physical performance. Finally, fat is a particularly essential part of your diet because it helps the body absorb vitamins A, D, E, and K, all of which are necessary for optimal health.

In addition to contributing to overall wellness, fats lend a hand in supporting your marathon training and running performance. As your endurance increases, the mitochondria within the muscles grow and become denser, which consequently gives you the opportunity to produce a greater amount of aerobic energy. This is the point at which both fats and carbohydrates can be utilized. Once the exercise intensity reaches 85 percent or higher, however, there isn't enough oxygen available to allow fat to be burned, so carbohydrates become the primary source. The good news is that, while the average person switches to burning carbohydrates at around 60 percent of their maximal intensity, endurance training can bring that percentage up a few more points. This means that your body will be able to burn fat at a higher intensity before carbohydrates take over; in practical terms, you'll be capable of running a little bit faster for a little bit longer. Despite this, we still don't need to eat large amounts of fat. For the best results, your diet should include about 20 percent fats, coming from sources such as nuts, fish, seeds, and avocados. Limit your consumption of fatty meats.

Protein

Protein should make up the smallest amount of your diet, about 10–15 percent. It plays a major role in repairing damaged muscles after running and also serves as an energy source. When you get to the point of drawing from those protein stores, however, it's a last-ditch effort to stay up and running. Additionally, protein assists in the manufacture of enzymes, antibodies, and hormones within the body, as well as serving as a transporter of vitamins, minerals, and fat in the blood. Last but not least, protein helps to maintain fluid balance both inside and outside the cells. This is important because certain proteins in the blood regulate the balance of water in our tissues as we sweat. Without that mechanism, a person could run into serious issues with fluid loss, as well as incur electrolyte imbalances as a result of too much sweat loss. That could lead to muscle cramping, loss of coordination, or other serious medical issues.

During exercise, your body relies on protein to a small extent, but the nutrient's reparative abilities are its most important benefit to you as a marathon runner. And timing is everything. By consuming protein at the same time as carbohydrates following exercise, you minimize the damage done to the muscles and speed the pace of recovery. Most importantly, protein helps you as an athlete preserve lean muscle mass, which translates into better recovery and therefore higher-quality training. When lean muscle mass is protected and maintained, there is a greater opportunity for carbohydrates to be stored, further preserving lean muscle mass and leading to better fuel utilization during prolonged exercise. In extreme situations, that protein can be drawn upon as an energy source; however, it will come from the running muscles, signaling your body's slow breakdown. If you fuel the right way, fats and carbohydrates will provide the energy you need to successfully finish the marathon, and protein will be left to assist in postrun repair.

NUTRITIONAL TAKEAWAY

We've given you a good idea of the number and type of calories you should be consuming. Later in this chapter, we'll go into further depth regarding when these calories need to be ingested. Remember these central points from this section:

- For weight balance and to maintain a high level of performance, it's important to know approximately how many calories you need daily.
- There is no reason to shy away from carbs, as long as the majority is complex in nature.
- Fat is OK in moderation, especially fats that come from seeds, nuts, and fish.
- Lean protein helps create and preserve muscle tissue and, if necessary, provides energy.
- Eat a balanced diet and you'll be well on your way to supporting optimal running performance.
- Where you get your calories is as important as the number of calories.

Marathon Hydration

The human body is comprised of two-thirds water, making hydration just as critical to a runner's performance as nutrition. The impact of even slight sweat loss on endurance performance may surprise you. Research has shown that a decrease in hydration stores as small as 2 percent, or a mere three pounds of sweat for a 150-pound runner, can negatively affect physical performance. Since sweat rates can reach up to 1–2 pounds per hour on a cool, dry day, imagine the loss in hot and humid conditions. The resulting physical response to dehydration is multifaceted. Many of the effects stem from impaired cardiovascular functions via increased heart rate, decreased stroke volume, and decreased cardiac output. As discussed when we took a close look at physiology in Chapter 2, all of these affect a runner's VO$_2$max and therefore pace. Indeed, a 3 percent loss of sweat for that same 150-pound runner means a 4–8 percent decrease in aerobic capacity.

Besides the cardiac implications, dehydration leads to a number of other problems. First, it impairs your body's ability to dissipate heat, increasing your body temperature. Not only will this throw cold water on your performance, it will increase your risk of serious heat-related illnesses, like heat exhaustion and heat stroke. Gastrointestinal distress is another symptom, which may lead you to avoid drinking more fluids, making the problem even worse. Adding insult to injury, it can also cause an imbalance in electrolytes, which are critical for muscle contractions, leading to cramps, weakness, and incomplete conduction between nerves and muscles. In addition, the decreased VO$_2$max will cause you to burn through your glycogen stores at a much higher rate. If this wasn't bad enough, dehydration can even result in cognitive impairment, so you may not even have the wits to pull over and stop running.

While we aren't looking to scare you, we do want to emphasize the importance of hydration. When determining appropriate fluid intake, take into account the following list of factors that affect fluid loss:

- **Higher ambient temperatures.** The hotter it is, the more you'll sweat. Also, the more fit you are, the more you will sweat.

- **Higher humidity.** In certain cases, this can have a larger impact than actual air temperature. Take a look at the 2008 Olympic marathon in Beijing: The temperatures were very warm, but it was not humid. The overall times were fast and even included a new Olympic record. However, two years prior, in Osaka, Japan, the World Championship marathon was run in similar heat, but with higher humidity, and race times suffered significantly. Remember, the level of humidity close to your body can increase if you're wearing nonwicking materials next to the skin. This means that the cotton shirt you like to run in is creating a more humid environment around your body.

- **Body surface area.** Bigger runners have a higher capacity to dissipate heat, but they also have increased surface area to gain heat, especially in hot weather. In essence, the bigger you are, the more likely you are to be hotter and sweat more.

- **Condition of the athlete.** Highly trained athletes have a much better cooling potential than nonconditioned athletes.

- **Original state of hydration.** If a runner is already slightly dehydrated going into an event, he or she will reach critical points of dehydration much sooner than an athlete who is well hydrated.

While it is important to understand how fluid is lost, you'll also want to know what factors impact fluid absorption. That is, once we ingest the fluid, how does it get from the stomach to the bloodstream where we can actually use it? Let's start with carbohydrates. We already mentioned that they aid in the absorption of water, but it's important to note that different types of carbs are absorbed at varying rates. Since carbohydrates are basically chains of molecules, the longer the chain, the more time it will take to exit the stomach. As scientists have begun to grasp the inner workings of this process, sports drink companies started including two lengths of chained carbohydrates in their beverages (usually dextrose and maltodextrin). With these drinks, you get the short chains that are quickly absorbed for immediate usage and the longer chains that assist in sustained absorption over time.

The amount of fluid you consume at any given time can also influence the rate of absorption. Although larger amounts of fluids ingested at one time are absorbed more quickly, for obvious reasons you aren't going to want to gulp down multiple cups of water at a single water stop during the marathon. Instead, start by consuming large amounts of fluids during the days leading up to the event and smaller quantities the day before and the morning of the race. Keep in mind that the temperature of the fluid can also increase or decrease absorption. At rest there appears to be no difference, but during exercise, cooler fluids seem to leave the stomach much faster, while room-temperature drinks are more effectively utilized.

Although you will have little control over the temperature of your beverages along the marathon course, you do have the ability to influence other absorption-related factors, such as your relative state of hydration at the start line. Once you begin running, there is no turning back to correct your hydration status. If you're dehydrated at mile 1, you will continue to be dehydrated for the entire race. The progressive nature of dehydration makes it increasingly difficult to catch up once you're at a deficit. Similarly, the faster you run, the harder it becomes for your body to absorb fluids into the bloodstream because the blood is pulled away from nonvital functions and directed toward the exercising muscles. Instead of circulating blood through the intestines and stomach, your system is working to pump blood to your legs to provide oxygen. Besides the physiological difficulties associated with absorbing fluids during fast running, there are also logistical challenges. Anyone who has ever tried to take a drink while running at 10K pace has probably found it's easier to spill water than to drink it.

It is clear that monitoring your hydration status is as important to your marathon performance as any other aspect of training. Your hydration will support you during easy runs, SOS days, and the race itself by keeping you healthy and allowing for consistent training. For the same reasons regular training is important, when it comes to mastering proper nutrition and hydration, practice makes perfect. It may take greater focus and attention in the beginning, but over time, your judgment will improve and your base of fuel-related knowledge will expand.

HYPONATREMIA

Although there has been a lot of media attention regarding hyponatremia and marathoning in recent years, the topic remains murky. The condition occurs when there is an imbalance between the sodium and water contents in the blood. It tends to surface when a runner is losing a significant amount of sweat and simultaneously consuming great amounts of water. Since sodium is involved in nerve impulses and proper muscle function, this condition represents the disruption of an important balance within the body. There are three types of hyponatremia: euvolemic, when the water content increases and the sodium content stays the same; hypervolemic, when both the sodium and water content increase, but the increase in water is far greater; and hypovolemic, when both sodium and water decrease, but sodium decreases faster. In all three instances, the concentration of sodium in the blood is diluted. It's like mixing a bottle of Gatorade, drinking half, and then refilling it with just water, weakening the original mixture.

The effects of hyponatremia are very serious, as it can affect brain and muscle function to the point of coma and death. However, despite the dangers, clear-cut guidelines are not readily available. In the end, remember that moderation in your hydration plan is important. Stick to these guidelines:

- If your exercise session will be more than an hour long, use a sports drink.
- Know your exercise sweat rate and drink to match it. Although most people replace about 65–80 percent of their fluid losses, some people do drink beyond that point. (You can figure out your sweat rate using the worksheet in Appendix C.)
- In recovery, choose drinks that contain electrolytes. There are plenty of varieties that offer low-carbohydrate options for daily replacement.

What and When to Eat and Drink

PREWORKOUT

The hours before your workout can be the toughest time to dial in nutrition and hydration, especially if you're trying to fit in early morning runs before work. While it would be ideal for you to get up an hour before your run to take in a bit of fuel, we understand that busy runners hold sleep in high regard, especially when you're recovering from daily hard training. Every minute counts, and that goes for both running and sleeping. When considering your preworkout or pre-race routine, you have to weigh the pros and cons of time-related factors. If you have to cut your slumber to five or six hours just to get up and fuel an hour before your run, I say don't worry about it. You're better off grabbing a healthy snack before bed and getting more sleep. I always tell runners to address pre-workout fueling on SOS workout days with particular focus because fuel depletion can compromise pace and performance. Easy days are less of a concern since you won't need as much fuel to execute the workout. If you're running later in the day, however, you have a greater number of fueling options from which to choose. Typically, the more time you have, the more you should eat. As your workout approaches, the goal is to get in what you need the most of, namely, carbohydrates and fluids, without filling up too much. Table 8.2 offers basic guidelines for fueling before workouts.

TABLE 8.2 GUIDELINES FOR FUELING BEFORE WORKOUTS

TIME BEFORE WORKOUT	OPTION	CONTENTS
3–4 hours	Meal	Carbs, fat, protein
2 hours	Snack	Carbs, protein
1 hour	Fluids	Carbs
5–10 minutes	Fluids or energy gel	Carbs

DURING WORKOUTS

A certain amount of trial and error is necessary as you fine-tune your overall fueling plan, but it is especially vital to test midrun nutrition during training. By getting this right, you'll avoid both dehydration and exhaustion of those precious carbohydrate stores. Since you'll be fueling throughout the marathon itself, practice drinking and refueling during workouts that exceed one hour. While there are times when you may have to force yourself to eat and drink during a hard effort, your body will thank you on race day. There is perhaps no greater performance booster than simple calories and hydration.

Hydration will undoubtedly give you the most bang for your buck in both training and races. Not only will fluids help maintain blood-volume levels, but sports drinks can also provide crucial calories without having to add another component to your plan. Your own sweat-loss rate may vary, but on average, we lose between 2 and 4 pounds of sweat per hour. If that's not replaced, muscles receive less oxygen, less heat is evaporated, and by-products (lactic acid) accumulate in greater amounts. Among other outcomes, the body tries to compensate by making the heart beat faster. Indeed, for every 1 percent of body weight lost as a result of sweating, your heart rate will increase by up to 7 beats per minute. Furthermore, for every 1 percent of body weight lost through dehydration, you will slow down by about 2 percent. The marathon is already hard enough, so the last thing you need is your heart thumping faster and your legs moving slower. At an 8:00-minute pace, a 2 percent loss in pace resulting from a 1 percent loss in body weight (as little as 1–2 pounds) translates into 5 lost seconds per mile. If you slow down by 2–4 percent, which is quite common, that 8:00-minute pace slows to closer to an 8:20 pace. That is the difference between a 3:29 and a 3:38 marathon finish.

The most recent research (Butler et al., *Clinical Journal of Sports Medicine*, 2006) says that when we drink solely based on thirst, somewhere between 68 and 82 percent of the lost fluid is recovered. These researchers suggest that the body compensates by basically pulling water from inside the cells to make up the difference, in addition to the natural formation of water through the combustion of fats and carbohydrates. While this undoubtedly occurs, they also discuss a major flaw in this line of thought. Their study indicated that all of the aforementioned stipulations are true up to a 3 percent reduction in body weight caused by sweat loss. The problem is that if we wait to drink until we are thirsty, we are already at about 2.3 percent (their calculation). While their subjects had unlimited access to fluid, in reality, you won't have the luxury of consuming 6–8 ounces whenever you feel like it. When I first read this study, I thought that perhaps everything we had been telling people was wrong. However, upon further examination, I realized that our hydration strategies remain appropriate and pertinent in terms of real-world endurance performance conditions. The following are the general rules of thumb about hydration we recommend to runners:

Start early. Drink within the first 10–20 minutes of running or at the first water stop. As mentioned, thirst may be a good indicator, but in the marathon scenario, you won't be able to drink enough soon enough to cover the deficit.

Drink 2–8 ounces of fluid every 15–20 minutes. For training workouts, this means carrying sufficient water with you, or placing it strategically beforehand. For races, this should work well with the water and sports-drink stations. Most races provide these stations approximately every 2 miles.

- Keep in mind that it's easier to drink more during the early stages of a run or race. If you drink more early on and keep replacing fluids regularly, you will keep the stores topped off. This creates the fastest gastric emptying, which means more rapid absorption of water, electrolytes, and carbohydrates.
- Count the gulps. One gulp is roughly equal to 1 ounce of fluid. Try for 4–6 gulps per water stop.
- Don't overdo it. Downing multiple cups of water will only make you sick.

◄ If you plan to use sports drinks and gels provided at the race, find
out ahead of time what products will be offered and practice using
them in workouts. If they cause distress, plan on bringing your own.

The guidelines for midrun nutrition are similar to those for hydration.
Gels are probably the most popular refueling product, but other options,
such as chews, are quickly gaining a following. Glucose tablets, which dia-
betics use to raise their blood-sugar levels, are another alternative. They
dissolve in your mouth and are a quick source of carbohydrates. Also,
sports drinks will add precious calories to your overall intake, relieving the
need to take in as many calories from solid foods. Here's what we suggest:

Consume 30–60 grams of carbohydrate per hour of exercise.

◄ The longer you're running, the more carbs you should consume.
For anything longer than 4 hours, take in 60 grams per hour.

◄ An 8-ounce sports drink supplies 50–80 calories.

◄ Gels provide 25 grams of carbohydrate.

Take in 200–300 total calories per hour.

◄ If you were to drink 8 ounces of sports beverage every 20 minutes,
you would get roughly 195 calories per hour. For most athletes,
this will be sufficient for most runs that last less than 2 hours.

◄ In addition to fluids and gels, some runners also find calories in
other types of food. It depends on what you prefer.

◄ If you use gels or something similar, chase with water, not a
sports drink.

◄ One gel every 30–45 minutes should provide enough calories.

A calculated fueling regimen can also play an important role in the
mental marathon game. Former Olympian and Hansons-Brooks Distance
Project team member Brian Sell used this strategy at the 2005 IAAF World

Championships marathon in Helsinki. Since it was a humid day, he knew refueling would be instrumental to his success because he'd be sweating more than usual. During the second half of the race, Brian kept saying to himself, "just get to the next bottle." He continued that mantra and envisioned his energy levels being boosted at each water stop every 5 kilometers. In addition to fueling his working muscles and keeping himself hydrated, he was simultaneously feeding his motivation to continue pushing onward.

POSTWORKOUT

Refueling after a workout is just as important to the quality of your next workout as your preworkout nutrition was to the effort you just completed. This part of your nutrition plan is the easiest to carry out, so be sure not to overlook its significance. When all is said and done, proper postworkout fueling will help you recover from the run, maintain high levels of training, and ultimately make you a better runner. We recommend the following plan for filling up after winding down:

The initial 15–30 minutes following exercise are the most important.

- For every pound of body weight lost, replenish with 20 ounces, or 2.5 cups, of water. To get an idea of how much water weight you tend to lose on a run, weigh yourself periodically throughout the first weeks of training, both before and after runs. With time you'll be able to make an educated guess about how much you should drink following a run. Check out the sweat-loss calculator in Appendix C to learn your specific needs.
- Immediately after your workout, take in 50–100 grams of carbohydrate. In particular, we recommend foods with a higher glycemic index, since they will get into the bloodstream and delivered to the muscles quickly. The glycemic index basically ranks foods on their rate of digestion. The quicker a food digests, the higher the

number. Try any of the following: bananas, orange juice, sports drinks, cornflakes, oatmeal, baked potato, cooked carrots, bread, beans, ice cream.

➥ Try to eat a meal within the two hours following those first 30 post-exercise minutes. Oatmeal, peanut butter and a bagel, or cereal are good choices, as is anything else that contains a large amount of healthy carbs and some protein to promote muscle repair. A protein-rich drink, like chocolate milk, is a great option.

➥ Plan ahead. If you are driving to your workout, pack something to consume when you are finished. Don't wait until you return home. Start the refueling process as soon as possible.

Fueling Plan Leading Up to Marathon Day

Once all the hard work is done and you have cut back on both the volume and intensity of your training, spend a little time fine-tuning your nutritional game plan. The following is a guide with tips for the final days leading up to the big race.

FINAL WEEK

➥ Although you have reduced your training volume, be sure to maintain a normal diet and avoid making any big changes.

➥ Seventy percent of your diet needs to be carbohydrates, primarily complex. The increased available capacity for storage in your muscles will allow for the replenishment of all deficits. Research has shown that endurance can increase by as much as 20 percent through the complete restoration of glycogen stores.

➥ Gaining weight is a sign that you are doing things right, so don't worry if you tip the scales an additional pound or two. Even gains of up to five pounds are common. While you may feel a bit sluggish, this is normal during the tapering period. Now is not the time to cut calories. Remember that every gram of stored carbohydrate is stored with three grams of water and you'll need every bit of that on race day.

- Hydrate throughout the week. Don't wait until the day prior to play catch-up.

THE DAY BEFORE

- Drink a healthy beverage with every snack and meal. Rather than sticking with water, mix it up with sports drinks.
- Avoid foods that cause gas or gastrointestinal disruption.
- Avoid high-fiber foods.
- Avoid sugar substitutes.
- Limit alcohol.
- Eat or drink a healthy bedtime snack, such as unbuttered popcorn, a bagel and peanut butter, or a sports bar.

RACE MORNING

- The primary goal the few hours before the start of the race is to top off fuel stores and stay hydrated.
- Consume carbohydrates via these guidelines:

  1 hour prior: 50 grams total

  2 hours prior: 100 grams total

  3 hours prior: 150 grams total

  4 hours prior: 200 grams total

- The optimal amount of time to allow between eating and the start of the race varies based on the individual. Remember, if you eat early, you can always go back to bed. If you have a sensitive stomach, a substantial bedtime snack may be preferable.

➡ Balance topping off reserves with having to stand in line for the bathroom. If you come into race day well fueled, you won't have to worry about any last-minute fueling measures.

Race-Fueling Strategy

We can't stress enough how important it is to take in calories and hydrate during the marathon. Despite your training efforts, it could mean the difference between an impressive personal best and not even being able to reach the finish line. When it comes to race nutrition and hydration, your two main goals should be to minimize fluid loss and maintain carbohydrate intake.

To figure out how and what you should consume, several factors should be considered. First, caloric expenditure is more closely aligned with the distance traveled than with pace. Although a faster runner is exercising at a higher intensity, he or she will burn about the same number of calories as a slower runner of the same weight. However, while pace might not matter, weight does. Put simply, for every kilogram of body weight, we burn one calorie for every kilometer we run (1 cal/kg/km). Since it's easy to check how much you weigh (to convert to kilograms, divide your weight by 2.2) and we know the distance of a marathon (42.295 km), we can easily calculate how many calories you will burn during the race.

Example: 150-lb. runner
150 lb. divided by 2.2 kg/lb. = 68.18 kg
calories burned: 42.195 × 68.18 = 2,877 calories

Those 2,877 calories will be a mixture of fat and carbohydrate calories. To figure out the ratio, you must consider how fast you will be traveling, because the faster you run, the more carbohydrates you use. Typical marathon pace for beginners is usually around 60 percent of VO_2max, 70 percent for advanced runners, and about 80 percent for elite runners. This information is enough to give us a general idea of what ratio of carbohydrates to fat will result. See Table 8.3 for the appropriate mix of carbs and fat calories at various running intensities.

The next step involves figuring out how many calories per mile (or kilometer) are being used. Consider the previous example of the runner who will expend 2,877 calories during the race. To figure out expenditure per mile, simply divide 2,877 by 26.2. The result is roughly 110 calories per mile. From here we can calculate the range of carbohydrate expenditure per mile. At 60 percent, the ratio would be 110 × 0.55 or 60.5 calories of carbohydrate per mile. At 70 percent, the ratio would be 110 × 0.65 or 71.5 calories per mile. Finally, at 80 percent, the carbohydrate expenditure would be 82.5 calories per mile. Given these values and depending on the pace the runner is attempting, the total caloric expenditure from carbohydrates would look like this:

cal/mile (60.5, 71.5, and 82.5) × 26.2 miles

or a range of 1,585.1–2,161.5 cals

This difference is about 600 calories, which may not seem like much, but actually equals about six extra gels (100 calories each). This also shows how imperative it is to run at an appropriate intensity during the race. Even a few seconds faster per mile for a significant amount of time could put you at a carbohydrate deficit from which you might not be able to recover. While

TABLE 8.3 CARBS AND FAT AT VARIOUS INTENSITIES

VO$_2$MAX	CARBOHYDRATE	FAT
60%	55%	45%
70%	65%	35%
80%	75%	25%

we want you to set your sights high and race to the best of your abilities on marathon day, some risks aren't worth taking.

Although we have calculated a range of necessary carbohydrates, we still haven't discussed how many you should actually replace, which largely depends on the amount that can be stored in your exercising muscles. Although the liver also stores glycogen, it would prefer to reserve it for the brain and central nervous system, so it's best if you can leave those stores alone. While trained athletes store somewhere around 80 calories per gram in their muscles, all of that glycogen is only available for local use. In other words, glycogen in your arms won't be available for use in your legs. On average, leg mass constitutes approximately 21 percent of total mass in males and 20 percent in females. With this information, we can figure out our potential carbohydrate storage. To calculate your needs, take your weight in kilograms and multiply it by 20 or 21 percent to calculate leg mass. From there, multiply by 80 cal/kg to determine your average glycogen storage. Tables 8.4 and 8.5 show the potential carbohydrate storage for males and females at various weights.

Example: 68.18 kg (0.21) = 14.32 kg
14.32 kg (80 cal/kg) = 1,146 cals of potential carbohydrate storage
(for running use)

Given our 68.18 kg example, we found that this runner has the storage of 1,146 calories available for use while running. We also know that this runner will expend 1,585–1,873 calories over the course of the entire race. This will create a deficit of 439–727 calories. By following the guidelines we have provided, this runner can develop a comprehensive plan to optimize fuel-storage potential and maintain energy throughout the race. Remember that this replacement plan will get you to the finish line, but there is no way to keep the tank completely full. It is about optimizing those stores and getting you through 26.2 without hitting empty.

TABLE 8.4 CARB STORAGE FOR MALES

BODY WEIGHT	LEG MUSCLE MASS	CARBOHYDRATE STORAGE
65 kg (143 lb.)	13.65 kg	1,092 kcals
70 kg (154 lb.)	14.7 kg	1,176 kcals
75 kg (165 lb.)	15.75 kg	1,260 kcals
80 kg (176 lb.)	16.8 kg	1,344 kcals
85 kg (187 lb.)	17.85 kg	1,428 kcals
90 kg (198 lb.)	18.9 kg	1,512 kcals
95 kg (209 lb.)	19.95 kg	1,596 kcals
100 kg (220 lb.)	21 kg	1,680 kcals
110 kg (242 lb.)	23.1 kg	1,848 kcals
120 kg (264 lb.)	25.2 kg	2,016 kcals

Potential carbohydrate storage in leg muscles for males given an average 21 percent of total mass.

TABLE 8.5 CARB STORAGE FOR FEMALES

BODY WEIGHT	LEG MUSCLE MASS	CARBOHYDRATE STORAGE
65 kg (143 lb.)	13 kg	1,040 kcals
70 kg (154 lb.)	14 kg	1,120 kcals
75 kg (165 lb.)	15 kg	1,200 kcals
80 kg (176 lb.)	16 kg	1,280 kcals
85 kg (187 lb.)	17 kg	1,360 kcals
90 kg (198 lb.)	18 kg	1,440 kcals
95 kg (209 lb.)	19 kg	1,520 kcals
100 kg (220 lb.)	20 kg	1,600 kcals
110 kg (242 lb.)	22 kg	1,760 kcals
120 kg (264 lb.)	24 kg	1,920 kcals

Potential carbohydrate storage in leg muscles for males given an average 21 percent of total mass.

As with most dietary guidelines and recommendations, these numbers are based on averages. If a runner is extremely fit, lean, and muscular with a high proportion of slow-twitch muscle fibers, the storage capabilities may be higher. Regardless of these factors, all runners should err on the side of caution. If your stomach can tolerate the calories, then there is no reason not to provide them. We can't emphasize enough the importance of nutritional dress rehearsals before race day. You should toe the line knowing exactly when and what you'll be eating and drinking the entire 26.2 miles.

9

RECOVERY

RECOVERY IS YET ANOTHER VITAL component of your training that's necessary to prompt required training adaptations. It is the combination of hard training and recovery that will ultimately lead to maximizing your racing ability. And yes, while you need to learn to run tired in order to employ the principle of cumulative fatigue, recovery is a key to keeping your fatigue at the level where it is useful, yet doesn't cross the line into overtraining.

The Overtraining Continuum

There is training hard, and then there is overtraining. It is important to understand the phases that build from fatigue to full-blown overtraining.

Stage 1: Fatigue. What you feel right after a workout. Recovery takes 24–48 hours. However, do not confuse recovery with time off. You can and will recover with easy running if you follow our guidelines.

Stage 2: Functional overreaching. This is also known as cumulative fatigue, where we aim to put you over the course of the training schedule. This stage is vital to the program and necessary to adapt to training and improve performance over the long term. Recovery takes up to two weeks.

Stage 3: Nonfunctional overreaching. In this stage, you've nudged past the fine line of hard training into training too hard. Performance suffers, recovery takes several weeks, and the negatives of the first two far outweigh any potential benefit.

Stage 4: Overtraining syndrome. When you reach this stage, you will know it because your training will be virtually nonexistent. Recovering from overtraining syndrome takes several months.

FIGURE 9.1 THE OVERTRAINING CONTINUUM

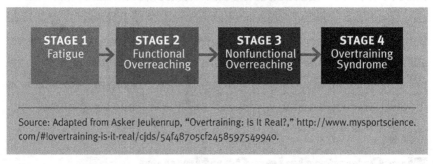

Source: Adapted from Asker Jeukenrup, "Overtraining: Is It Real?," http://www.mysportscience.com/#!overtraining-is-it-real/cjds/54f48705cf2458597549940.

Symptoms of Overtraining

There are several signs of overtraining, some of which we can monitor ourselves, while others require more invasive methods of detection (such as blood work). We will focus here on the indicators you can monitor yourself. These include:

- Early onset of fatigue
- Chronic muscle soreness

- Incomplete workouts
- Insufficient recovery
- Frequent infections
- Frequent colds
- Irritability
- Motivation loss
- Loss of enthusiasm
- Loss of competitive spirit

One element must be present for you to cross the line from cumulative fatigue to overtraining: Your performances have to be suffering. If you feel some of the above symptoms but your performance is not actually compromised, then you are in the stage of cumulative fatigue, where we want you. However, that is not to say that you shouldn't be monitoring the situation closely. You want to make sure you are doing what you can to ensure recovery so that cumulative fatigue doesn't turn into anything more serious.

Recovery Aids

The rest of this chapter explores key ways to aid your recovery so that you don't slip into overtraining syndrome.

SLEEP

When I discuss recovery in training, I always start with sleep because it gives you the largest return on investment. Sleep costs us only time, and the gains we see from quality sleep are well worth it. A good night's sleep offers two major benefits. One, protein synthesis (or the making of protein) occurs at a high level overnight. Letting that happen allows muscles to repair faster. Two, during a deep phase of sleep called Rapid Eye Movement (REM) sleep, growth hormone is released. This anabolic compound triggers adaptation in exercised muscles while promoting growth even during recovery.

How much sleep do you need? According to Sage Rountree's *The Athlete's Guide to Recovery*, eight hours of sleep per night should be our baseline. After that, we need more based on how much training we are doing. For 10 hours of training in a week, add an extra hour per day (nine hours). For 15 hours of training, aim for 9.5 hours a night, and for 20 hours of training per week, 10 hours a night. These time frames are ideal for optimal recovery, but we understand that life intervenes and you sometimes get less than the ideal amount. If the recommended volume of sleep is not going to be attainable, at least do everything you can to maximize the sleep that you can get. Here are some tips to help you reach REM sleep quicker:

- Make sure your room is cool, dark, and quiet.
- Create a good routine (in bed at the same time, up at the same time).
- Avoid watching TV in bed.
- Don't consume caffeine 4–5 hours before bed.
- Be careful of fluid consumption prior to sleep.

Naps are also beneficial. Rountree suggests that naps should either be 20 minutes or more than 90 minutes. Ideally, if you can sneak a longer nap in every so often, do it! That's when growth hormone is released to spur recovery and adaptation. She suggests avoiding naps in the 45-minute range, as we often wake up groggy after that amount of sleep, so it's tougher to return to work or workouts.

NUTRITION

Nutrition also offers a high return on investment. Simply eating a balanced diet and hydrating will help speed your recovery along. We discuss nutrition and hydration in detail in Chapter 8, but in this section, we will focus on basic fuel and fluid for immediate recovery from workouts.

The first thing to focus on is refueling. We have an extremely limited stored amount of carbohydrate, and the longer and more intense a workout is, the more is depleted. Your goal is to get 1.2 grams of carbs per kilogram of body weight ingested as soon as possible after that workout. For a 150-pound person, this is about 82 grams, which might be in the form of a sports bar and fluids, or chocolate milk and a banana. This gets the recovery process moving right away. We suggest you consume this amount of carbohydrate a couple more times over the next two hours.

Rehydrating is as important as refueling. Within five hours of completing a tough workout, or on a hot day, try to replace about 150 percent of the fluid lost. So, if you lose two pounds on the run, take in three pounds of fluid within the next five hours. To maximize your rehydration strategy, space out this intake. If you attempt to drink the total amount immediately after your workout, you'll quickly urinate out what the intestine cannot absorb. Breaking the intake into two or three rounds should result in more of that fluid staying in your body. Also, ensure you have some sodium in the fluid, as this will aid in retaining the fluid and not just urinating the excess.

STRETCHING/FLEXIBILITY

We discuss stretching as part of your overall training strategy in Chapter 7. As far as recovery, stretching has its place; however, it is not right after your workout. Focus instead on hydration and refueling in the short window of time after your workout, and save stretching for either several hours before or after the workout. If you just can't break that habit of stretching postworkout, then keep it very light and as soon as you feel the slightest discomfort, back off.

ICE BATHS

Ice baths (or anything cold for that matter) promote vasoconstriction. This "closing off" of the arteries prevents blood from entering injured tissue. The short-term effect is a reduced amount of inflammation and pain. While this sounds great, we actually need inflammation to heal tissue. We also need inflammation to promote long-term adaptation. If we block inflammation, there's nothing telling our body that we need to adapt to the stress it's being placed under because the markers that trigger adaptation are being blocked. So save the ice baths for a "special treat." Perhaps after a weekend long run, do a cold soak as a way of resetting for the upcoming week. Something like that is fine. Just do not get in the habit of doing them several times per week.

Here are other tips to make your ice bath effective:

- Soak for 10–15 minutes after a two-plus-hour long run or an intense 90-minute SOS.
- Use 50–55 degree water.
- Perform within 60 minutes of your run (within 15 minutes of completion is best).

COMPRESSION GEAR

The jury is still out as to whether compression gear truly aids in recovery or performance. But many runners swear by it, and we think there is a place for it, especially when it comes to practical items such as compression socks. In an ideal world, you'd be able to get off your feet and relax after a hard workout, but most of us cannot. Wearing a pair of compression socks can certainly help you feel better, if nothing else. And if they do improve our recovery after a hard workout, then that is a bonus. If you choose to wear compression socks, we recommend that you wear them for twice as long as your workout. So, if you did a two-hour long run, then wear the socks for about four hours. This is true especially if you are going straight from a workout to a situation in which you'll be on your feet for a significant amount of time.

MASSAGE

Massage releases the tension of worked muscles and helps manage inflammation. A longer-term approach to massage includes breaking down scar tissue and muscle adhesions. One session won't change the structure of your muscles, but if you have the time and can afford it, a good deep-tissue massage every few weeks is excellent. If not, try to get one once a month. If you make massage a regular part of your routine, you'll find that your muscles are more resilient, you'll bounce back from workouts quicker, and you'll have fewer aches and pains.

Recovery from the training we do is as vital as the training we are trying to recover from. There are a lot of options out there and luckily for us, the simplest ones (sleeping, rehydrating, and refueling) give us the biggest return on investment. When you start to reach that point of uncertainty between training hard and overtraining, take stock of what your recovery has been like. You may just need to make a few small tweaks to keep the training at a high level.

10

MARATHON GEAR

WHEN KEVIN AND KEITH AREN'T coaching, they spend a lot of time thinking about shoes for their Michigan-based chain of running stores, Hansons Running Shops. So we can't very well discuss their methods for marathon training without devoting some time to gear, especially footwear. Aside from errors in training, improper footwear is the most common cause of running injury. That's right, running itself doesn't usually cause injuries: It's the mistakes made by runners and coaches that can cause trouble. This is a good thing because it means that the majority of injuries can be avoided if you arm yourself with the knowledge you need to stay healthy.

Shoes

Shoes are really an extension of your personal biomechanics. While there are a lucky few runners with textbook-perfect bone and muscle structure, chances are you aren't one of them. Most runners have at least a couple minor imperfections that predispose them to injury, like a leg that's a little longer than the other, a fallen arch, or a weak pelvis. This is where shoes come into play. Getting fitted in the right pair of shoes is as important as training smart and eating right. To help you with shoe selection, we will discuss stride biomechanics, foot type, and the various components that make up a shoe. After reading this chapter, you should be ready to go to your local running specialty store, confer with an expert, and choose the best shoe for you.

RUNNING STRIDE BIOMECHANICS

When it comes to selecting the right shoe, several factors must be considered. One is the point of impact of the foot on the ground, referred to as the foot strike. A related consideration is how long the foot stays on the ground during each step. With foot strike, the goal is to make the moment of impact brief enough that braking forces are minimized (which slows you down and is jarring to your body), but not so brief that the maximal force used to move the body forward is compromised. It may not seem like foot strike could have a significant overall impact on performance, but over the long term it makes a big difference. Over the course of 5 kilometers, a runner finishing in 30 minutes will take a whopping 5,400 steps. If that runner could decrease foot-strike time by just 1/100th of a second, he or she would run those 5 kilometers a whole minute faster. Extrapolate that to the marathon and you're talking about potentially shaving 8 minutes off your time, merely by striking more efficiently.

Though there are certain universal truths that are widely accepted concerning foot-strike biomechanics, there's still much debate over the ideal place to land: the heel, midfoot, or forefoot. For all the controversy, there is relatively little research on the topic, and the studies that have been conducted should be approached with extreme caution, as there is much speculation about the results. One of the more reliable studies (Hasegawa et al., *Journal of Strength and Conditioning*, 2007) looked at the foot-strike patterns of elite runners during a half-marathon race. The results showed that nearly 75 percent of the runners landed on their heels, while 24 percent landed midfoot and just 1 percent were forefoot strikers. It should also be noted that 60 percent of the first 50 finishers of the race were midfoot strikers.

Since the research is somewhat unreliable in even categorizing the various types of foot strike, it is more productive to look at the matter in terms of where the foot is landing relative to your body, not what part of the foot hits the ground first. The biggest mistake runners make is attempting to increase stride length. This often leads to overstriding, which means you're likely landing on your heels, creating a braking motion and forcing your legs to absorb more shock. Since this increases the amount of time you are in contact with the ground, your pace also slows. If you focus on landing underneath your center of gravity, however, you'll avoid these issues.

While the verdict is still out in the academic world, we recommend simply proceeding with your training and not becoming too preoccupied with altering your natural form. There are, however, a couple practical tips concerning foot strike that may help you run more efficiently. First, as we just suggested above, avoid overstriding. Instead of trying to develop monster strides, think about lifting your legs with the quads and pulling the lower leg underneath the quad upon each landing. This will cause you to strike under your center of gravity and on the middle of your foot. The other variable that you can tinker with to develop a more efficient foot strike is posture. When you hear a coach tell a runner to "run tall," that means keeping the shoulders pulled back, with a slight bend at the waist; avoid slouching your shoulders and view your entire torso and head as a single entity. The slight forward lean will keep you from overdoing posture and ending up looking like a drum major in a marching band. Remember, your pelvis should be beneath your center of gravity and your feet striking under you, with neither foot extending further forward than your chest.

FOOT TYPE

In addition to the way you strike the ground with each step, the actual shape of your feet should also play a role in your shoe selection process. Among the many shapes and sizes of human beings, there are three major foot types, distinguished by the type of arch: flat, high, and medium.

Flat Arch

Through coaching and working at Hansons Running Shops, we have found that the flat foot, although not the most common, is definitely the most troublesome. In addition to having a flatter arch, flat feet are often accompanied by ankles that lean inward toward one another. When running, individuals with this foot type tend to land on the outsides of their feet, and as they proceed through the foot strike, the foot and ankle roll inward. This is referred to as overpronation. It is important to note that some amount of pronation is normal, as the foot naturally rolls inward, providing some attenuation of shock and giving the body leverage to push off from the ground. However, a flat-footed runner who overpronates, or rolls inward too much, tends to experience an increase in certain overuse injuries. The main problem is that this runner's feet tend to be too flexible, cushioning the blow of the foot slamming into the ground but also providing little leverage to carry the body through the striking motion to assist in pushing off from that step. This excessive motion leads to a host of rotational forces applied to the foot, ankle, shin, and knee, creating issues like tendonitis, plantar fasciitis, and Achilles' tendonitis. As you may have guessed, this foot type requires a very specific shoe to alleviate these problems and allow for normal running.

High Arch

The second type of foot is one that has a high arch, which is, unsurprisingly, the exact opposite of the flat foot. A runner with this foot type also lands on the outside of the foot, but remains there all the way through toe-off (the point at which the toes propel the runner forward as the foot is pushed off from the ground). While the flat foot offers great natural cushioning but is a poor lever for pushing off, the reverse is true for the high-arched foot. Along with high arches comes inflexibility, so the feet are unable to do a good job of absorbing the forces that running imposes on the body. Since all of the weight is put on the outside of the foot during ground contact, even the toe-off is somewhat limited, because it can't take full advantage of the big toe as a lever to push off.

Ironically, this motion, called underpronation or supination, can lead to some of the same injuries as overpronation but for different reasons. While rotational forces tend to be the cause of injuries in flat-footed runners, poor shock absorption is the plight of supinators. In addition, this foot type may lead to a greater number of issues with the iliotibial band, the long band of tissue that stretches from the pelvis down to the knee joint.

Medium Arch

The third foot type, the medium (neutral) arch, is somewhere in the middle. Although it is often labeled as "normal," after working in running stores and fitting thousands of athletes, I can safely say that the medium arch is the least common. The lucky runner with this foot type will have a foot strike that likely begins at the middle to the outside of the heel, gently rolls to the middle of the foot, then continues along the middle of the foot to use the leverage of the big toe, therefore maximizing toe-off. Although the biomechanics may be better, a medium-arched runner still risks injury by running in a shoe that is too supportive or not supportive enough. As we have mentioned, each biomechanical difference comes with its own set of unique problems, making it particularly important to choose a shoe that is made for your arch type. For a more accurate assessment of your foot type and accompanying shoe category, seek advice from a professional at a running specialty store or from a gait-analysis expert. You can do tests at home to determine foot type, but they don't always guarantee a proper shoe prescription. When choosing a shoe, it is important not only to consider your foot type, but also to understand the motion of your feet when running, as well as other biomechanical issues.

SHOE CONSTRUCTION

In order to understand what type of shoe may be best for your feet, you should be familiar with the various components used to create running-specific footwear. The main pieces are the outsole, midsole, last, heel counter, and upper.

The Outsole

Let's start at the bottom with the outsole of a shoe, also known as the tread. Until recently, the outsole of the shoe did little more than provide traction, and the only variation among shoes was in the type of rubber used. Now, however, there are a growing number of technologies used for outsoles. Instead of one piece of rubber, the outsoles are often broken into basic pods for the heel and forefoot, which saves weight. Also, rather than rubber, today's companies are relying on new materials, like silica, which are said to provide better traction in wet conditions, and are more environmentally friendly because they are biodegradable. Outsole technology has also improved in terms of the general wear of the shoe, so you can get more miles out of a pair of shoes. In fact, for most runners nowadays, the midsole (a.k.a. cushioning) breaks down well before the outsole.

The Midsole

From a biomechanical standpoint, the midsole is where most of the action occurs. In recent years, once-popular midsole materials, like ethylene vinyl acetate (EVA) and air pockets, have been replaced with new technologies that are more resilient, lighter, and biodegradable. For example, Brooks, the shoe company that outfits the Hansons-Brooks elite squad, currently has a product that biodegrades within 25 years, not the centuries it takes traditional materials. Cushioning technology has also improved, allowing the shoes to absorb forces more readily and last up to 15 percent longer.

While all midsoles contain some amount of cushioning, the amount of support varies. Depending on how much stability a runner needs, some shoes contain a denser midsole to provide more support, including dual-density and tri-density materials. This type of midsole helps to keep an overpronating foot in a more neutral position, but it also adds weight to the shoe. Different shoe models contain varying amounts of these materials, leading to a wide variety of stability and weight options. To spot a shoe that contains a denser midsole, look for a gray area that comprises part of the medial side (inside) of the midsole. Other pieces are sometimes added for extra support: One example is roll bars, which make for an even stiffer, controlled shoe. The more a person pronates, the more such extra components will help.

When you buy a good pair of running shoes, your money is going to the midsole. Instead of looking at the tread to determine if your shoes need to be replaced, it is more important to consider the number of miles you've run in the shoe (most max out at 300–500 miles) and the wear and tear on the midsole. Despite all the technological advances, shoes still break down and as soon as the midsole is past its prime, you're at risk for injury.

The Last
The last is the actual shape of the shoe. There are three basic lasts: straight, curved, and semicurved. Each of these three varieties correlates to a specific foot type to control motion and to provide optimal cushioning. For instance, a straight last is the best foundation for an overpronating runner because it helps control the excessive inward rolling that characterizes the motion of a flat-footed runner, and also provides for better toe-off. The curved last is the opposite of the straight last. Instead of being symmetrical, it is markedly curved along the medial side of the shoe where the arch sits. A curved last is built for supinators to help deal with the poor natural cushioning by promoting a slight inward roll. Finally, the semicurved last can be viewed as a hybrid between the curved and the straight varieties. It is tailored to runners with a medium (neutral) arch, offering some rigidity, but also allowing for natural pronation.

The Heel Counter
You can't see the heel counter, but it is a unit that hugs the heel to minimize motion in the ankle. Since some runners need this type of control and others don't, there are varying levels of heel-counter stability, with the most flexible shoes having no heel counter at all.

The Upper

The lightweight material that covers the top of the foot is known as the upper. Usually made of a highly breathable nylon mesh, the upper permits sweat and water to be wicked away from the feet, keeping them cool and dry. You'll also notice the various lacing patterns of different uppers; many of the newest versions help to hug the arch and provide a bit of extra support. And if you live in an area with cold, wet weather, you'll want uppers that provide more weather-resistant capabilities to keep snow and slush out of the shoe.

SHOE TYPE

Despite the seemingly endless array of options, running shoes can be categorized, making the choices easier to sift through. Just as there are three foot types, there are three main classes of shoes. Even so, there are several subtypes; a fourth and perhaps a fifth and sixth category have recently been added. The shoe types we will discuss are as follows: motion-control, neutral, stability, lightweight, minimalist, and maximalist.

Motion-Control

This shoe is designed for the flattest of feet. A typical motion-control shoe is build atop a straight last, has a dual-density midsole from the heel to beyond the arch, a plastic roll bar in the heel and arch, and a stiff heel counter. With all of the extras, these shoes aren't your lightest option, but they are good at their main job, which is to prevent overpronation.

Neutral

These shoes are best suited for a runner who has high arches. They are built on a curved last with loads of cushioning, no dual-density midsole materials, and a minimal heel counter. The goal of this type of footwear is to provide cushioning and flexibility while weighing as little as possible.

Stability

The stability category is for neutral and mildly overpronating "normal" runners. The last is typically semicurved, with some dual-density midsole technology, a flexible forefoot, ample cushioning, and a mild heel counter. This type of shoe provides a nice middle-of-the-road option for a runner who needs a slight amount of support but doesn't want to sacrifice cushioning.

Lightweight

While lighter-weight shoes have been around for a long time, they are becoming increasingly mainstream, falling somewhere between a regular running shoe and a racing flat. They are akin to a lightweight version of a neutral shoe, with certain exceptions that include supportive features. Although these shoes are a couple ounces lighter than the other categories, most runners shouldn't wear them exclusively in training. They are, however, a good option for certain runners to wear for certain SOS workouts, especially speed and strength work.

Minimalist

Minimalist footwear offers little if any cushioning or true protection for the feet, allowing you to feel as if you're running barefoot. While this type of footwear has gained plenty of notoriety in recent years, the recommendations on wearing them have sparked much argument. From Olympic coaches to weekend warriors, it seems that everyone has an opinion. In the beginning, the Hansons wouldn't sell the trend-driven minimalist models, not so much because they thought they were simply a fad, but because people just aren't very good at following directions. Consumers wanted these shoes because they were lightweight and trendy. Although instructions on the shoe box usually gave specific advice on how to begin using the shoes—that is, very gradually—people would lace them up and head out for 5 miles right off the bat.

After a week of running in them, they'd end up injured without understanding why. We saw enough ailing runners to know this was happening, and thus decided to avoid selling such footwear altogether.

Today, however, it is nearly impossible to ignore the minimalist movement. To help you decide if such a shoe is right for you, let's take a serious look at the origins as well as the pros and cons of minimalism. First, you must understand the premise of minimalism, which includes two basic ideas: (1) You should wear the least amount of shoe that you can tolerate without getting hurt and (2) by wearing less shoe, you strengthen your feet and improve your running stride. Minimalist advocates often argue that our ancestors ran barefoot, so we should get back to basics and do the same. The key word here is "ancestors." These folks didn't wear shoes for 20 years and then decide to go out and run 10 miles barefoot. Living in a world much different than our Paleolithic forefathers and foremothers, we wear shoes from the time we are very young, so a transition from wearing shoes to going barefoot is necessary. Most proponents of minimalism suggest taking a gradual approach to decreasing the amount of shoe over the course of several months. If you are wearing a stability model, for instance, you should not go directly to a minimalist shoe, but perhaps transition with a lightweight trainer before moving to the minimalist or "barefoot" footwear. This allows the bones and soft tissues to gradually adjust to the minimalist footwear. Even after you have fully transitioned, we don't recommend wearing this type of shoe every day for regular training, but rather as a training supplement to be worn periodically.

Another argument supplied by the minimalist movement states that running in less shoe helps strengthen your feet. While not many will argue against this notion, the idea should be approached with prudence. For those of you who have run in racing flats, track spikes, or even done speed work, think about how sore your calves are the following day. Running in minimalist shoes elicits similar strain and resulting fatigue and soreness.

Now imagine that you place this same stress on your calves day after day by continuing to use this type of footwear. How long would you guess it takes for injuries to arise? The current research says about two weeks (Lieberman et al., *Nature*, 2010). The point is that most people don't take the time to safely transition from regular shoes to minimalist footwear, causing a seemingly endless list of issues.

The final contention made by minimalist supporters is that wearing less of a shoe will improve running form, because it encourages forefoot or midfoot striking over heel striking. The basic thought is that landing on the midfoot reduces impact forces, reducing not only the risk of injury, but also the need for shoe cushioning. Studies have shown that barefoot runners who land on the forefoot display significantly lower impact forces than runners who wear shoes and land on their heels. This information is certainly interesting; nevertheless, the available research on the subject is limited, making it important to dissect each new study. The primary findings of current research are that if runners are accustomed to running barefoot, or in minimalist shoes, then they usually land on the midfoot and forefoot. They also tend to land with significantly less impact force than runners wearing shoes. On the other hand, runners who aren't adapted to running barefoot or in minimal footwear will most likely land on their heels when they go shoe-free. The result of this is a landing force that is nearly seven times greater than landing on the heel when wearing shoes. So for many runners, it's best to stick with their normal shoes (Lieberman et al., *Nature*, 2010).

One of the main arguments against wearing shoes is the contention that they don't reduce the risk of injury. It is true that injury rates among runners have hovered around 70 percent for the last four decades. However, the statistics potentially offer alternate explanations that don't involve the issue of footwear. According to Running USA, the average male finisher of a marathon was 34 in 1980, while the average age of female finishers was 31. In 2014 those ages rose to 40 and 36, respectively. Beyond that, the number of marathon finishers in 1980 totaled 143,000, and in 2014 there were 550,637 finishers. So in addition to the fact that the marathoning population has more than tripled, people who run the 26.2-mile distance are also, on average, older. Along with that, given the general trends in obesity, one could assume that the weight of the average marathoner has also increased. Without question, the demographic of American marathon finishers is drastically different than it was 30 years ago. It is then safe to postulate that, perhaps, traditional running shoes and the new technologies introduced over the years have actually helped keep more runners healthy, rather than the opposite. There is simply no way of knowing with certainty, but this is what many coaches believe.

In deciding what is best for you as a runner, consider the research, along with your own biomechanics and injury history. Minimalist running will work for some, but not for others. If you want to try it, be patient and allow yourself a considerable amount of time to make the transition, especially if you are running high mileage. Using this footwear will require a significant reduction in your training, so experimenting with this at the beginning of a marathon cycle isn't a good idea. Our suggestion is first to wear something like a lightweight trainer for SOS workouts (other than long runs) and regular trainers the other days to see how your body responds. As always, pay attention to what your body is telling you, read the research for yourself, and ignore ostentatious claims made by the media.

Maximalist

The term "maximalist" relates to the thickness of a shoe's midsole created on a "dynamic" footbed—the part of the shoe your foot rests on. This combination is designed to work well with any type of foot. There are claims regarding reduced soreness after runs as well as efficacy for long runs and recovery or easy runs, although there are no definitive studies that prove these claims at this point. If you are interested in this type of shoe, we can recommend their use for recovery runs, but we caution against wearing them for long runs when fatigued legs is one of the desired training effects. Minimizing that training stress on a day when it is part of the workout only delays training adaptations. As with minimalist shoes, there is a time and a place for the shoe, but as a consumer, you'll have to decide if a shoe you'll wear only once or twice a week is worth the cash.

FOOTWEAR PRICING

One of the most common questions runners ask about shoes relates to price. Indeed, not all shoes are created equal. Just as with buying a car, the more features you want or need, the more you're going to pay. Remember, however, that shoe type should guide your decision, not cost. So when you head to the store, be sure to consider your specific needs and make an informed decision. There are three basic price points that we generally refer to: entry-level, midgrade, and high-end.

Entry-Level

Your cheapest option, these shoes offer the basics, but not much else. They are great for someone just getting into the sport, especially those who aren't even sure they'll continue running. Most entry-level shoes are made with cushioning in the heel but not the forefoot. They are noticeably less responsive and just don't feel as comfortable as higher-end models. Even so, these shoes are reliable, well constructed, and get the job done. They will also be the cheapest way to get out of a running shop. While there are even less expensive sneakers that can be found at big-box athletic stores, we never recommend choosing anything below this category.

Midgrade

Regardless of the shoe type, models that fall into this category offer the basics, plus a few extras, like full-length cushioning, better midsole material, a more responsive feel, and an enhanced overall fit. A blend of luxury and functionality, this category of shoe will be able to withstand a few more miles than the entry-level shoes.

Should I rotate shoes?

While owning more than one pair of shoes costs you up front, in the long run, it just might save you money. How? If you rotate between two pairs of shoes, each shoe can recover on its "off day." The cushioning gets compressed and when the shoe is used every day, or close to it, the cushioning doesn't have a chance to bounce all the way back. That means the shoe breaks down a little quicker and you end up buying new shoes sooner.

A common scenario for two pairs of shoes would be to have one pair of everyday training shoes, plus one pair of lightweight trainers or racing flats in which to do speed or strength and tempo runs. This way, your trainers last a touch longer, and you have the bonus of having run several fast runs in the shoes you plan to wear on race day. Another option, this one for newer runners, is to have a regular pair of trainers and also a pair of maximalist shoes to wear a couple days per week when you feel like you need a little extra recovery.

If you plan to rotate two pairs of shoes, make sure they play a consistent role in your week and that you get equal use out of both. Otherwise, you'll burn through your primary shoe and be left with a pair you can't wear every day.

High-End

Shoes in this category have all the bells and whistles in terms of the latest technology and are often a company's premier model. You may get a little more wear out of these shoes, but runners need to weigh whether the higher price tag is worth it for their individual needs.

HOW TO CHOOSE A SHOE

With a firm understanding of the various types of running shoes on the market, you are now ready to move forward with selecting a pair that is right for you.

Probably the most important step you can take is to go to your local running specialty store rather than making a purchase at an online superstore. While some get lucky selecting shoes off the Internet, you are far more likely to get it right the first time if you have a knowledgeable employee assist you with the fitting process. Selecting the right shoes is like putting together the pieces of a puzzle; a well-trained employee will help you connect the dots and make a good choice. When you go to the store, be sure to bring along your old running shoes and come ready to answer questions about your training and past running experience, such as:

- "Have you had any injuries?"
- "How did your last shoes treat you?"
- "Have you been fitted for running shoes before?"

A running-shop specialist may examine the wear pattern on the bottom of your old shoes, from which a general idea of foot strike can be garnered. For instance, if you tend to grind down the entire medial (inside) side of the tread, you're most likely overpronating and need more support than that shoe offers. Conversely, if the outside edge is worn, you're probably supinating and need less support and more cushioning. If your wear pattern is even, you're probably already in the correct shoe category. It is important to keep in mind that this isn't an exact science. If you've gone through 10 versions of the same model and haven't had any issues with injuries, stick with what you know works, regardless of the wear pattern.

In most running specialty shops, the employee will also ask to observe your gait. Many running establishments have treadmills and cameras that capture images of the motion of your feet when walking and running. Once the images are slowed down on the screen, you can see exactly how you are striking. Even without the technology, an experienced employee can watch you walk or run and get a good idea of what type of shoe you should be in. If you're looking to go a step beyond, you can visit a sports performance lab and get a gait analysis with the use of special software for about $100. Another new technology that is becoming more popular is a basic force pad that the runner stands on without shoes. This force, or pressure, pad shows the outline of the foot and gives a fairly accurate idea of arch type. It also shows where you place the most pressure. This can help determine where you might need more cushioning and whether you need any stability in the shoes. This usually includes a printout of your foot scan, along with recommendations on shoe type.

Once you are presented with several options of shoes that are appropriate for your feet, it's your responsibility to decide which pair is the most comfortable. Be sure to select the appropriate size; your dress shoes might be a 9, but your running shoes might be a different size. When you put the shoes on, consider these factors:

- **Heel:** The heel should provide a snug fit, preventing any slippage.
- **Toe box:** There should be a bit of room in the toe box, both in terms of length and width. Your toes should have room to splay out and push off when you're running, but you don't want so much room that your feet slide around.
- **Timing:** If you can arrange it, go to the store around the same time of day you'd normally run, because your feet swell over time. What feels like the right size in the morning can be too tight after a day spent on your feet.

The final decision comes down to how the shoe fits your feet. When given three shoes from the same category and price range, it is likely you'll find that any of them will do the job. It's up to you to choose the one that feels the best. Remember to select your shoes based on function, not fashion. By understanding foot types and shoe categories and by working with a knowledgeable employee at a running specialty store, you'll end up with a pair of shoes that will serve you well during marathon training.

WHEN TO REPLACE SHOES

We have found that most runners who are new to our training programs assume they can purchase a new pair of shoes at the beginning of training and wear them all the way through race day. The flaw in this reasoning is made apparent when the runner realizes that a pair of shoes can carry a person only 350–500 miles, depending on the shoe, body type, and running style. The Beginner Program has you running about 700 total miles over 18 weeks of training, putting any shoe used during our plans well beyond its expiration date. In reality, you will need two pairs to get you through training and the race itself.

In most cases, we suggest getting fit for one pair, trying them out for a few weeks, and then deciding whether to purchase an identical pair or a different model. If you end up loving the first pair you bought, make sure that the model hasn't changed when you go to buy the next pair. Although the name may be the same, models can differ from one season to the next, bringing along significant issues with fit that may not jibe with your preferences and overall comfort.

RACE-DAY KICKS

Your first run in a new pair of shoes most certainly should not be on race day. While shoes are ready to be worn right out of the box, requiring little to no break-in time, it is important to make sure that the specific pair of shoes that you'll be wearing for 26.2 tough miles will be comfortable. While you could wear multiple pairs of the same model with no issues, you still need to give your body time to react to the shoe when it is new. If you think about it, it makes perfect sense. As a shoe slowly breaks down, your foot adjusts to its slightly changing makeup. However, when you lace up the same model fresh off the store shelves, your feet have to make an immediate adjustment to the more substantial thickness of the midsole and the shape of the upper. This goes for runners who wear orthotics, too. Just as your feet need to adapt to the new shoe, so do your inserts. The shoes you race in should have enough mileage to have that familiar feel, but not so many miles that they are beginning to break down. For most runners, this falls between 50 and 100 miles, or two to three weeks before the race.

When selecting a race-day shoe, the majority of runners will choose a model in which they can also log plenty of training miles. However, some runners look for a lighter shoe for race day. When deciding whether or not to lighten up for the big day, consider that you're going to be on your feet for a long time, significantly longer than for any of your training runs. That means your feet are going to swell and be in need of a slightly bulkier shoe that has adequate cushioning to take the brunt of the force upon each foot strike. Keep in mind that racing flats are lighter for a reason; they trade cushioning and support for a lighter weight and faster feel. Since fatigue will have a detrimental effect on running mechanics and running economy, you become more susceptible to injury as you tire. We ask most runners considering flats, "Why sacrifice a couple ounces that may ultimately take a toll on your biomechanics?"

We generally suggest that the cutoff for wearing racing flats is about 3:10 for the marathon, male or female. This means that anyone slower should be wearing regular shoes and anyone faster may choose to try racing flats. For those who will finish after 3:10, I would be concerned about the aforementioned issues with biomechanics and injury. Some runners simply need that extra cushioning and support, especially during the later stages of the race. If you are in this camp but are interested in going even lighter, consider the lightweight trainer category. In recent years these shoes have emerged as a great transitional option between a regular training shoe and a racing flat. While they aren't as substantial as your everyday training shoe, they will offer enough support and cushioning for limited use, like a marathon. This allows you to save a couple ounces of shoe weight without running the risk of injury.

In my own running experience, I have found that running in regular training shoes works for most of my daily runs. However, for long runs when I'm looking to pick up the pace, I often choose a lighter-weight, more flexible shoe that still supports my low arches. It isn't much, but that decreased weight makes me feel faster and I still get the protection I need to keep me from getting injured, especially since I only wear them for certain workouts. If you decide to purchase a second pair of lightweight trainers, be sure to wear them for a few workouts before racing in them. This way you'll know whether they will work for the big day.

Apparel

While apparel and accessories are also important to marathon training, this is simply too vast a category for the focus of this book. What you wear on race day will depend on both weather and what you have worn in training. For instance, a running cap may be a perfect accessory for a rainy, cool race in March, but on a steamy July day, it may do nothing but trap heat. The following are some basic guidelines to keep in mind when choosing your ensemble:

- **Avoid cotton:** No cotton socks, shorts, pants, or shirts. Instead of helping to wick moisture and heat away from your body, cotton traps heat and absorbs sweat, creating a humid environment close to your skin. This can lead to both chafing and blisters.
- **Dress down:** Pretend it's 20 degrees warmer than it actually is when choosing your outfit. So if it's 40 degrees out, dress like it is 60. You may be chilly for the first mile, but once you start generating heat, you will warm up quickly.
- **Consider cost:** Calculate cost per wear when purchasing running clothing. It's not about the initial investment but rather how much wear you'll get out of it. Good running apparel can be pricey, but it is quite durable and should last several seasons.
- **Try it on:** Seams can rub, shorts can ride up, shirts can feel too baggy or too tight. When you find what you want to wear on race day, be sure to try it on first and see how it fits and feels.

Whatever you choose to wear on race day, make sure you have taken it for a few test runs first. Ideally, wear the outfit on a longer run so you know that with time and increased sweat output, the materials won't cause you any problems. After all the hard training you've put in, the last thing you want is to have a wardrobe malfunction on the big day.

11

RACE TACTICS

OVER THE YEARS THE HANSONS coaches have adopted the saying "worry early." What we mean is that it is important to tend to race-day details in advance to limit unnecessary stress on the big day. You've committed to 18 weeks of hard training, early mornings, skipped social events, and other sacrifices; don't blow it by neglecting to iron out the particulars of the race well in advance. Of course there is no strategy under the sun that will completely eliminate race-day nerves, but there are certain steps that can put you ahead of those who aren't prepared. From your pre-race meal to where you'll meet your family at the finish to what shoes you're going to wear, planning ahead will go a long way toward keeping you calm when it matters. Going into race weekend, Plan A, along with Plan B and Plan C, should be well rehearsed and ready to be put into motion. When you're relaxed at the start line, you're less likely to make silly mistakes in the early stages of the race, keeping you focused and ready to follow protocol. We often caution runners not to underestimate the amount of planning a marathon requires. Consider the following factors as you make arrangements prior to race morning, remembering that your marathon will only be as good as your pre-race preparation, whether that is the training itself or getting to the start line on time.

Pre-Race Preparation

TRAVEL

If you are headed to a destination race, you'll probably need to arrange your travel plans months ahead of time. Besides needing to decide how to get to the race, you have to secure a place to stay. For the most part, cities that put on marathons with 35,000 or more runners will sell out of decent hotel rooms soon after race registration closes. Believe me, you'll want a reasonably comfortable bed both before and after the race.

Many marathoners, especially first-timers, choose to sign up for a local race to avoid the extra costs and hassle associated with traveling. But even if your race is local, you still might want to consider getting a room. While sleeping in familiar surroundings is attractive to some, others would rather stay at a hotel downtown the night before so they can easily walk to the start line the next morning. There are a couple of advantages to this strategy. You are able to get a bit more shut-eye before rising for the big day. And if you tend to get stressed by the influx of crowds and chaos surrounding race morning, you might find walking just those few blocks to the start line eases your anxiety. If you prefer to sleep in your own bed the night before, be sure to leave early enough to get to the start. While you may live only 15 minutes from where the race begins, traffic and parking can be challenging in any city during marathon morning. Consider having someone drop you off so you don't have to figure out where to park your car.

FAMILY SPECTATING

Most marathoners welcome a friendly face along the course. Not only does it break up the monotony, it also gives you something to look forward to as you grind through 26.2 miles. Despite this, don't spend time worrying about where and when you'll meet family and friends. The best strategy here is to put someone else in charge. For the Olympic Trials marathon, I reserved hotel rooms and purchased flights for my parents, but beyond that, my wife took care of the details. She set up itineraries, flew down to Houston with my parents, and made sure they got to their hotel. Beforehand she helped figure out where to find me along the course and the spot we would meet at the finish. She knew that I needed to focus on my race during the days leading up to marathon weekend, so she picked up a bit of slack and allowed me to forgo dealing with certain arrangements that were likely to stress me out. Delegate chores to someone you can depend on, consider this person your captain, and allow him or her to take control of details you need not be bothered by.

In terms of where to direct your personal cheering squad along the course, Kevin often recommends having someone meet you at mile 17. Having heard him dispense this advice to many runners over the years, we like to refer to this as "The Kevin Hanson Feelin' Fresh Rule." Basically, the rule suggests having a friend or family member wait at mile 17 (or a good spectating spot nearby) with a dry shirt for you to throw on for the last third of the race. He reasons that by the time you get to this stage, things really start to get hard. You're tired and sweaty, and your form is beginning to falter. Having someone stand at a predetermined spot with a dry shirt or even a clean hat, gloves, or singlet allows you to swap out the sweat-soaked garment for a fresh one and presto! You're feelin' fresh again! It may seem trivial, but it really can help. Just remember, pin your number on your shorts if you plan on following the "Feelin' Fresh Rule."

STUDY THE COURSE

Knowing the course you're racing on is a big advantage. If your race is local, consider running sections of the course periodically so you know what to expect come race day. Training on the route lets you learn the turns, the hills, and various other details of the course, and establish a sense of familiarity. With familiarity comes calm and control. In the same way, the athletes in the Hansons-Brooks Distance Project will often take a trip to where we are racing to run the course a few times. Doing this early in the training segment allows us to alter what and where we do our training to be fully prepared for the course. If you don't have the luxury of running the course prior to competition, check the official marathon website, YouTube, and the blog-o-sphere for course tours.

Race Weekend

THE RACE EXPO

Most race expos are akin to bustling flea markets. I'll admit that I sometimes love wandering the aisles, browsing the latest running shoes, gear, and goodies. Despite this, I urge you to avoid spending any length of time on your feet at the expo, a common mistake I see many runners make. They are in awe of the pageantry surrounding the big event, so they stand around on hard concrete floors in the convention hall instead of sitting on their couch or hotel bed, resting. For most Sunday marathons, the expo is open Friday and Saturday. If this is the case and you are able, go during your lunch hour on Friday and pick up your packet. This keeps you from lingering too long, and you can have a relaxed pre-race day. If you can't make it to the expo until the day before the race, go as early as possible to avoid the crowds and then get the heck out of there so you can go home and put your feet up.

PRE-RACE DINNER

Whether you're attending the race's organized pre-race pasta dinner or staying home with your family to eat, the guidelines are the same. Most important, carbo-loading doesn't mean having four plates of spaghetti and three loaves of bread. Eat a regular-sized meal, but make sure it's healthy and high in easily digestible carbohydrates. The main goal is to top off those glycogen stores prior to the race. This meal should cap off a week of balanced eating as suggested in the nutrition chapter; otherwise your pre-race dinner won't make much difference. Test your meal choices ahead of time by eating the same meals leading up to your long runs so you know what to expect on race day. Additionally, while hydration is an ongoing process, make sure you use the day before the race to continue taking in water and sports drinks. Proper hydration takes time and should be tended to throughout the week.

BEFORE BED

Use the evening prior to the race to make sure all your T's are crossed and I's dotted. Your race bag should be packed and ready to go, the timing chip fastened to your shoelaces, your clothes laid out, and your water bottle full. When you head to bed, chances are that sleep will be fairly hard to come by. Don't fret if you are tossing and turning; you should have banked plenty of rest over the past 10 days. If you do find yourself awake, consider grabbing a midnight snack, like an energy bar or piece of fruit. While this isn't necessary, the body burns through about half of the glycogen stored in the liver during the overnight hours. By eating a late-night snack, you further reduce how much you need to replace in the morning, potentially avoiding stomach upset. If you tend to get especially nervous right before a race, this is a good way to consume calories before the jitters set in. Instead of needing 300–500 calories in the morning, you may be able to reduce that to just 100–200 calories to top off glycogen stores.

RACE MORNING

If you wake up three hours or more before the race, you can get away with eating a normal breakfast, such as a bagel with peanut butter, a banana, and coffee or juice. Any closer to gun time and you need to be conservative. Within a few hours of the start, eat less solid food and mostly carbohydrates. With an hour to go, stick with something like an energy gel, which will satiate you for a short time, but won't give you a full feeling. Furthermore, begin measuring your liquid intake by sips, not ounces. The last thing you want is to have water sloshing around in your stomach the first half of the race. Try to have an idea of how long you are going to be standing in the corral at the start. Sometimes runners can be there upward of an hour waiting to cross the start line. Bring your fluids with you to the corral, sip to keep things topped off, and know where the port-a-johns are.

In addition to what you're putting in your body, you must consider what you're putting on your body. Check the weather forecast for both before and during the race. If you end up standing in the corrals for 30 minutes or more, you'll want to be prepared. At the Detroit Marathon, which is held in October, the weather can vary from 80-degree heat to blizzard-like conditions whipping across the Detroit River. Most years, the temperatures hover between 30 and 40 degrees, making wardrobe choices particularly tricky during the early hours of the morning. While your legs may go numb as you stand around before the sun fully rises, you'll feel fine once you begin running. This means that you'll need to layer in order to stay warm prior to the start, but then be able to easily shed garments as you warm up during the race. One of the most common worries we hear from runners in our training programs concerns whether they should wear nice gear that they'll have to carry with them or something old they don't mind tossing to the curb. The Hansons solution is simple: Wear something you're willing to lose. For your bottom layer, sport your regular running gear with the race number attached, but over the top, wear an old pair of sweatpants that have been sitting at the bottom of your dresser drawer or the sweatshirt you wore to paint the living room. When you begin to warm up, which you will, you can throw off the top layer without a second thought.

MENTAL PREP

In my experience, the best way to mentally prepare yourself prior to a marathon is simply to be calm. Getting your heart rate up before you even start running is never a good idea. Step back and spend a moment thinking about your training, reassuring yourself that you are fit and ready to race. Training doesn't lie: 2 + 2 = 4. We call it "cautious confidence," which means being realistic about the difficulty of the race ahead, but also reminding yourself that all your training has prepared you to handle it.

Why does this approach work? For one, it forces you to slow down and accept that the task at hand is going to be hard and hurt at times. This keeps you cautious to the point of avoiding overzealous pacing right out of the gate. In addition, when the going gets tough during the race, you are prepared for it. You knew it wasn't going to be a cakewalk. By preparing this way, you will have positive and motivating thoughts ready and waiting to help you endure. Indeed, as you are able to continue moving forward, despite the discomfort, you will likely be encouraged by your stamina and ability to persevere.

RACE PROTOCOL

Once the starting gun goes off, it's time to cash in all those hard-earned chips. The most common question we get about race strategy regards mile splits. We have already discussed the physiological reasons behind pulling back on the reins and running a conservative pace the first half of the race, but there is more to it than that. Throughout training, many of your workouts are focused on running specific paces. We strongly believe in the truth attached to the old adage "race the way you train," and have emphasized even pacing during workouts in hopes of getting the same result on race day. More specifically, the training is meant to prepare you to run fairly predictable splits throughout but with the second half of the race slightly faster than the first, a strategy called a negative split. Kevin often reminds runners, "You can't really mess anything up if you go out too slow, but you certainly can if you go out too fast." In other words, going out slow will almost never cause lasting damage to your overall pace, but starting too fast might. If you go out ahead of pace and then start fading, not only will your body feel the strain, but your mind also takes a beating as you get passed by other runners who started slower.

What's more, every world record has been set via negative splits. Most PRs are set that way, too. When you start out at a pace you can maintain and then find yourself passing other runners who overestimated their abilities, you'll discover a newfound confidence in the later stages of the race. While many runners say that they feel the best at the beginning of the race and want to capitalize on that by banking time early on, this approach nearly always ends in disaster. A marathon is a long haul, and what feels like a comfortable pace at mile 2 probably won't feel so great at mile 20.

While you should remain steadfast in your race plan in most circumstances, flexibility may be required. Sometimes a fast marathon depends on getting lucky with a few variables—the weather in particular. It can be disappointing to train your hardest only to be met by 80-degree heat, hurricane winds, or even a monsoon. These are not things you can control, and yes, they will probably affect your race performance. In these situations, it is easy to feel that all is lost. While there are plenty of quantifiable gains from training for a marathon, even if the stars don't align for a great race day, not being able to run your best performance can be heartbreaking. If you encounter this, step back and look at the real reasons you decided to train for the marathon and the numerous benefits and personal growth that have resulted from training. Surely it is not a total loss, even if you have to adjust for a slower pace. In the same way we have emphasized smart training, you also must be wise about your race strategy. If the forecast has thrown a wrench into your original plans, alter the course of action accordingly to ensure you reach the finish line in one piece.

From a temperature standpoint, you can expect to slow down anywhere from 5 to 8 seconds per mile when the temps reach the 60s and higher. Generally speaking, you would likely run 5 seconds slower per mile at 60 degrees, 10 seconds slower at 70 degrees, and 15 seconds slower at 80 degrees. This, of course, can depend on a number of factors. For instance, if you have been training in the heat for months, it's not going to affect you as much. The same goes for smaller runners, as well as highly trained harriers. When it comes down to it, weather-related adjustments of expected finishing times can vary depending on the individual.

RACE FUEL

I've never understood why so many races put their one and only gel station at the 18-mile mark. If you haven't fueled up before you get there, you're probably already far past the point of having those calories make a difference. The importance of starting your calorie and fluid replacement early cannot be stressed enough. For elite runners, bottles of fluid containing each runner's own concoctions are placed every 5 kilometers. Physiologists tell us that the stomach can handle about 8 ounces of fluid every 15 minutes or so, which is about 5 kilometers for elite men. With that said, for the other 99.9 percent of runners who don't have access to their own special bottles, there are water stops every 2 miles or so in most marathons. This means that if you take a cup of water or sports drink at every water stop, you'll be taking in fluids at about the same rate as the elites. The cups that are offered are usually 6–8 ounces and are generally filled with about 4–6 ounces of fluid. When you take into account average spillage, a runner can get 2–3 ounces of sports drink at each station. We suggest getting a cup at one of the first tables at the station and then perhaps a second cup at the last table. While the sports drink is the best option in most cases, get your hands on whatever you can. If you are using a gel, try to grab a cup of water.

MID-RACE PACE ADJUSTMENTS

Over the years we've witnessed many runners who have gotten either significantly ahead or behind the desired pace early in the race. This is often a side effect of the crowded streets at the beginning of the race. Once runners make it out of the first few miles, they speed up in hopes of getting back on track, making for extremely inconsistent mile splits. For instance, a marathoner with a 9:00-minute-per-mile goal pace may be slowed by the mob of runners leading the pack, resulting in a pace closer to 9:20 for the first several miles. As the crowds thin out around the 10K mark, the runner may feel a need to make up for lost time and increase speed to 8:45 pace instead of getting back to the original plan of running 9:00-minute miles. As you have probably guessed from what we've said about pacing, this is the wrong time to try to gain time. Get settled back into race pace and gradually pick it up over the next several miles to conserve energy and set yourself up for a strong second half.

Although you may feel great during the first half of the race, that doesn't give you the green light to pick up the pace whenever you see an opening. I can't tell you how many runners I have seen cross the halfway point far ahead of schedule, only to crash and burn in the later miles. If adrenaline gets the best of you in the early stages of the race, prompting your pace to be faster than planned, don't panic. Just fix it. Slow down to goal pace and find the rhythm that will carry you for miles on end. Focus on your own race and try not to get caught up in what other runners are doing. If a few runners breeze past you, assume you'll catch them later on; in most cases, that's exactly what will happen.

Race-Day Checklist

- Shoes and socks
- Singlet and/or sports bra
- Shorts
- Water/sports drink
- Race number
- Timing chip
- Pins or race-number belt
- Energy gels
- Watch
- Sunglasses
- Hat
- Lip balm and/or sunscreen
- Pre- and post-race clothes
- Towel
- Toilet paper or tissues
- Anti-chafing lubricant (Body Glide or petroleum jelly)
- Band-Aids to protect nipples (for the guys)
- Gloves/arm warmers
- Throwaway shirt and/or pants
- Money
- Equipment check bag containing post-race gear
- Directions to start and pre-race instructions

12

POST-RACE
What Now and What Next?

FOR THE HANSONS-BROOKS DISTANCE PROJECT team, two weeks of no running is the cardinal rule after a marathon. When I first joined the team, it was 10 days; however, Kevin and Keith found that wasn't quite long enough. Regardless of whether you met your goals or fell short, you need to take a couple weeks of down time. When you cross that finish line, it's like a race-car driver praying that there's just enough fuel to take him past the checkered flags. While you'll be fueling and hydrating throughout the race, there is no way to keep your stores topped off. By the time the finish line is in sight, you're probably running on empty. Taking a break from running after the marathon is important because it gives your body time to bring glycogen and hydration levels back to normal.

In addition to being depleted of all fuel sources, your exercising muscles also feel the burn. I have run 10 marathons, ranging from 2:14 to 2:20, and the pain the following day is always the same. I'm stiff, sore, and supremely worn out. The marathon breaks down your muscles on a microscopic level, leaving them in dire need of time for rest and repair.

Plan of Action

By taking a couple weeks of rest, you'll ensure that you'll be healthy and prepared for your next endeavor. Consider the following your plan of action as soon as you cross that finish line.

IMMEDIATELY POST-RACE

It often happens that a runner reaches the finish line and then wonders, "Okay, now what?" We spend so much time focusing on training that it's easy to forget to plan for what comes after you finish your 26.2-mile goal. No matter what the clock says, as long as you gave the race your best shot, you can count your marathon a success. So first, take a few moments after the race to revel in the fact that you took your body to the edge and made it to the finish. Allow yourself a moment to be proud of this major accomplishment. Along with those positive feelings will most certainly come soreness and exhaustion. I remember standing in the finishing chute after my first marathon thinking, "There is no way I will ever do that again." That was 10 marathons ago. Sure it can hurt, but after that first race, many marathoners are hooked.

FIRST 30 MINUTES

The same general rules you follow post-workout apply post-marathon. While you may wince at the thought of eating, you need to try to consume some calories right away. The good news is that you can pretty much eat anything you are craving. One of my teammates always wants a bowl of chicken broth, while my wife absolutely has to have a Coke. Personally, I am partial to chocolate chip cookies. At this point, it is the calories that are important, not the source from which they are coming. This is a good thing because you usually can't be picky when it comes to finish-line fare. Whatever they are offering, take it. Since you have depleted nearly all of your available muscle and liver glycogen, your body will bounce back far sooner if you do. What's more, your blood glucose is low, you're dehydrated, and you have only a few remaining electrolytes. The faster you start replacing these nutrients, the sooner you'll be back to feeling normal. That window of optimal recovery time is short, so take advantage of the goodies in the finish chute during those first 30 minutes after the race.

THE FIRST 2 HOURS

Once you gather your hardware and snacks, you can leave the finish chute and find your family and friends. As long as you have had something to eat and drink, you don't need to worry about consuming a full meal until your stomach settles down. If it isn't a hometown race, go back to your hotel, get cleaned up, and put on some comfortable clothes (and shoes!). By that point you may be ready to sit down for lunch. Although you are probably tired of pasta, focus on taking in a high percentage of carbohydrates to replace all of that lost glycogen. If you still aren't ready for a feast, steadily consume calories to get in a good amount over time. At this point, try to choose more nutritious snacks to get your system back on track. Fruits, vegetables, and whole grains are all great options for food, along with water, fruit juice, or sports drinks.

THE REST OF THE DAY

Continue to hydrate and replace calories as desired. Put your feet up and relax for a few hours; no one will argue that you don't deserve it. Although I'm always stiff and tired, I like to get up and walk around later in the evening to loosen up my legs. As you probably know from talking to anyone who has finished a marathon, mobility can be tricky for the next couple of days. Those first steps out of bed the following morning will be labored, and walking up and down stairs may seem a challenge akin to climbing Mount Everest. From elites to weekend warriors, no one escapes a marathon without at least a little soreness. Besides the glycogen depletion, the structural integrity of the muscles has been compromised, so don't plan any big outings right after the marathon. In my experience, the first marathon dishes out the most difficult recovery. The more you run over time, however, the easier recovery seems. After my first marathon it took nearly two months before I felt back to normal. Today, however, I feel 100 percent after only a few days.

THE NEXT 3–5 DAYS

Don't run at all during this period of time. Just focus on navigating stairs and getting through the workday without too much trouble. We have learned that taking a break from running is generally very beneficial. Not only should you not run, but also you should take time away from putting any other races on the calendar. Some runners fall into a cycle of jumping back into mileage just a few days after the marathon, often leaving their legs feeling stale a month or two down the line. Instead, take the time off now, recover completely, and then go back to running. Use this time to catch up on the things that took a backseat during training and enjoy the break. Instead of worrying about your next workout or fitting in your long run, you can sleep in, read the newspaper, and regain some balance in your life.

THE NEXT 2 WEEKS

Many runners dislike taking a few weeks off training, worrying they might lose precious fitness. It's important, however, to understand how a break fits into the bigger picture of training. A planned break most certainly can prevent a forced break due to injury or overtraining. You are better off allowing yourself the time off now, even though it feels like a major deviation from the routine you established over the past few months. Some people will take the entire two weeks away from exercise altogether; others will incorporate some crosstraining. Either option is fine, as long as the crosstraining isn't too intense. A light resistance training program or a cycling regimen is a reasonable choice. The benefit of jumping into crosstraining is that it helps to maintain the routine you worked so hard to build, making it easier to resume running again. The bottom line is to refrain from running for these two weeks to let your body completely recover before getting out and pounding the pavement again.

AFTER 2 WEEKS

Following your two-week vacation, it's time to start running again. If you're a first-time marathon finisher, we don't want to put a timeline on your return, other than to advise you to be cautious. Most veterans are itching to get running again after a fortnight of rest. While we love to see this enthusiasm, one of the problems we often encounter is that some runners want to begin planning their next race before they are even two weeks out from the marathon. It is good to have goals, and we are always glad that a runner wants to continue training, but make sure you are flexible with these plans. For both newbies and veterans alike, it is important to wait and see how recovery goes in order to avoid rushing back to running too soon.

Getting Back to Your Routine

Once you have established that you're fully recovered and ready to get back into your routine, we advise starting with an easy running regimen. Upon your return, those first few runs may feel stiff and more difficult than usual. Don't worry: You haven't lost as much ground as you think. Two weeks off will have decreased your fitness by about 5 percent, a small number at this point in the training cycle. For new runners, try starting with about 30 minutes every other day. The first week might look like this:

BEGINNER: FIRST WEEK BACK TO RUNNING	
Monday	20–30 minutes of slow running
Tuesday	OFF (crosstrain/resistance training)
Wednesday	25–30 minutes of slow running
Thursday	OFF (same as Tuesday)
Friday	30 minutes of slow running
Saturday	OFF (same as Tuesday)
Sunday	30 minutes of slow running

Veteran runners can be more aggressive in their return, but their effort should still be based on how the body reacts to the return to training. An experienced runner's body is probably more accustomed to marathon training, making the comeback somewhat easier. Even so, every runner is different, and you should be cognizant of what your body is telling you after the marathon. A sample week for a veteran runner returning to running might look like this:

ADVANCED: FIRST WEEK BACK TO RUNNING	
Monday	Easy 30 minutes of slow running
Tuesday	Easy 30 minutes of slow running
Wednesday	OFF
Thursday	Easy 40 minutes of slow running
Friday	Easy 50 minutes of slow running
Saturday	Easy 50 minutes of slow running
Sunday	Easy 60 minutes of slow running

For all runners, resistance training can be resumed, two or three times each week. This should be done on days that you won't be doing SOS workouts in the upcoming weeks, allowing you to get into a routine. For example, if you know that in the future you'll be doing SOS workouts on Tuesday, Thursday, and Sunday, establish your resistance-training days on Monday, Wednesday, and/or Friday. By starting the regimen at this time, you can build running-specific strength without doing a single workout for several weeks.

After following the aforementioned mileage for the first week back to training, you might consider bringing things up a notch for the second week, although it should still be all easy mileage. This depends on how your body responded to that first week. If you are feeling refreshed and looking forward to getting back on track, add a bit of mileage. The beginner should add two days with 30-minute runs, bringing the weekly total to five days of 30-minute runs each. Advanced runners can add time to each of their running days, aiming for 45–60 minutes of easy running, six days a week. If you are still feeling sore and tired, however, give yourself another week to linger at the lower mileage and let your body and mind recover.

4 TO 6 WEEKS POST-MARATHON

After those first two weeks of easy running, you should spend the next two weeks building mileage, allowing for a slow return to typical training volume. The Advanced Program peaks at 60–70 miles, but the average mileage is between 35 and 45 miles per week and the Beginner Program is slightly less, at 30–35 miles per week on average. Once you are comfortably running "average" weekly mileage again, you can begin structured training and start to draw up plans for new goal races or more general ambitions. Whatever it is you choose to do, a training segment doesn't always need to adhere to an 18-week time frame. You may find that as you become more experienced, the length of time you need to prepare for a marathon can be shortened by a few weeks. In most cases, a speed or base-building segment can be 10–14 weeks. The more weekly mileage a person is able to tolerate, the shorter those training segments often need to be.

THE GREAT BEYOND

The question at this point is where to go from here. Many runners feel they need to get right back into marathon training, although this isn't the optimal choice for a lot of runners. Case in point, we limit the runners in our Elite Program to three marathons in two years. If you just completed a fall marathon, it might be a good idea to build a strong base before entering training for a spring marathon. This is a sensible plan if you qualified for Boston or have another spring marathon in mind. That gap of time from November through January is great for base fitness running, especially since it tends to be a time of year that includes holiday plans and family obligations. For runners who just completed the Beginner or Just Finish Programs, this can be an ideal time to build up mileage and perhaps gradually enter a more ambitious training regimen for the spring marathon. This time gives you the chance to safely and slowly put mileage on your legs, preparing you for the increased training.

Some runners decide to capitalize on the fitness base they have just built by dedicating a training segment to shorter races. From 5Ks to the half-marathon, this is a great way to build speed and keep your legs feeling fresh, rather than simply going right back into long marathon training. Many of the runners we work with are stuck in a marathon rut and simply need to take a step back and work on some of the types of training they abandoned long ago. Sure it's nice to be at ease with the marathon distance, but sometimes it is beneficial to break out of your comfort zone. A 10-week speed section is especially beneficial for runners who have just finished a spring marathon but want to do a fall marathon as well. After two weeks off, they can focus on shorter races for a couple of months and then go straight back into marathon training. After a speed-focused season of training, runners inevitably feel fresher, faster, and ready for a breakthrough at 26.2.

Assessing Race Success and Determining Future Direction

Every training cycle, regardless of the race-day result, contains value for an athlete. Identifying patterns of success and failure are crucial to long-term success. Hopefully, race day brings a nice payout for your hard work, but sometimes it doesn't. Either way, it is important to review the training cycle as a whole, and try to find the components that increased fitness and those that inhibited it. Good questions to ask after a training cycle include:

- Was I able to complete all of the training as scheduled? If not, did I run more than scheduled or less?

- Was I able to hit all the prescribed workout paces? If not, were there specific workout types that gave me trouble?
- Did I run any of the workouts, easy days, or long runs faster than prescribed?
- Was this training cycle at a higher level of weekly mileage than usual? Higher than I've ever done?
- Was the goal pace faster than I've ever run? Was goal pace too aggressive?
- Were my goals appropriate relative to recent performances and fitness?
- What was my pre-race routine like compared to past cycles?
- How well did I execute my race plan? Did I start too fast? Too slow?
- Did I have people to race? Was the crowd support good?
- What was going on in my life during this training cycle?
- Was my life more stressful or less stressful than past training cycles?
- Did I get sick during this training cycle?
- Was I dealing with any injuries this training cycle?
- What was my sleep like this training cycle?
- What was the weather like this training cycle? Did I adjust for weather?

The goal is to look for parameters that correlate with success and failure. From there you work to incorporate those associated with success and mindfully eliminate or adjust those that seem to factor in failure. Teasing apart the factors related to both will allow you to progress through higher levels of fitness more quickly than those who do not do so.

Once you've identified some success and failure factors, where do you go next? First, take your scheduled downtime as outlined earlier in the chapter. This is especially important if you're carrying any injuries or excess fatigue. After this well-deserved downtime, thoughtfully consider your options. Need help deciding? Check out the decision tree in Figure 12.1.

FIGURE 12.1 DECISION TREE

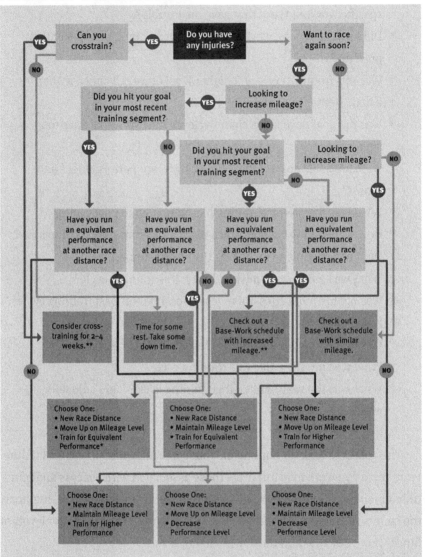

*"Train for equivalent performance" means focus on shorter distances. For example, if you want to break 3 hours in the marathon but haven't broken 1:30 in the half-marathon, consider a training cycle to work on bringing your half-marathon time down to an equivalent 3-hour marathon performance before going back to attempt that marathon goal time.
**The Hansons base-building and crosstraining programs can be found at www.hansons coachingservices.com.

Appendix A

The Elite Program: Hansons-Brooks Distance Project

Having honed their coaching philosophies and training methods via the Beginner and Advanced Programs, Keith and Kevin decided to take their experience and expertise to the elite running world in 1999. At the time, a shift was at hand within the sport, as several competitive training groups sprang up across the country with a shared mission of supporting American postcollegiate runners. Over the years, the African nations had begun to dominate distance running, leaving other countries, such as the United States, to step back and reevaluate how they trained their Olympic hopefuls. The Hansons, already highly successful coaches, knew they had the necessary tools and training methods to assist elite runners in their pursuit of international success. Thus the Hansons-Brooks Distance Project came to fruition. Having been a member of the group for more than a decade, I have seen firsthand how valuable elite coaches and an established group can be. If I had entered the sport even five years earlier, the options would have been significantly more limited and my competitive running career cut short. A number of runners, including me, owe a debt of gratitude to the Hansons for both starting and maintaining this world-class development program.

When one scrolls through the Hansons-Brooks roster of current and former runners, a pattern emerges: Only a few of them were truly great runners in college. With a long-term plan for development, however, the accomplishments of the athletes in this group rival those of any other elite program in the country. In the years since first forming, the squad has had nine women run under 2:45 in the marathon, including three under 2:33. Similarly, the men's program has seen 24 of its runners dip under 2:20 in the marathon, eight of them under 2:15. The lesson here is that development and success take time. While the majority of the runners recruited by the Hansons-Brooks Distance Project were only average-to-good collegiate athletes, many have gone on to achieve great success under the same training principles used to develop the 18-week programs in this book. To understand the building blocks on which your training will rest, you may find it interesting to explore the related elements that are important to the elite runners we train. Not only will this dispel any myths about the way high-level runners actually train, it will also reveal the similarities between your own training and that of Olympic hopefuls.

In the same way we have stressed long-term development in the Beginner and Advanced Programs, we do the same in the Elite Program. In fact, setting our sights on success far down the road is our goal when runners first join the team. Kevin and Keith seek to develop a runner over months and years, not cultivate a one-hit wonder who is prone to overtraining and burnout. Because most of our athletes enter the program lacking the credentials to be threats on the national—let alone world—stage, they often have no choice but to embrace patience as they work and wait for the development process to pay off. Consider the fact that U.S. marathon runners tend to peak, on average, when they are around 29–30 years old. Runners coming into our program are typically 23–25 years old, giving them several years to grow and progress before they reach their peak marathon potential. When you look at the runners who have had success in the Hansons-Brooks program, they are generally those who gave the training more than a year or two to take hold. Olympian Brian Sell, who joined the program in 2001, slowly improved in every marathon he ran over several years before competing at the Olympics in 2008. His marathon time dropped from the low 2:20 range to 2:10:30. Olympian Desiree Davila followed a similar path. Between the ages of 23 and 28, she went from being a marathoner running in the 2:30s to the 2:22 Boston Marathon runner-up in 2011. Since the 2012 Olympics, she has finished in the top five at Berlin, New York, and again at Boston. In 2016 she'll again be a favorite to make the Olympic team.

While the underlying principle of long-term development underscores all of our marathon training programs, there are also some outward differences between the programs in this book and the Elite Program. Indeed, the lives of most runners vary greatly from the existence of elite athletes, and the training plans appropriately reflect those differences. Despite the distinctions, you may be surprised to discover that your training isn't as different from that of an elite runner as you may have thought.

ELITE PROGRAM COMPONENTS

Nine-day training cycle. When I joined the Hansons-Brooks Distance Project in 2004, our weekly training cycle was similar to the plans within these pages. We ran a track workout on Tuesday, a tempo-type workout on Thursday, and then a long run on Sunday. But along the way, we switched to a nine-day training cycle that looks something like this:

Sunday: Long, 18–20 miles

Monday: a.m.: Easy, 12–14 miles; p.m.: Easy, 4–6 miles

Tuesday: Same as Monday

Wednesday: Tempo run, 8–12 miles

Thursday: Same as Monday

Friday: Same as Monday

Saturday: Track, 5 miles' worth of speed (20 seconds faster than marathon pace)

Sunday: Same as Monday

Monday: Same as previous Monday

The training mileage for a runner in the Elite Program remains fairly steady all year. For example, when I train for a marathon, my weekly volume ranges from 110 to 140 miles per week; when I am preparing for shorter races, my volume is still 100–120 miles per week. Within this mileage, traditional long runs every week are not always necessary. Since the volume of the easy days is between 12 and 14 miles, or 1:18–1:35 in terms of time, runners gain many of the same desired aerobic adaptations for marathon performance as a regular long run would offer. This high mileage makes the nine-day cycle particularly advantageous because it allows for adequate rest while still working all the systems that are important to marathon development.

Weekly volume. In looking at the example of a nine-day training stint in the Elite Program, you may notice that the mileage is significantly higher than in the other training plans in this book. While the Advanced Program peaks at around 70 miles per week, a male runner following the Elite Program will reach 120–140 miles per week and female elites hit 120–130 miles per week. When it comes to the elite training, there are a number of factors built into the plan that make such high mileage tolerable and productive.

The first factor is time. We aren't referring to 24 hours in a day or seven days in a week, but rather the years of previous training that have slowly allowed for an increased volume of mileage. While most runners entering the development program aren't running more than 100 miles per week, the majority of them are logging 80–100 miles. The increased mileage makes the nine-day cycle especially important because instead of asking a 22-year-old runner to jump into 120-mile weeks with three hard workouts a week, the frequency of SOS workouts is cut to every third day, giving that runner the chance to increase volume through easy days. Sometimes the extra mileage hurts a runner's performances initially, but over time, adaptations occur, leading to steady improvements.

The second factor concerns recovery. In addition to fitting in more mileage at easier paces, the nine-day cycle also allows for steady recovery between SOS workouts. Even with these extra recovery days, cumulative fatigue plays an important role in the Elite Program, but it is balanced with injury prevention. When the volume of an easy day reaches between 16 and 20 miles, that extra day between SOS workouts is necessary to provide added recovery. Although these days are classified as "easy" in the Elite Program, they are often run at approximately marathon pace. For example, during peak mileage of marathon training, easy runs are typically completed at a pace of 6:00–6:30 per mile and long runs are around 5:30–6:00 per mile. If marathon goal pace is 5:05 per mile, then the majority of runs are 25 seconds to 1:15 slower than that pace.

A third factor is the layout of the training segment. The Beginner and Advanced training schedules in this book have a clear break between weeks. First there is speed with an introduction to tempo runs. Then there is a clear shift to strength workouts as we move to race-specific workouts. The Elite Program builds differently. We don't spend weeks doing tempo runs, long runs, or the other components, as we have already been doing these throughout the previous months. Rather those workouts are sprinkled in to maintain balance. Also, since we are training at a high level most of the time, we don't require an 18-week training block. I personally feel that I race my best with a 12–14 week training block that includes a few weeks of returning to running, 8–10 weeks of high mileage and intense workouts, and then a few weeks of gradual taper. Anything longer, and I felt like I plateau and begin to become overtrained.

The other factors that make this higher-volume program manageable are the inherent benefits that go along with being a part of a structured training group like the Hansons-Brooks Distance Project. While all of the runners in the program have a job in some capacity (besides running), their schedules allow them to take naps throughout the week, in addition to getting 8–10 hours of sleep a night. Let's face it: If you had the opportunity to take a two-hour nap a couple times per week, you'd probably be able to handle more weekly mileage too. The high mileage is also made easier by having running shoes from Brooks. Members of the Distance Project go through a lot of shoes when they are logging 140 miles per week; that steady supply of footwear eases the financial burden. Additionally, our athletes have the advantage of access to chiropractors, physical therapists, and other medical professionals who understand runners and the unique injuries and issues related to the sport.

SOS workouts. Along with a higher overall volume of mileage, the mileage contained within SOS workouts is also higher. This means that the volume of SOS mileage is proportionate to the overall training plan, whether you're looking at the Beginner, Advanced, or Elite Program. By breaking down each SOS workout, you'll see how similar the Elite Program really is to the ones we recommend in this book.

■ **The Long Run:** After all of our preaching about the 16-mile long run, it may surprise you to discover that the runners following the Elite Program complete 20- to 22-mile long runs. When it comes down to it, however, it really isn't about 16 miles or 22 miles, but rather the percentage of weekly volume and the time it actually takes to complete the long run. In a typical 120-mile week, a 20-miler represents about 16–17 percent of the weekly volume. For me, a 20-mile long run takes between 1:55 and 2:10, which falls well within the guidelines we have described. On the other hand, a 16-mile long run completed by athletes running 70 miles per week will account for approximately 23 percent of their total weekly volume. Typically, that 16-mile long run will take around the same two-hour duration, eliciting virtually identical metabolic and physiological adaptations despite the difference in actual miles.

■ **Speed Sessions:** In the Beginner and Advanced Programs, the speed sessions total 3 miles of fast running. Generally you'll be running around 50 miles per week when you do these workouts, so that means that speed will account for 6 percent of the weekly volume. Meanwhile, the absolute volume of a speed session in the Elite Program is typically around 6 miles. With a weekly volume of 120 miles, the percentage is 5 percent of the total weekly volume. Again, the principle is the same; speed represents a small percentage of weekly training while we focus on developing aerobic capabilities through sub-lactate threshold work.

- **Strength Sessions:** Strength sessions are a vital part of marathon development, regardless of the level of training. In the Beginner and Advanced Programs, these sessions include 6 miles of hard running to be completed during 55- to 70-mile weeks, accounting for 9–10 percent of weekly volume. In the Elite Program, strength workouts are usually between 9 and 12 miles, which is 8–10 percent of total weekly volume within a 120-mile week. Once again, absolute volume is greater, but the percentage of SOS mileage completed during the training week is proportionate across programs.

- **Tempo Runs:** At its peak, the 10-mile tempo run is about 15 percent of weekly volume in the Beginner and Advanced Programs. The Elite Program also includes 10-mile tempo runs, so this work makes up 12 percent of the weekly volume. The percentage here is slightly less as a result of the variations in the tempo runs that the elite runners complete; these will be discussed later in this appendix.

ELITE PROGRAM WORKOUTS

Over the years, a number of the workouts we assign to our elite runners have gained national attention. These workouts are unique to the Elite Program, and for the most part (like the Bread and Butter and The Simulator) shouldn't be attempted by runners in either the Beginner or Advanced Programs. For most of these workouts, the volume is simply too high.

Long-Run Variations

- **The Steady-State Effort:** This is one of my personal favorites because it involves a high level of concentration, reduces boredom associated with repetitive training, and also stimulates important aerobic adaptations. I use this with runners who are experienced but can't feasibly increase their mileage because of life's other obligations and constraints. Scheduled well into training, when a runner's fitness is established, this workout begins like any other long run. But then you'll gradually increase the pace to about 30 seconds slower than goal marathon pace, and hold that speed for 50–75 percent of the run. By forcing your body to run at a significant effort, nearing the tipping point between using mostly fat and drawing upon those highly coveted carbohydrates, you stimulate your aerobic threshold. Because your body wants to conserve carbohydrates, it begins to adapt to that pace and maximize its fat-burning capabilities. Pacing precision is important here because if you go too hard, you'll hit the wall prematurely, but if you run too slow, you'll miss out on some of the desired effects. This workout is also a good mental exercise because it is a long, tough effort that requires an athlete to maintain focus for an extended period of time, just like the marathon itself.

- **Last 3 GO!:** Kevin and Keith came up with this variation to help us run fast on tired legs. As with other long runs, you maintain a moderate pace throughout the majority of the run. The difference comes at the end. When the going gets tough, the tough are forced to run faster. In this workout, you increase your speed to marathon pace or faster during the last 3 miles of the long run, right when your legs are the most fatigued. The point is to teach the body to run even when it is tired, pushing that breaking point farther and farther down the road. Physiologically, it puts an emphasis on recruiting intermediate muscle fibers and maybe even some fast-twitch fibers. This is an especially good workout for competitive marathoners because it simulates that point in a marathon when you're digging deep and expending your last energy stores, but you're still forced to keep moving forward. This one can be a great tool for advanced runners attempting to qualify for races or compete on a local level.

- **The Depletion:** I use this workout only once or twice during a marathon cycle because we coaches are big proponents of practicing marathon nutrition during long runs and this run abandons that practice. Some coaches strongly encourage runners to regularly avoid taking in fluids or carbohydrates on long runs because they believe it teaches the body to burn fat better. You aren't, however, going to do that in a race, so nutrition intake needs to be practiced during the majority of long runs, with a couple of exceptions. This is where the Depletion run comes in. For this particular long run, pace is less important, and is slower than the other long runs because the runner doesn't eat anything prior and ingests only water throughout. This workout is meant to burn through the majority of the glycogen stores, triggering the body to store more glycogen. Our runners who implement this workout use it as their last significant long run. When they enter the taper period immediately following the Depletion workout, the muscles have something to store as the glycogen-loading phase kicks in to replace those stores. Although this may not seem like a big deal, it can mean the difference between hitting the wall and busting right through it.

Tempo-Run Variations

- **The Cutdown:** This workout, between 10 and 12 miles, starts at a pace of 6:00 minutes per mile for the elite men in the program, which is within our easy range, and decreases by 10-second increments down to half-marathon pace. A typical cutdown workout looks like this: 6:00, 6:00, 5:50, 5:40, 5:30, 5:20, 5:10, 5:00,

4:50. This workout often feels easy at the beginning, but it becomes increasingly challenging with each passing mile.

- **Five and GO!:** The first half of this 10-mile tempo run is done at marathon pace and the second half hits either a designated faster pace, usually half-marathon pace, or is simply run as fast as we can go.

- **The Simulator:** This workout was first introduced into the Elite Program in 2006 as we prepared for the Boston Marathon. I clearly remember this because Kevin and Keith put out poster boards of Boston landmarks at their designated mile markers and Wellesley was marked with pictures of bikini models. It must have worked, because that year the team managed to finish in 4th, 10th, 11th, 15th, 18th, 19th, and 22nd places. This Simulator is 26.2 kilometers at marathon goal pace run on a course that represents the race for which you are training. If an athlete is preparing for the hilly TCS New York City Marathon, it is important to execute it on a similar course and not one that resembles, say, the flat Bank of America Chicago Marathon. Some of the "magical" qualities of this simulation are lost if the right terrain can't be located. Besides providing a significant effort run at goal pace, the idea of this workout is to let you visualize the course, develop a plan for racing, and get a feel for what you want to do on race day. Including warm-up and cooldown, this workout tops out around 20 miles, and therefore should be approached with caution. If an athlete is logging low mileage, attempting this workout is a flat-out bad idea. Runners should try this only if they are putting in at least 100 miles per week and also have a course on which to properly simulate the goal race. The Simulator is generally done about four weeks prior to the goal marathon and is the first in a series of quite difficult workouts.

Strength-Workout Variations

▰ **The Bread-and-Butter Workout:** This 2 × 6-mile workout has been around as long as the Elite Program has existed and was the first of the Hansons' training innovations to gain national attention. Quite similar to other strength workouts, the Bread and Butter Workout is scheduled for 10 days after the Simulator. After a warm-up, the first 6 miles are run at 5 seconds faster than goal marathon pace, followed by 10 minutes of light jogging. Then comes the second 6 miles, which are run 5–10 seconds per mile faster than goal pace. Success in this workout has also typically led to optimal marathon performances. Completed less than 3 weeks before the big day, the Bread and Butter Workout marks the beginning of the taper portion of the Elite Program. While there are still other workouts and mileage volume remains fairly high, the hardest work is complete. From this point until race day, the emphasis is on smart training, fitness maintenance, and recovery.

THE THREE TWO RULE

In addition to all of the above training principles, Kevin and Keith have one very strict rule they require all of the Elite team members to follow: the Three Two Rule. Basically this rule states that no runner in the program can run more than three marathons every two years. The reason for this is that when runners start chasing marathon goals, they tend to fall into a never-ending cycle of spring and fall marathons. Athletes often end up abandoning certain training elements, speed work in particular. By upholding this rule, the runners in the Hansons-Brooks Distance Project are encouraged to spend whole seasons focused on improving leg speed, which will ultimately aid in marathon performance. The same goes for runners adhering to our other training programs; if you are stuck in a cycle of poor marathon results, try dedicating a segment of your year to working on 5K and 10K racing and you'll come back to marathon training refreshed and ready to break through that plateau.

SAMPLE TRAINING LOG FOR ELITE PROGRAM

The following program (Table A.1) is a log of my training for the 2011 Rock 'n' Roll San Diego Marathon, from February to June. While this is tailored to my individual needs, it is a typical training program for a veteran runner who is part of the Hansons-Brooks Distance Project. The only real difference in

TABLE A.1 TRAINING LOG: ROCK 'N' ROLL SAN DIEGO 2011

WEEK	MON	TUES	WED	THURS
1	8 mi., 56:00 (7:00/mi.)	8 mi., 56:00 (7:00/mi.)	8 mi., 56:00 (7:00/mi.)	9 mi., 63:00 (7:00/mi.)
2	10 mi., 70:00 (7:00/mi.)	AM: 8 mi., 56:00 (7:00/mi.) PM: 4 mi., 28:00 (7:00/mi.)	10 mi., 1:08:46 (6:48/mi.)	Tempo run, 8-mi. cutdown from 6:00 to 5:10/mi. (45:30/5:41/mi.); warm-up and cool-down: 12 mi. total
3	AM: 10 mi., 70:00 (7:00/mi.) PM: 4 mi., 28:00 (7:00/mi.)	AM: 10 mi., 70:00 (7:00/mi.) PM: 6 mi., 41:00 (6:50/mi.)	AM: 10 mi., 70:00 (7:00/mi.) PM: 6 mi., 41:00 (6:50/mi.)	3 × 2 mi. @ goal MP with 0.5-mi. jog recovery (6 mi.: 30:10, 5:01/mi.); warm-up and cooldown: 13 mi. total
4	16 mi. long, 1:35:00 (5:56/mi.)	AM: 10 mi., 1:08:00 (6:48/mi.) PM: 6 mi., 40:00 (6:40/mi.)	AM: 12 mi., 1:20:00 (6:40/mi.) PM: 4 mi., 27:30 (6:52/mi.)	2 × 3 mi. @ 5:01/ mi. with 1-mi. jog recovery; warm-up and cooldown: 13 mi. total
5	18 mi. long, 1:45:00 (5:50/mi.)	AM: 12 mi., 1:20:00 (6:40/mi.) PM: 4 mi., 27:00 (6:45/mi.)	AM: 12 mi., 1:22:00 (6:50/mi.) PM: 4 mi., 28:00 (7:00/mi.)	AM: 12 mi., 1:22:00 (6:50/mi.) PM: 4 mi., 28:00 (7:00/mi.)

what our elite women runners do relates to pace as they also run 120 or more miles per week. You'll notice that there are no big secrets when it comes to training an elite runner. In fact, the principles used are the same for everyone.

FRI	SAT	SUN	WEEKLY TOTAL
8 mi., 56:00 (7:00/mi.)	10 mi., 70:00 (7:00/mi.)	AM: 8 mi., 56:00 (7:00/mi.) PM: 4 mi., 28:00 (7:00/mi.)	63 mi.
AM: 7 mi., 46:30 (6:38/mi.) PM: 6 mi., 41:00 (6:50/mi.)	AM: Easy 9 mi., 63:00 (7:00/mi.) PM: 4 mi., 27:00 (6:45/mi.)	Easy 10 mi., 68:30 (6:51/mi.)	80 mi.
14 mi., 1:35:00 (6:47/mi.)	AM: 10 mi., 1:08:00 (6:48/mi.) PM: 4 mi., 27:00 (6:45/mi.)	Day off	87 mi.
AM: 12 mi., 1:20:00 (6:40/mi.) PM: 4 mi., 28:00 (7:00/mi.)	AM: 10 mi., 1:08:00 (6:48/mi.) PM: 6 mi., 40:00 (6:40/mi.)	AM: 10 mi., 1:08:00 (6:48/mi.) PM: 6 mi., 41:00 (6:50/mi.)	109 mi.
5 × 2 mi. with 0.5-mi. jog recovery 10:08, 10:02, 10:00, 10:00, 10:01: 18 mi. total	AM: 10 mi., 1:07:00 (6:42/mi.) PM: 6 mi., 41:40 (6:56/mi.)	AM: 12 mi., 1:16:30 (6:22/mi.) PM: 4 mi., 26:45 (6:41/mi.)	116 mi.

CONTINUES

TABLE A.1 CONTINUED

WEEK	MON	TUES	WED	THURS
6	20 mi. long, 1:51:30 (5:34/mi.)	AM: 12 mi., 1:18:00 (6:30/mi.) PM: 6 mi., 42:00 (7:00/mi.)	AM: 12 mi., 1:17:30 (6:27/mi.) PM: 6 mi., 42:00 (7:00/mi.)	AM: 10-mi. cutdown, 56:00 (5:36/mi.): 16 mi. total
7	AM: 12 mi., 1:21:30 (6:47/mi.) PM: 6 mi., 40:30 (6:45/mi.)	20 mi. long, 2:09:30 (6:28/mi.)	AM: 14 mi., 1:33:00 (6:38/mi.) PM: 6 mi., 40:00 (6:40/mi.)	AM: 14 mi., 1:32:00 (6:32/mi.) PM: 6 mi., 39:00 (6:30/mi.)
8	Strength: 3-2-3 @ 5:02/mi. with 1-mi. jog recovery 10:00, 15:00, 9:58: 15 mi. total	AM: 15 mi., 1:38:00 (6:32/mi.) PM: 6 mi., 38:40 (6:28/mi.)	AM: 14 mi., 1:31:00 (6:30/mi.) PM: 6 mi., 39:15 (6:32/mi.)	20 mi. long, 1:51:30 (6:34, 5:51, 5:45, 5:47, 5:45, 5:43, 5:31, 5:40, 5:23, 5:30, 5:29, 5:24, 5:18, 5:23, 5:32, 5:26, 5:20, 5:15, 5:29, 5:10)
9	AM: 14 mi., 1:30:00 (6:25/mi.) PM: 6 mi., 42:00 (7:00/mi.)	AM: 14 mi., 1:30:00 (6:25/mi.)	Tempo: 10 mi., first 5 @ goal MP and second 5 @ 4:58–5:02/mi., 50:48 (5:04/mi.): 16 mi. total	AM: 14 mi., 1:31:00 (6:30/mi.) PM: 6 mi., 40:00 (6:40/mi.)
10	AM: 14 mi., 1:30:30 (6:27/mi.) PM: 6 mi., 39:30 (6:35/mi.)	Tempo: 10 mi. first 5 mi. at 5:12/mi., second 5 mi. @ 5:02/mi. 50:48 (5:04/mi.): 16 mi. total	AM: 14 mi., 1:31:30 (6:32/mi.) PM: 6 mi., 38:45 (6:27/mi.)	AM: 14 mi., 1:31:30 (6:32/mi.) PM: 6 mi., 39:00 (6:30/mi.)

FRI	SAT	SUN	WEEKLY TOTAL
AM: 12 mi., 1:20:00 (6:40/mi.) **PM:** 6 mi., 40:00 (6:40/mi.)	**AM:** 12 mi., 1:18:30 (6:32/mi.) **PM:** 6 mi., 39:00 (6:30/mi.)	**AM:** 12 mi., 1:22:00 (6:50/mi.) **PM:** 6 mi., 39:00 (6:30/mi.)	**126** mi.
4 × 1 mi. @ MP: 20 (4:52) sec. on track, 400-m jog recovery: 13 mi. total	**AM:** 14 mi., 1:31:30 (6:32/mi.) **PM:** 6 mi., 38:30 (6:25/mi.)	**AM:** 14 mi., 1:31:30 (6:32/mi.) **PM:** 6 mi., 38:30 (6:25/mi.)	**131** mi.
AM: 14 mi., 1:31:00 (6:30/mi.) **PM:** 6 mi., 40:00 (6:30/mi.)	**AM:** 14 mi., 1:35:00 (6:47/mi.) **PM:** 6 mi., 40:00 (6:40/mi.)	Strength: 3 × 3 mi. @ 5:02/mi. with 1-mi. jog recovery: 17 mi. total	**133** mi.
AM: 14 mi., 1:31:00 (6:30/mi.) **PM:** 6 mi., 40:00 (6:40/mi.)	21 mi. long, 1:57:00 (5:34/mi.)	**AM:** 14 mi., 1:32:30 (6:36/mi.) **PM:** 6 mi., 40:30 (6:45/mi.)	**131** mi.
AM: Track 8 × 1K @ 4:40/mi. pace with 400-m jog recovery **PM:** 6 mi., 39:00 (6:30/mi.)	**AM:** 14 mi., 1:34:00 (6:42/mi.) **PM:** 6 mi., 39:30 (6:35/mi.)	**AM:** 14 mi., 1:32:00 (6:34/mi.) **PM:** 6 mi., 40:00 (6:40/mi.)	**130** mi.

TABLE A.1 CONTINUED

WEEK	MON	TUES	WED	THURS
11	Strength: 5 × 2 mi., all between 9:41 and 9:44 with 0.5-mi. jog recovery: 18 mi. total	AM: 14 mi., 1:32:00 (6:34/mi.) PM: 6 mi., 40:00 (6:40/mi.)	AM: 14 mi., 1:31:40 (6:32/mi.) PM: 4 mi., 27:00 (6:45/mi.)	Strength: 3 × 3 mi. @ 4:52/mi. with 1-mi. jog recovery (14:36, 14:42, 14:40): 17 mi. total
12	AM: 14 mi., 1:31:00 (6:30/mi.) PM: 6 mi., 40:00 (6:40/mi.)	18 mi. long, Depletion run 1:55:00 (6:23/mi.)	AM: 14 mi., 1:31:00 (6:30/mi.) PM: 6 mi., 40:00 (6:40/mi.)	AM: 14 mi., 1:32:00 (6:34/mi.) PM: 6 mi., 40:00 (6:40/mi.)
13	20 mi. long, 1:50:19 with last 3 mi. @ 4:55, 4:56, 4:52	AM: 14 mi. 1:32:00 (6:34/mi.) PM: 6 mi., 40:00 (6:40/mi.)	AM: 12 mi., 1:20:00 (6:40/mi.) PM: 6 mi., 40:00 (6:40/mi.)	Strength: 2 × 6 mi. (29:39, 10-min. jog, 29:36): 19 mi. total
14	AM: 12 mi., 1:20:00 (6:40/mi.) PM: 4 mi., 28:00 (7:00/mi.)	AM: 14 mi., 1:33:00 (6:38/mi.) PM: 6 mi., 40:00 (6:40/mi.)	20 mi. long, 2:05:00 (6:15/mi.)	AM: 14 mi., 1:33:00 (6:38/mi.) PM: 6 mi., 40:00 (6:40/mi.)
15	16 mi., 1:43:00 (6:26/mi.)	AM: 12 mi., 1:20:00 (6:40/mi.) PM: 4 mi., 28:00 (7:00/mi.)	AM: 10 mi., 1:10:00 (7:00/mi.) PM: 4 mi., 28:00 (7:00/mi.)	12 mi., 1:20:00 (6:40/mi.)

CONTINUES

FRI	SAT	SUN	WEEKLY TOTAL
AM: 14 mi., 1:30:30 (6:27/mi.) **PM:** 6 mi., 41:00 (6:50/mi.)	**AM:** 15 mi., 1:40:00 (6:40/mi.)	Simulator (half-marathon) 1:06:39 for half-marathon in Kalamazoo, MI (5:05/mi.): 20 mi. total	**128** mi.
Track: 5 × 1 mi. @ 4:40/mi. with 800-m jog: 16 mi. total	**AM:** 14 mi., 1:31:00 (6:30/mi.) **PM:** 6 mi., 40:00 (6:40/mi.)	**AM:** 14 mi., 1:31:00 (6:30/mi.) **PM:** 6 mi., 39:50 (6:38/mi.)	**134** mi.
AM: 14 mi., 1:32:00 (6:34/mi.) **PM:** 6 mi., 40:00 (6:40/mi.)	**AM:** 14 mi., 1:32:00 (6:34/mi.) **PM:** 6 mi., 40:00 (6:40/mi.)	Tempo: 8 mi. tempo (40:15–5:01/mi.): 14 mi. total	**131** mi.
14 mi., 1:34:00 (6:42/mi.)	Tempo: 3 × 2 mi. at MP with 0.5-mi. jog recovery: 14 mi. total	**AM:** 12 mi., 1:20:00 (6:40/mi.) **PM:** 4 mi., 28:00 (7:00/mi.)	**120** mi.
AM: 8 mi., 56:00 (7:00/mi.)	**AM:** 6 mi., 42:00 (7:00/mi.)	MARATHON! 2:14:37, a new personal best, second-fastest last 10K in the field, 5th place	**99** mi., counting race

Appendix B
Training Plans Annotated with Supplemental Work

Chapter 7, on supplemental training, gave you a lot of information; now let's take a closer look at how you can put it into action. Below is an example of what your overall training program might look like if you add stretching, flexibility, and strength training into the mix.

We have annotated calendars for the Beginner (Table B.1) and Advanced (Table B.2) Programs only. We assume that runners choosing the Just Finish Program are new to running and just establishing a baseline. For new runners, adding more to the schedule might not be wise, considering that the schedule as it stands may already be a significant increase in what they are doing.

TABLE B.1 BEGINNER PROGRAM

WEEK	MON	TUES	WED	THURS
1	—	—	OFF	DWU1 Easy 3 mi. (5 km) LS/Flex
2	OFF	Easy 2 mi. (3 km)	OFF	DWU1 Easy 3 mi. (5 km) LS/Flex
3	OFF	Easy 4 mi. (7 km)	OFF	DWU1 Easy 4 mi. (7 km) LS/Flex
4	OFF	DWU1 Easy 5 mi. (8 km) BWM, LS	OFF	DWU1 Easy 3 mi. (5 km) LS/Flex
5	OFF	DWU1 Easy 5 mi. (8 km) BWM, LS	OFF	DWU1 Easy 4 mi. (7 km) LS/Flex
6	DWU1 Easy 4 mi. (7 km) LS/Flex	SPEED: DWU1, WU, DWU2, 12 × 400/ 400R, CD	DWU1 BWM LS/Flex	TEMPO: DWU1, WU, DWU2, TEMPO 5 mi. (8 km), CD
7	DWU1 Easy 4 mi. (7 km) BWM, LS/Flex	SPEED: DWU1, WU, DWU2, 8 × 600/ 400R, CD	DWU1 RT LS/Flex	TEMPO: DWU1, WU, DWU2, TEMPO 5 mi. (8 km), CD
8	DWU1 Easy 6 mi. (10 km) BWM, LS/Flex	SPEED: DWU1, WU, DWU2, 6 × 800/ 400R, CD	DWU1 RT LS/Flex	TEMPO: DWU1, WU, DWU2, TEMPO 5 mi. (8 km), CD
9	DWU1 Easy 5 mi. (8 km) BWM, LS/Flex	SPEED: DWU1, WU, DWU2, 5 × 1km/ 400R, CD	DWU1 RT LS/Flex	TEMPO: DWU1, WU, DWU2, TEMPO 8 mi. (13 km), CD
10	DWU1 Easy 7 mi. (11 km) BWM, LS/Flex	SPEED: DWU1, WU, DWU2, 4 × 1200/ 400R, CD	DWU1 RT LS	TEMPO: DWU1, WU, DWU2, TEMPO 8 mi. (13 km), CD

SPEED WORKOUTS
See pace charts, pp. 68–74

STRENGTH WORKOUTS
See pace charts, pp. 78–81

TEMPO WORKOUTS
See pace chart, p. 86

FRI	SAT	SUN	WEEKLY TOTAL
OFF	Easy 3 mi. (5 km)	DWU1 Easy 4 mi. (7 km) LS/Flex	10 mi. (17 KM)
DWU1 Easy 3 mi. (5 km) LS	DWU1 Easy 3 mi. (5 km) LS/Flex	DWU1 Easy 4 mi. (7 km) LS/Flex	15 mi. (25 KM)
Easy 4 mi. (7 km) LS	DWU1 Easy 4 mi. (7 km) LS/Flex	DWU1 Easy 5 mi. (8 km) LS/Flex	21 mi. (36 KM)
DWU1 Easy 3 mi. (5 km) LS	DWU1 Easy 5 mi. (8 km) LS/Flex	DWU1 Easy 5 mi. (8 km) LS/Flex	23 mi. (34 KM)
DWU1 Easy 5 mi. (8 km) LS	DWU1 Easy 4 mi. (7 km) LS/Flex	DWU1 Easy 6 mi. (10 km) LS/Flex	24 mi. (40 KM)
DWU1 Easy 4 mi. (7 km) BWM, LS/Flex	DWU1 Easy 8 mi. (13 km) BWM, LS/Flex	DWU1 Easy 8 mi. (13 km) LS/Flex	39 mi. (68 KM)
DWU1 Easy 4 mi. (7 km) BWM, LS/Flex	DWU1 Easy 6 mi. (10 km) BWM, LS/Flex	DWU1 Long 10 mi. (16 km) LS/Flex	38 mi. (64 KM)
DWU1 Easy 5 mi. (8 km) BWM, LS/Flex	DWU1 Easy 6 mi. (10 km) BWM, LS/Flex	DWU1 Long 10 mi. (16 km) LS	41 mi. (66 KM)
DWU1 Easy 6 mi. (10 km) BWM, LS/Flex	DWU1 Easy 5 mi. (8 km) BWM, LS/Flex	DWU1 Long 15 mi. (24 km) LS	47 mi. (80 KM)
DWU1 Easy 5 mi. (8 km) BWM, LS/Flex	DWU1 Easy 8 mi. (13 km) BWM, LS/Flex	DWU1 Long 10 mi. (16 km) LS	46 mi. (71 KM)

Continues

Key: DWU1: Dynamic warm-up level 1; DWU2: Dynamic warm-up level 2; R: recovery; LS: Light static stretch; Flex: Stretching for flexibility; BWM: Body weight/movement strength; RT: Resistance strength training; WU: Warm-up 1–3 miles; CD: Cooldown 1–3 miles

TABLE B.1 CONTINUED

WEEK	MON	TUES	WED	THURS
11	DWU1 Easy 5 mi. (8 km) BWM, LS/Flex	DWU1, WU, DWU2, 6 × 1 mi. (2 km)/400R, CD	DWU1 RT LS	DWU1, WU, DWU2, TEMPO 8 mi. (13 km), CD
12	DWU1 Easy 5 mi. (8 km) BWM, LS/Flex	DWU1, WU, DWU2, 4 × 1.5 mi. (2.5 km)/800R, CD	DWU1 RT LS	DWU1, WU, DWU2, TEMPO 9 mi. (14 km), CD
13	DWU1 Easy 7 mi. (11 km) BWM, LS/Flex	DWU1, WU, DWU2, 3 × 2 mi. (3 km)/800R, CD	DWU1 RT LS	DWU1, WU, DWU2, TEMPO 9 mi. (14 km), CD
14	DWU1 Easy 5 mi. (8 km) BWM, LS/Flex	DWU1, WU, DWU2, 2 × 3 mi. (5 km)/1 mi. (2 km)R, CD	DWU1 RT LS	DWU1, WU, DWU2, TEMPO 9 mi. (14 km), CD
15	DWU1 Easy 7 mi. (11 km) BWM, LS/Flex	DWU1, WU, DWU2, 3 × 2 mi. (3 km)/800R, CD	DWU1 RT LS	DWU1, WU, DWU2, TEMPO 10 mi. (16 km), CD
16	DWU1 Easy 5 mi. (8 km) BWM, LS/Flex	DWU1, WU, DWU2, 4 × 1.5 mi. (2.5 km)/800R, CD	DWU1 RT LS	DWU1, WU, DWU2, TEMPO 10 mi. (16 km), CD
17	DWU1 Easy 7 mi. (11 km) BWM, LS/Flex	DWU1, WU, DWU2, 6 × 1 mi. (2 km)/400R, CD	DWU1 RT LS	DWU1, WU, DWU2, TEMPO 10 mi. (16 km), CD
18	DWU1 Easy 5 mi. (8 km) LS	DWU1 Easy 5 mi. (8 km) LS	OFF	DWU1 Easy 6 mi. (10 km)

SPEED WORKOUTS
See pace charts, pp. 68–74

STRENGTH WORKOUTS
See pace charts, pp. 78–81

TEMPO WORKOUTS
See pace chart, p. 86

FRI	SAT	SUN	WEEKLY TOTAL
DWU1 Easy 5 mi. (8 km) BWM, LS/Flex	DWU1 Easy 8 mi. (13 km) LS/Flex	DWU1, Long 16 mi. (27 km) LS	**54 mi.** (91 KM)
DWU1 Easy 5 mi. (8 km) BWM, LS/Flex	DWU1 Easy 8 mi. (13 km) RT, LS/Flex	DWU1, Long 10 mi. (16 km) LS	**49 mi.** (80 KM)
DWU1 Easy 6 mi. (10 km) BWM, LS/Flex	DWU1 Easy 6 mi. (10 km) RT, LS/Flex	DWU1, Long 16 mi. (27 km) LS	**56 mi.** (91 KM)
DWU1 Easy 5 mi. (8 km) BWM, LS/Flex	DWU1 Easy 8 mi. (13 km) RT, LS/Flex	DWU1, Long 10 mi. (16 km) LS	**49 mi.** (81 KM)
DWU1 Easy 6 mi. (10 km) BWM, LS/Flex	DWU1 Easy 6 mi. (10 km) RT, LS/Flex	DWU1, Long 16 mi. (27 km) LS	**57 mi.** (93 KM)
DWU1 Easy 5 mi. (8 km) BWM, LS/Flex	DWU1 Easy 8 mi. (13 km) RT, LS/Flex	DWU1, Long 10 mi. (16 km) LS	**50 mi.** (82 KM)
DWU1 Easy 6 mi. (10 km) BWM, LS/Flex	DWU1 Easy 6 mi. (10 km) LS	Easy 8 mi. (13 km) LS	**49 mi.** (82 KM)
DWU1 Easy 5 mi. (8 km) BWM, LS/Flex	DWU1 Easy 3 mi. (5 km) LS	RACE!	**50 mi.** (81 KM)

Key: DWU1: Dynamic warm-up level 1; DWU2: Dynamic warm-up level 2; R: recovery; LS: Light static stretch; Flex: Stretching for flexibility; BWM: Body weight/movement strength; RT: Resistance strength training; WU: Warm-up 1–3 miles; CD: Cooldown 1–3 miles

TABLE B.2 ADVANCED PROGRAM

WEEK	MON	TUES	WED	THURS
1	—	—	OFF	DWU1 Easy 6 mi. (10 km)
2	DWU1 Easy 6 mi. (10 km) LS/Flex	DWU1, WU, DWU2, 12 × 400/ 400R, CD	OFF	DWU1 Easy 6 mi. (10 km)
3	DWU1 Easy 6 mi. (10 km) LS/Flex	DWU1, WU, DWU2, 8 × 600/ 400R, CD	OFF	DWU1, WU, DWU2, TEMPO 6 mi. (10 km), CD
4	DWU1 Easy 6 mi. (10 km) LS/Flex	DWU1, WU, DWU2, 6 × 800/ 400R, CD	OFF	DWU1, WU, DWU2, TEMPO 6 mi. (10 km), CD
5	DWU1 Easy 6 mi. (10 km) LS/Flex	DWU1, WU, DWU2, 5 × 1 km/ 400R, CD	DWU1, BWM, LS/Flex	DWU1, WU, DWU2, TEMPO 6 mi. (10 km), CD
6	DWU1 Easy 6 mi. (10 km) LS/Flex	DWU1, WU, DWU2, 4 × 1200/ 400R, CD	DWU1, BWM, LS/Flex	DWU1, WU, DWU2, TEMPO 7 mi. (11 km), CD
7	DWU1 Easy 6 mi. (10 km) LS/Flex	DWU1, WU, DWU2, 400-800- 1200-1600-1200- 800/400R, CD	DWU1, BWM, LS/Flex	DWU1, WU, DWU2, TEMPO 7 mi. (11 km), CD
8	DWU1 Easy 6 mi. (10 km) BMW, LS/Flex	DWU1, WU, DWU2, 3 × 1600/ 600R, CD	DWU1, BWM, LS/Flex	DWU1, WU, DWU2, TEMPO 7 mi. (11 km), CD
9	DWU1 Easy 8 mi. (13 km) BMW, LS/Flex	DWU1, WU, DWU2, 6 × 800/ 400R, CD	DWU1, BWM, LS/Flex	DWU1, WU, DWU2, TEMPO 8 mi. (13 km), CD
10	DWU1 Easy 6 mi. (10 km) BMW, LS/Flex	DWU1, WU, DWU2, 3 × 1600/ 600R, CD	DWU1, BWM, LS/Flex	DWU1, WU, DWU2, TEMPO 8 mi. (13 km), CD

(Column labels in shaded vertical bands: SPEED under TUES; TEMPO under THURS)

SPEED WORKOUTS
See pace charts, pp. 68–74

STRENGTH WORKOUTS
See pace charts, pp. 78–81

TEMPO WORKOUTS
See pace chart, p. 86

FRI	SAT	SUN	WEEKLY TOTAL
DWU1 Easy 6 mi. (10 km) LS/Flex	DWU1 Easy 6 mi. (10 km) LS/Flex	DWU1 Easy 8 mi. (13 km) LS/Flex	**26** mi. (43 км)
DWU1 Easy 6 mi. (10 km) LS/Flex	DWU1 Easy 6 mi. (10 km) LS/Flex	DWU1 Easy 8 mi. (13 km) LS/Flex	**41** mi. (59 км)
DWU1 Easy 7 mi. (11 km) LS/Flex	DWU1 Easy 6 mi. (10 km) LS/Flex	DWU1 Long 10 mi. (16 km) LS/Flex	**46** mi. (77 km)
DWU1 Easy 6 mi. (10 km) LS/Flex	DWU1 Easy 8 mi. (13 km) LS/Flex	DWU1 Easy 8 mi. (13 km) LS/Flex	**45** mi. (75 km)
DWU1 Easy 7 mi. (11 km) BMW, LS/Flex	DWU1 Easy 6 mi. (10 km) LS/Flex	DWU1 Long 12 mi. (20 km) LS/Flex	**47** mi. (80 km)
DWU1 Easy 6 mi. (10 km) BMW, LS/Flex	DWU1 Easy 10 mi. (16 km) LS/Flex	DWU1 Easy 8 mi. (13 km) LS/Flex	**47** mi. (78 km)
DWU1 Easy 7 mi. (11 km) BMW, LS/Flex	DWU1 Easy 8 mi. (13 km) LS/Flex	DWU1 Long 14 mi. (23 km) LS	**54** mi. (88 km)
DWU1 Easy 6 mi. (10 km) BMW, LS/Flex	DWU1 Easy 10 mi. (16 km) LS/Flex	DWU1 Easy 10 mi. (16 km) LS/Flex	**49** mi. (82 km)
DWU1 Easy 7 mi. (11 km) BMW, LS/Flex	DWU1 Easy 8 mi. (13 km) LS/Flex	DWU1 Long 15 mi. (25 km) LS	**57** mi. (94 km)
DWU1 Easy 6 mi. (10 km) BMW, LS/Flex	DWU1 Easy 10 mi. (16 km) LS/Flex	DWU1 Easy 10 mi. (16 km) LS/Flex	**50** mi. (84 km)

Continues

Key: DWU1: Dynamic warm-up level 1; DWU2: Dynamic warm-up level 2; R: recovery; LS: Light static stretch; Flex: Stretching for flexibility; BWM: Body weight/movement strength; RT: Resistance strength training; WU: Warm-up 1–3 miles; CD: Cooldown 1–3 miles

TABLE B.2 CONTINUED

WEEK	MON	TUES	WED	THURS
11	DWU1 Easy 8 mi. (13 km) BMW, LS/Flex	DWU1, WU, DWU2, 6 × 1 mi. (2 km)/400R, CD	DWU1, RT, LS/Flex	DWU1, WU, DWU2, TEMPO 8 mi. (13 km), CD
12	DWU1 Easy 6 mi. (10 km) BMW, LS/Flex	DWU1, WU, DWU2, 4 × 1.5 mi. (2 km)/800R, CD	DWU1, RT, LS/Flex	DWU1, WU, DWU2, TEMPO 9 mi. (14 km), CD
13	DWU1 Easy 8 mi. (13 km) BMW, LS/Flex	DWU1, WU, DWU2, 3 × 2 mi. (3 km)/800R, CD	DWU1, RT, LS/Flex	DWU1, WU, DWU2, TEMPO 9 mi. (14 km), CD
14	DWU1 Easy 6 mi. (10 km) BMW, LS/Flex	STRENGTH DWU1, WU, DWU2, 2 × 3 mi. (5 km)/1 mi. (2 km)R, CD	DWU1, RT, LS/Flex	TEMPO DWU1, WU, DWU2, TEMPO 9 mi. (14 km), CD
15	DWU1 Easy 8 mi. (13 km) BMW, LS/Flex	DWU1, WU, DWU2, 3 × 2 mi. (3 km)/800R, CD	DWU1, RT, LS/Flex	DWU1, WU, DWU2, TEMPO 10 mi. (16 km), CD
16	DWU1 Easy 6 mi. (10 km) BMW, LS/Flex	DWU1, WU, DWU2, 4 × 1.5 mi. (2 km)/800R, CD	DWU1, RT, LS/Flex	DWU1, WU, DWU2, TEMPO 10 mi. (16 km), CD
17	DWU1 Easy 8 mi. (13 km) BMW, LS/Flex	DWU1, WU, DWU2, 6 × 1 mi. (2 km)/400R, CD	DWU1, RT, LS/Flex	DWU1, WU, DWU2, TEMPO 10 mi. (16 km), CD
18	DWU1 Easy 6 mi. (10 km) BMW, LS/Flex	DWU1 Easy 5 mi. (8 km)	OFF	DWU1 Easy 6 mi. (10 km) LS

SPEED WORKOUTS
See pace charts, pp. 68–74

STRENGTH WORKOUTS
See pace charts, pp. 78–81

TEMPO WORKOUTS
See pace chart, p. 86

FRI	SAT	SUN	WEEKLY TOTAL
DWU1 Easy 7 mi. (11 km) BMW, LS/Flex	DWU1 Easy 8 mi. (13 km) LS/Flex	DWU1 Long 16 mi. (27 km) LS	61 mi. (103 KM)
DWU1 Easy 6 mi. (10 km) BMW, LS/Flex	DWU1 Easy 10 mi. (16 km) LS/Flex	DWU1 Easy 10 mi. (16 km) LS/Flex	55 mi. (89 KM)
DWU1 Easy 7 mi. (11 km) BMW, LS/Flex	DWU1 Easy 8 mi. (13 km) RT, LS/Flex	DWU1 Long 16 mi. (27 km) LS	62 mi. (101 KM)
DWU1 Easy 6 mi. (10 km) LS	DWU1 Easy 10 mi. (16 km) RT, LS/Flex	DWU1 Easy 10 mi. (16 km) LS/Flex	55 mi. (92 KM)
DWU1 Easy 7 mi. (11 km) LS	DWU1 Easy 8 mi. (13 km) RT, LS/Flex	DWU1 Long 16 mi. (27 km) LS	63 mi. (103 KM)
DWU1 Easy 6 mi. (10 km) LS	DWU1 Easy 10 mi. (16 km) RT, LS/Flex	DWU1 Easy 10 mi. (16 km) LS/Flex	56 mi. (91 KM)
DWU1 Easy 7 mi. (11 km) BMW, LS/Flex	DWU1 Easy 8 mi. (13 km) LS/Flex	DWU1 Easy 8 mi. (13 km) LS	55 mi. (92 KM)
DWU1 Easy 6 mi. (10 km) LS	DWU1 Easy 3 mi. (8 km) LS	RACE!	52 mi. (88 KM)

Key: DWU1: Dynamic warm-up level 1; DWU2: Dynamic warm-up level 2; R: recovery; LS: Light static stretch; Flex: Stretching for flexibility; BWM: Body weight/movement strength; RT: Resistance strength training; WU: Warm-up 1–3 miles; CD: Cooldown 1–3 miles

Appendix C
Sweat-Loss Calculator

1	**Check weight* before and after training to calculate weight loss.** Weight before [ ] Weight after [ ] Amount of weight lost [ ] oz. (ml) * Check weight without clothing, if possible. Time period (1 hour preferable) [ ]
2	**Convert amount of weight loss to ounces (milliliters) of fluid.** e.g., a 2-lb. weight loss = 30 oz. of fluid / e.g., a 1-kg weight loss = 1,000 ml of fluid [ ] oz. (ml) of fluid lost
3	**Record amount of fluid consumed during training session.** e.g., squeeze bottles are 20–24 oz./600–720 ml [ ] oz. (ml) of fluid consumed
4	**Add amount of fluid lost and fluid consumed.** Fluid lost + fluid consumed = [ ] oz. (ml)
5	**Divide total oz. (ml) of weight loss by number of hours of training to determine amount of oz. lost in sweat per hour.** Total fluid lost ffi hours of training = [ ] Fluid losses in oz. (ml) per hour

Example:

1–2. Weight before training: 165 lb. (75 kg); Weight after training: 164 lb. (74 kg)
Total weight loss: 1 lb. (0.5 kg) = 15 oz. (500 ml) fluid
3. Consumed 30 oz. (960 ml) fluid during 1-hour bike ride: 30 oz. (960 ml) fluid
4. Add fluid lost and fluid consumed: 15 oz. (500 ml) + 30 oz. (960 ml) = 45 oz. (1,460 ml)
5. Divide total sum of weight loss by hours of training: 45 oz. (1,060 ml) ffi 1 hour of training = 45 oz. per hour for sweat losses

Source: Adapted with permission from Monique Ryan, *Sports Nutrition for Endurance Athletes*, 3rd ed. (Boulder, CO: VeloPress, 2012).

Index

Tables and figures are denoted by *t* and *f*, respectively.

About the Authors

LUKE HUMPHREY began running track in middle school and hasn't slowed down since. After several all-state performances in high school, Luke ran for Central Michigan University from 1999 to 2004. There he was a member of several NCAA Division I top-25 cross country teams, including a 9th place team in 2002. In fall of 2004 Luke competed in his first marathon at the LaSalle Bank Chicago Marathon for the Hansons-Brooks Distance Project. He ran a debut time of 2:18:46 and was

18th overall. Since then Luke has gone on to finish 11th in the 2006 Boston Marathon, 11th in the 2008 ING New York City Marathon, and 12th in the 2010 Bank of America Chicago Marathon and has also qualified for three U.S. Olympic Trials for the marathon (2008, 2012, and 2016). Luke holds a personal best of 2:14:38 in the marathon. He has a B.A.A. in exercise science from Central Michigan University and an M.S. in exercise science from Oakland University. Luke began Hansons Coaching Services in May 2006 to help runners of all abilities reach their running goals. He and his wife, Nicole, have a daughter, Josephine.

KEITH AND KEVIN HANSON are cofounders of the Hansons-Brooks Distance Project, together coaching the Olympic development team to victories on national and international stages. They also co-own the Hansons Running Shops and avidly support, build, and encourage the running community, coaching hundreds of local runners to their first or hundredth marathon.